Spring Boot in Action

CRAIG WALLS

MANNING
Shelter Island

For online information and ordering of this and other Manning books, please visit
www.manning.com. The publisher offers discounts on this book when ordered in quantity.
For more information, please contact

    Special Sales Department
    Manning Publications Co.
    20 Baldwin Road
    PO Box 761
    Shelter Island, NY 11964
    Email: orders@manning.com

Manning Publications Co.
20 Baldwin Road
PO Box 761
Shelter Island, NY 11964

Development editor:	Cynthia Kane
Technical development editor:	Robert Casazza
Copyeditor:	Andy Carroll
Proofreader:	Corbin Collins
Technical proofreader:	John Guthrie
Typesetter:	Gordan Salinovic
Cover designer:	Marija Tudor

ISBN 9781617292545
Printed in the United States of America
1 2 3 4 5 6 7 8 9 10 – EBM – 20 19 18 17 16 15

contents

foreword

In the spring of 2014, the Delivery Engineering team at Netflix set out to achieve a lofty goal: enable end-to-end global continuous delivery via a software platform that facilitates both extensibility and resiliency. My team had previously built two different applications attempting to address Netflix's delivery and deployment needs, but both were beginning to show the telltale signs of monolith-ness and neither met the goals of flexibility and resiliency. What's more, the most stymieing effect of these monolithic applications was ultimately that we were unable to keep pace with our partner's innovation. Users had begun to move around our tools rather than with them.

It became apparent that if we wanted to provide real value to the company and rapidly innovate, we needed to break up the monoliths into small, independent services that could be released at will. Embracing a microservice architecture gave us hope that we could also address the twin goals of flexibility and resiliency. But we needed to do it on a credible foundation where we could count on real concurrency, legitimate monitoring, reliable and easy service discovery, and great runtime performance.

With the JVM as our bedrock, we looked for a framework that would give us rapid velocity and steadfast operationalization out of the box. We zeroed in on Spring Boot.

Spring Boot makes it effortless to create Spring-powered, production-ready services without a lot of code! Indeed, the fact that a simple Spring Boot Hello World application can fit into a tweet is a radical departure from what the same functionality required on the JVM only a few short years ago. Out-of-the-box nonfunctional features like security, metrics, health-checks, embedded servers, and externalized configuration made Boot an easy choice for us.

Yet, when we embarked on our Spring Boot journey, solid documentation was hard to come by. Relying on source code isn't the most joyful manner of figuring out how to properly leverage a framework's features.

It's not surprising to see the author of Manning's venerable *Spring in Action* take on the challenge of concisely distilling the core aspects of working with Spring Boot into another cogent book. Nor is it surprising that Craig and the Manning crew have done another tremendously wonderful job! *Spring Boot in Action* is an easily readable book, as we've now come to expect from Craig and Manning.

From chapter 1's attention-getting introduction to Boot and the now legendary 90ish-character tweetable Boot application to an in-depth analysis of Boot's Actuator in chapter 7, which enables a host of auto-magical operational features required for any production application, *Spring Boot in Action* leaves no stone unturned. Indeed, for me, chapter 7's deep dive into the Actuator answered some of the lingering questions I've had in the back of my head since picking up Boot well over a year ago. Chapter 8's thorough examination of deployment options opened my eyes to the simplicity of Cloud Foundry for cloud deployments. One of my favorite chapters is chapter 4, where Craig explores the many powerful options for easily testing a Boot application. From the get-go, I was pleasantly surprised with some of Spring's testing features, and Boot takes advantage of them nicely.

As I've publicly stated before, Spring Boot is just the kind of framework the Java community has been seeking for over a decade. Its easy-to-use development features and out-of-the-box operationalization make Java development fun again. I'm pleased to report that Spring and Spring Boot are the foundation of Netflix's new continuous delivery platform. What's more, other teams at Netflix are following the same path because they too see the myriad benefits of Boot.

It's with equal parts excitement and passion that I absolutely endorse Craig's book as the easy-to-digest and fun-to-read Spring Boot documentation the Java community has been waiting for since Boot took the community by storm. Craig's accessible writing style and sweeping analysis of Boot's core features and functionality will surely leave readers with a solid grasp of Boot (along with a joyful sense of awe for it).

Keep up the great work Craig, Manning Publications, and all the brilliant developers who have made Spring Boot what it is today! Each one of you has ensured a bright future for the JVM.

ANDREW GLOVER
MANAGER, DELIVERY ENGINEERING AT NETFLIX

preface

At the 1964 New York World's Fair, Walt Disney introduced three groundbreaking attractions: "it's a small world," "Great Moments with Mr. Lincoln," and the "Carousel of Progress." All three of these attractions have since moved into Disneyland and Walt Disney World, and you can still see them today.

My favorite of these is the Carousel of Progress. Supposedly, it was one of Walt Disney's favorites too. It's part ride and part stage show where the seating area rotates around a center area featuring four stages. Each stage tells the story of a family at different time periods of the 20th century—the early 1900s, the 1920s, the 1940s, and recent times—highlighting the technology advances in that time period. The story of innovation is told from a hand-cranked washing machine, to electric lighting and radio, to automatic dishwashers and television, to computers and voice-activated appliances.

In every act, the father (who is also the narrator of the show) talks about the latest inventions and says "It can't get any better," only to discover that, in fact, it does get better in the next act as technology progresses.

Although Spring doesn't have quite as long a history as that displayed in the Carousel of Progress, I feel the same way about Spring as "Progress Dad" felt about the 20th century. Each and every Spring application seems to make the lives of developers so much better. Just looking at how Spring components are declared and wired together, we can see the following progression over the history of Spring:

- When Spring 1.0 hit the scene, it completely changed how we develop enterprise Java applications. Spring dependency injection and declarative transactions meant no more tight coupling of components and no more heavyweight EJBs. It couldn't get any better.

- With Spring 2.0 we could use custom XML namespaces for configuration, making Spring itself even easier to use with smaller and easier to understand configuration files. It couldn't get any better.

- Spring 2.5 gave us a much more elegant annotation-oriented dependency-injection model with the `@Component` and `@Autowired` annotations, as well as an annotation-oriented Spring MVC programming model. No more explicit declaration of application components, and no more subclassing one of several base controller classes. It couldn't get any better.

- Then with Spring 3.0 we were given a new Java-based configuration alternative to XML that was improved further in Spring 3.1 with a variety of `@Enable`-prefixed annotations. For the first time, it become realistic to write a complete Spring application with no XML configuration whatsoever. It couldn't get any better.

- Spring 4.0 unleashed support for conditional configuration, where runtime decisions would determine which configuration would be used and which would be ignored based on the application's classpath, environment, and other factors. We no longer needed to write scripts to make those decisions at build time and pick which configuration should be included in the deployment. How could it possibly get any better?

And then came Spring Boot. Even though with each release of Spring we thought it couldn't possibly get any better, Spring Boot proved that there's still a lot of magic left in Spring. In fact, I believe Spring Boot is the most significant and exciting thing to happen in Java development in a long time.

Building upon previous advances in the Spring Framework, Spring Boot enables automatic configuration, making it possible for Spring to intelligently detect what kind of application you're building and automatically configure the components necessary to support the application's needs. There's no need to write explicit configuration for common configuration scenarios; Spring will take care of it for you.

Spring Boot starter dependencies make it even easier to select which build-time and runtime libraries to include in your application builds by aggregating commonly needed dependencies. Spring Boot starters not only keep the dependencies section of your build specifications shorter, they keep you from having to think too hard about the specific libraries and versions you need.

Spring Boot's command-line interface offers a compelling option for developing Spring applications in Groovy with minimal noise or ceremony common in Java applications. With the Spring Boot CLI, there's no need for accessor methods, access modifiers such as `public` or `private`, semicolons, or the `return` keyword. In many cases, you can even eliminate `import` statements. And because you run the application as scripts from the command line, you don't need a build specification.

Spring Boot's Actuator gives you insight into the inner workings of a running application. You can see exactly what beans are in the Spring application context, how Spring MVC controllers are mapped to paths, the configuration properties available to your application, and much more.

With all of these wonderful features enabled by Spring Boot, it certainly can't get any better!

In this book, you'll see how Spring Boot has indeed made Spring even better than it was before. We'll look at auto-configuration, Spring Boot starters, the Spring Boot CLI, and the Actuator. And we'll tinker with the latest version of Grails, which is based on Spring Boot. By the time we're done, you'll probably be thinking that Spring couldn't get any better.

If we've learned anything from Walt Disney's Carousel of Progress, it's that when we think things can't get any better, they inevitably do get better. Already, the advances offered by Spring Boot are being leveraged to enable even greater advances. It's hard to imagine Spring getting any better than it is now, but it certainly will. With Spring, there's always a great big beautiful tomorrow.

about this book

Spring Boot aims to simplify Spring development. As such, Spring Boot's reach stretches to touch everything that Spring touches. It'd be impossible to write a book that covers every single way that Spring Boot can be used, as doing so would involve covering every single technology that Spring itself supports. Instead, *Spring Boot in Action* aims to distill Spring Boot into four main topics: auto-configuration, starter dependencies, the command-line interface, and the Actuator. Along the way, we'll touch on a few Spring features as necessary, but the focus will be primarily on Spring Boot.

Spring Boot in Action is for all Java developers. Although some background in Spring could be considered a prerequisite, Spring Boot has a way of making Spring more approachable even to those new to Spring. Nevertheless, because this book will be focused on Spring Boot and will not dive deeply into Spring itself, you may find it helpful to pair it with other Spring materials such as *Spring in Action, Fourth Edition* (Manning, 2014).

Roadmap

Spring Boot in Action is divided into seven chapters:

- In chapter 1 you'll be given an overview of Spring Boot, including the essentials of automatic configuration, starter dependencies, the command-line interface, and the Actuator.
- Chapter 2 takes a deeper dive into Spring Boot, focusing on automatic configuration and starter dependencies. In this chapter, you'll build a complete Spring application using very little explicit configuration.

- Chapter 3 picks up where chapter 2 leaves off, showing how you can influence automatic configuration by setting application properties or completely overriding automatic configuration when it doesn't meet your needs.
- In chapter 4 we'll look at how to write automated integration tests for Spring Boot applications.
- In chapter 5 you'll see how the Spring Boot CLI offers a compelling alternative to conventional Java development by enabling you to write complete applications as a set of Groovy scripts that are run from the command line.
- While we're on the subject of Groovy, chapter 6 takes a look at Grails 3, the latest version of the Grails framework, which is now based on Spring Boot.
- In chapter 7 you'll see how to leverage Spring Boot's Actuator to dig inside of a running application and see what makes it tick. You'll see how to use Actuator web endpoints as well as a remote shell and JMX MBeans to peek at the internals of an application.
- Chapter 8 wraps things up by discussing various options for deploying your Spring Boot application, including traditional application server deployment and cloud deployment.

Code conventions and downloads

There are many code examples throughout this book. These examples will always appear in a fixed-width code font like this. Any class name, method name, or XML fragment within the normal text of the book will appear in code font as well. Many of Spring's classes and packages have exceptionally long (but expressive) names. Because of this, line-continuation markers (➥) may be included when necessary. Not all code examples in this book will be complete. Often I only show a method or two from a class to focus on a particular topic.

Complete source code for the applications found in the book can be downloaded from the publisher's website at www.manning.com/books/spring-boot-in-action.

Author Online

The purchase of *Spring Boot in Action* includes free access to a private web forum run by Manning Publications, where you can make comments about the book, ask technical questions, and receive help from the author and from other users. To access the forum and subscribe to it, point your web browser to www.manning.com/books/spring-boot-in-action. This page provides information on how to get on the forum once you are registered, what kind of help is available, and the rules of conduct on the forum.

Manning's commitment to our readers is to provide a venue where a meaningful dialogue between individual readers and between readers and the author can take place. It is not a commitment to any specific amount of participation on the part of the author whose contribution to the forum remains voluntary (and unpaid). We suggest you try asking the author some challenging questions lest his interest stray!

The Author Online forum and the archives of previous discussions will be accessible from the publisher's website as long as the book is in print.

About the cover illustration

The figure on the cover of *Spring Boot in Action* is captioned "Habit of a Tartar in Kasan," which is the capital city of the Republic of Tatarstan in Russia. The illustration is taken from Thomas Jefferys' *A Collection of the Dresses of Different Nations, Ancient and Modern* (four volumes), London, published between 1757 and 1772. The title page states that these are hand-colored copperplate engravings, heightened with gum arabic. Thomas Jefferys (1719–1771) was called "Geographer to King George III." He was an English cartographer who was the leading map supplier of his day. He engraved and printed maps for government and other official bodies and produced a wide range of commercial maps and atlases, especially of North America. His work as a mapmaker sparked an interest in local dress customs of the lands he surveyed and mapped, which are brilliantly displayed in this collection.

Fascination with faraway lands and travel for pleasure were relatively new phenomena in the late eighteenth century, and collections such as this one were popular, introducing both the tourist as well as the armchair traveler to the inhabitants of other countries. The diversity of the drawings in Jefferys' volumes speaks vividly of the uniqueness and individuality of the world's nations some 200 years ago. Dress codes have changed since then, and the diversity by region and country, so rich at the time, has faded away. It is now often hard to tell the inhabitant of one continent from another. Perhaps, trying to view it optimistically, we have traded a cultural and visual diversity for a more varied personal life. Or a more varied and interesting intellectual and technical life.

At a time when it is hard to tell one computer book from another, Manning celebrates the inventiveness and initiative of the computer business with book covers based on the rich diversity of regional life of two centuries ago, brought back to life by Jeffreys' pictures.

acknowledgments

This book will show how Spring Boot can automatically deal with the behind-the-scenes stuff that goes into an application, freeing you to focus on the tasks that make your application unique. In many ways, this is analogous to what went into making this book happen. There were so many other people taking care of making things happen that I was free to focus on writing the content of the book. For taking care of the behind-the-scenes work at Manning, I'd like to thank Cynthia Kane, Robert Casazza, Andy Carroll, Corbin Collins, Kevin Sullivan, Mary Piergies, Janet Vail, Ozren Harlovic, and Candace Gillhoolley.

Writing tests help you know if your software is meeting its goals. Similarly, those who reviewed *Spring Boot in Action* while it was still being written gave me the feedback I needed to make sure that the book stayed on target. For this, my gratitude goes out to Aykut Acikel, Bachir Chihani, Eric Kramer, Francesco Persico, Furkan Kamaci, Gregor Zurowski, Mario Arias, Michael A. Angelo, Mykel Alvis, Norbert Kuchenmeister, Phil Whiles, Raphael Villela, Sam Kreter, Travis Nelson, Wilfredo R. Ronsini Jr., and William Fly. Special thanks to John Guthrie for a final technical review shortly before the manuscript went into production. And extra special thanks to Andrew Glover for contributing the foreword to my book.

Of course, this book wouldn't be possible or even necessary without the incredible work done by the talented members of the Spring team. It's amazing what you do, and I'm so excited to be part of a team that's changing how software is developed.

Many thanks to all of those involved in the No Fluff/Just Stuff tour, whether it be my fellow presenters or those who show up to hear us talk. The conversations we've had have in some small way contributed to how this book was formed.

A book like this would not be possible without an alphabet to compose into words. So, just as in my previous book, I'd like to take this opportunity to thank the Phoenicians for the invention of the first alphabet.

Last, but certainly not least...my love, devotion, and thanks go to my beautiful wife Raymie and my awesome girls, Maisy and Madi. Once again, you've tolerated another writing project. Now that it's done, we should go to Disney World. Whatdya say?

Bootstarting Spring

This chapter covers

- How Spring Boot simplifies Spring application development
- The essential features of Spring Boot
- Setting up a Spring Boot workspace

The Spring Framework has been around for over a decade and has found a place as the de facto standard framework for developing Java applications. With such a long and storied history, some might think that Spring has settled, resting on its laurels, and is not doing anything new or exciting. Some might even say that Spring is legacy and that it's time to look elsewhere for innovation.

Some would be wrong.

There are many exciting new things taking place in the Spring ecosystem, including work in the areas of cloud computing, big data, schema-less data persistence, reactive programming, and client-side application development.

Perhaps the most exciting, most head-turning, most game-changing new thing to come to Spring in the past year or so is Spring Boot. Spring Boot offers a new paradigm for developing Spring applications with minimal friction. With Spring Boot, you'll be able to develop Spring applications with more agility and be able to focus on addressing your application's functionality needs with minimal (or possibly no) thought of configuring Spring itself. In fact, one of the main things that Spring Boot does is to get Spring out of your way so you can get stuff done.

Throughout the chapters in this book, we'll explore various facets of Spring Boot development. But first, let's take a high-level look at what Spring Boot has to offer.

1.1   Spring rebooted

Spring started as a lightweight alternative to Java Enterprise Edition (JEE, or J2EE as it was known at the time). Rather than develop components as heavyweight Enterprise JavaBeans (EJBs), Spring offered a simpler approach to enterprise Java development, utilizing dependency injection and aspect-oriented programming to achieve the capabilities of EJB with plain old Java objects (POJOs).

But while Spring was lightweight in terms of component code, it was heavyweight in terms of configuration. Initially, Spring was configured with XML (and lots of it). Spring 2.5 introduced annotation-based component-scanning, which eliminated a great deal of explicit XML configuration for an application's own components. And Spring 3.0 introduced a Java-based configuration as a type-safe and refactorable option to XML.

Even so, there was no escape from configuration. Enabling certain Spring features such as transaction management and Spring MVC required explicit configuration, either in XML or Java. Enabling third-party library features such as Thymeleaf-based web views required explicit configuration. Configuring servlets and filters (such as Spring's `DispatcherServlet`) required explicit configuration in web.xml or in a servlet initializer. Component-scanning reduced configuration and Java configuration made it less awkward, but Spring still required a lot of configuration.

All of that configuration represents development friction. Any time spent writing configuration is time spent not writing application logic. The mental shift required to think about configuring a Spring feature distracts from solving the business problem. Like any framework, Spring does a lot for you, but it demands that you do a lot for it in return.

Moreover, project dependency management is a thankless task. Deciding what libraries need to be part of the project build is tricky enough. But it's even more challenging to know which versions of those libraries will play well with others.

As important as it is, dependency management is another form of friction. When you're adding dependencies to your build, you're not writing application code. Any incompatibilities that come from selecting the wrong versions of those dependencies can be a real productivity killer.

Spring Boot has changed all of that.

1.1.1   Taking a fresh look at Spring

Suppose you're given the task of developing a very simple Hello World web application with Spring. What would you need to do? I can think of a handful of things you'd need at a bare minimum:

- A project structure, complete with a Maven or Gradle build file including required dependencies. At the very least, you'll need Spring MVC and the Servlet API expressed as dependencies.
- A web.xml file (or a WebApplicationInitializer implementation) that declares Spring's DispatcherServlet.
- A Spring configuration that enables Spring MVC.
- A controller class that will respond to HTTP requests with "Hello World".
- A web application server, such as Tomcat, to deploy the application to.

What's most striking about this list is that only one item is specific to developing the Hello World functionality: the controller. The rest of it is generic boilerplate that you'd need for any web application developed with Spring. But if all Spring web applications need it, why should you have to provide it?

Suppose for a moment that the controller is all you need. As it turns out, the Groovy-based controller class shown in listing 1.1 is a complete (even if simple) Spring application.

Listing 1.1 A complete Groovy-based Spring application

```
@RestController
class HelloController {

  @RequestMapping("/")
  def hello() {
    return "Hello World"
  }

}
```

There's no configuration. No web.xml. No build specification. Not even an application server. This is the entire application. Spring Boot will handle the logistics of executing the application. You only need to bring the application code.

Assuming that you have Spring Boot's command-line interface (CLI) installed, you can run HelloController at the command line like this:

```
$ spring run HelloController.groovy
```

You may have also noticed that it wasn't even necessary to compile the code. The Spring Boot CLI was able to run it from its uncompiled form.

I chose to write this example controller in Groovy because the simplicity of the Groovy language presents well alongside the simplicity of Spring Boot. But Spring Boot doesn't require that you use Groovy. In fact, much of the code we'll write in this book will be in Java. But there'll be some Groovy here and there, where appropriate.

Feel free to look ahead to section 1.21 to see how to install the Spring Boot CLI, so that you can try out this little web application. But for now, we'll look at the key pieces of Spring Boot to see how it changes Spring application development.

1.1.2   *Examining Spring Boot essentials*

Spring Boot brings a great deal of magic to Spring application development. But there are four core tricks that it performs:

- *Automatic configuration*—Spring Boot can automatically provide configuration for application functionality common to many Spring applications.
- *Starter dependencies*—You tell Spring Boot what kind of functionality you need, and it will ensure that the libraries needed are added to the build.
- *The command-line interface*—This optional feature of Spring Boot lets you write complete applications with just application code, but no need for a traditional project build.
- *The Actuator*—Gives you insight into what's going on inside of a running Spring Boot application.

Each of these features serves to simplify Spring application development in its own way. We'll look at how to employ them to their fullest throughout this book. But for now, let's take a quick look at what each offers.

AUTO-CONFIGURATION

In any given Spring application's source code, you'll find either Java configuration or XML configuration (or both) that enables certain supporting features and functionality for the application. For example, if you've ever written an application that accesses a relational database with JDBC, you've probably configured Spring's JdbcTemplate as a bean in the Spring application context. I'll bet the configuration looked a lot like this:

```
@Bean
public JdbcTemplate jdbcTemplate(DataSource dataSource) {
  return new JdbcTemplate(dataSource);
}
```

This very simple bean declaration creates an instance of JdbcTemplate, injecting it with its one dependency, a DataSource. Of course, that means that you'll also need to configure a DataSource bean so that the dependency will be met. To complete this configuration scenario, suppose that you were to configure an embedded H2 database as the DataSource bean:

```
@Bean
public DataSource dataSource() {
  return new EmbeddedDatabaseBuilder()
          .setType(EmbeddedDatabaseType.H2)
          .addScripts('schema.sql', 'data.sql')
          .build();
}
```

This bean configuration method creates an embedded database, specifying two SQL scripts to execute on the embedded database. The build() method returns a Data-Source that references the embedded database.

Neither of these two bean configuration methods is terribly complex or lengthy. But they represent just a fraction of the configuration in a typical Spring application. Moreover, there are countless Spring applications that will have these exact same methods. Any application that needs an embedded database and a `JdbcTemplate` will need those methods. In short, it's boilerplate configuration.

If it's so common, then why should you have to write it?

Spring Boot can automatically configure these common configuration scenarios. If Spring Boot detects that you have the H2 database library in your application's classpath, it will automatically configure an embedded H2 database. If `JdbcTemplate` is in the classpath, then it will also configure a `JdbcTemplate` bean for you. There's no need for you to worry about configuring those beans. They'll be configured for you, ready to inject into any of the beans you write.

There's a lot more to Spring Boot auto-configuration than embedded databases and `JdbcTemplate`. There are several dozen ways that Spring Boot can take the burden of configuration off your hands, including auto-configuration for the Java Persistence API (JPA), Thymeleaf templates, security, and Spring MVC. We'll dive into auto-configuration starting in chapter 2.

STARTER DEPENDENCIES

It can be challenging to add dependencies to a project's build. What library do you need? What are its group and artifact? Which version do you need? Will that version play well with other dependencies in the same project?

Spring Boot offers help with project dependency management by way of starter dependencies. Starter dependencies are really just special Maven (and Gradle) dependencies that take advantage of transitive dependency resolution to aggregate commonly used libraries under a handful of feature-defined dependencies.

For example, suppose that you're going to build a REST API with Spring MVC that works with JSON resource representations. Additionally, you want to apply declarative validation per the JSR-303 specification and serve the application using an embedded Tomcat server. To accomplish all of this, you'll need (at minimum) the following eight dependencies in your Maven or Gradle build:

- `org.springframework:spring-core`
- `org.springframework:spring-web`
- `org.springframework:spring-webmvc`
- `com.fasterxml.jackson.core:jackson-databind`
- `org.hibernate:hibernate-validator`
- `org.apache.tomcat.embed:tomcat-embed-core`
- `org.apache.tomcat.embed:tomcat-embed-el`
- `org.apache.tomcat.embed:tomcat-embed-logging-juli`

On the other hand, if you were to take advantage of Spring Boot starter dependencies, you could simply add the Spring Boot "web" starter (`org.springframework.boot:spring-boot-starter-web`) as a build dependency. This single dependency will transitively pull in all of those other dependencies so you don't have to ask for them all.

But there's something more subtle about starter dependencies than simply reducing build dependency count. Notice that by adding the "web" starter to your build, you're specifying a type of functionality that your application needs. Your app is a web application, so you add the "web" starter. Likewise, if your application will use JPA persistence, then you can add the "jpa" starter. If it needs security, you can add the "security" starter. In short, you no longer need to think about what libraries you'll need to support certain functionality; you simply ask for that functionality by way of the pertinent starter dependency.

Also note that Spring Boot's starter dependencies free you from worrying about which versions of these libraries you need. The versions of the libraries that the starters pull in have been tested together so that you can be confident that there will be no incompatibilities between them.

Along with auto-configuration, we'll begin using starter dependencies right away, starting in chapter 2.

THE COMMAND-LINE INTERFACE (CLI)

In addition to auto-configuration and starter dependencies, Spring Boot also offers an intriguing new way to quickly write Spring applications. As you saw earlier in section 1.1, the Spring Boot CLI makes it possible to write applications by doing more than writing the application code.

Spring Boot's CLI leverages starter dependencies and auto-configuration to let you focus on writing code. Not only that, did you notice that there are no import lines in listing 1.1? How did the CLI know what packages RequestMapping and RestController come from? For that matter, how did those classes end up in the classpath?

The short answer is that the CLI detected that those types are being used, and it knows which starter dependencies to add to the classpath to make it work. Once those dependencies are in the classpath, a series of auto-configuration kicks in and ensures that DispatcherServlet and Spring MVC are enabled so that the controller can respond to HTTP requests.

Spring Boot's CLI is an optional piece of Spring Boot's power. Although it provides tremendous power and simplicity for Spring development, it also introduces a rather unconventional development model. If this development model is too extreme for your taste, then no problem. You can still take advantage of everything else that Spring Boot has to offer even if you don't use the CLI. But if you like what the CLI provides, you'll definitely want to look at chapter 5 where we'll dig deeper into Spring Boot's CLI.

THE ACTUATOR

The final piece of the Spring Boot puzzle is the Actuator. Where the other parts of Spring Boot simplify Spring development, the Actuator instead offers the ability to inspect the internals of your application at runtime. With the Actuator installed, you can inspect the inner workings of your application, including details such as

- What beans have been configured in the Spring application context
- What decisions were made by Spring Boot's auto-configuration
- What environment variables, system properties, configuration properties, and command-line arguments are available to your application
- The current state of the threads in and supporting your application
- A trace of recent HTTP requests handled by your application
- Various metrics pertaining to memory usage, garbage collection, web requests, and data source usage

The Actuator exposes this information in two ways: via web endpoints or via a shell interface. In the latter case, you can actually open a secure shell (SSH) into your application and issue commands to inspect your application as it runs.

We'll explore the Actuator's capabilities in detail when we get to chapter 7.

1.1.3　*What Spring Boot isn't*

Because of the amazing things Spring Boot does, there has been a lot of talk about Spring Boot in the past year or so. Depending on what you've heard or read about Spring Boot before reading this book, you may have a few misconceptions about Spring Boot that should be cleared up before continuing.

First, Spring Boot is not an application server. This misconception stems from the fact that it's possible to create web applications as self-executable JAR files that can be run at the command line without deploying applications to a conventional Java application server. Spring Boot accomplishes this by embedding a servlet container (Tomcat, Jetty, or Undertow) within the application. But it's the embedded servlet container that provides application server functionality, not Spring Boot itself.

Similarly, Spring Boot doesn't implement any enterprise Java specifications such as JPA or JMS. It does support several enterprise Java specifications, but it does so by automatically configuring beans in Spring that support those features. For instance, Spring Boot doesn't implement JPA, but it does support JPA by auto-configuring the appropriate beans for a JPA implementation (such as Hibernate).

Finally, Spring Boot doesn't employ any form of code generation to accomplish its magic. Instead, it leverages conditional configuration features from Spring 4, along with transitive dependency resolution offered by Maven and Gradle, to automatically configure beans in the Spring application context.

In short, at its heart, Spring Boot is just Spring. Inside, Spring Boot is doing the same kind of bean configuration in Spring that you might do on your own if Spring Boot didn't exist. Thankfully, because Spring Boot does exist, you're freed from dealing with explicit boilerplate configuration and are able to focus on the logic that makes your application unique.

By now you should have a general idea of what Spring Boot brings to the table. It's just about time for you to build your first application with Spring Boot. First things first, though. Let's see how you can take your first steps with Spring Boot.

1.2   Getting started with Spring Boot

Ultimately, a Spring Boot project is just a regular Spring project that happens to leverage Spring Boot starters and auto-configuration. Therefore, any technique or tool you may already be familiar with for creating a Spring project from scratch will apply to a Spring Boot project. There are, however, a few convenient options available for kickstarting your project with Spring Boot.

The quickest way to get started with Spring Boot is to install the Spring Boot CLI so that you can start writing code, such as that in listing 1.1, that runs via the CLI.

1.2.1   Installing the Spring Boot CLI

As we discussed earlier, the Spring Boot CLI offers an interesting, albeit unconventional, approach to developing Spring applications. We'll dive into the specifics of what the CLI offers in chapter 5. But for now let's look at how to install the Spring Boot CLI so that you can run the code we looked at in listing 1.1.

There are several ways to install the Spring Boot CLI:

- From a downloaded distribution
- Using the Groovy Environment Manager
- With OS X Homebrew
- As a port using MacPorts

We'll look at each installation option. In addition, we'll also see how to install support for Spring Boot CLI command completion, which comes in handy if you're using the CLI on BASH or zsh shells (sorry, Windows users). Let's first look at how you can install the Spring Boot CLI manually from a distribution.

MANUALLY INSTALLING THE SPRING BOOT CLI

Perhaps the most straightforward way to install the Spring Boot CLI is to download it, unzip it, and add its bin directory to your path. You can download the distribution archive from either of these locations:

- http://repo.spring.io/release/org/springframework/boot/spring-boot-cli/ 1.3.0.RELEASE/spring-boot-cli-1.3.0.RELEASE-bin.zip
- http://repo.spring.io/release/org/springframework/boot/spring-boot-cli/ 1.3.0.RELEASE/spring-boot-cli-1.3.0.RELEASE-bin.tar.gz

Once you've downloaded the distribution, unpack it somewhere in your filesystem. Inside of the unpacked archive, you'll find a bin directory that contains a spring.bat script (for Windows) and a spring script for Unix. Add this bin directory to your system path and you're ready to use the Spring Boot CLI.

SYMBOLICALLY LINKING TO SPRING BOOT   If you're using the Spring Boot CLI on a Unix machine, it may be helpful to create a symbolic link to the unpacked archive and add the symbolic link to your path instead of the actual directory. This will make it easy to upgrade to a newer version of Spring Boot later (or even to flip between versions) by simply reassigning the symbolic link to the directory of the new version.

You can kick the tires a little on the installation by verifying the version of the CLI that was installed:

```
$ spring --version
```

If everything is working, you'll be shown the version of the Spring Boot CLI that was installed.

Even though this is the manual installation, it's an easy option that doesn't require you to have anything additional installed. If you're a Windows user, it's also the only choice available to you. But if you're on a Unix machine and are looking for something a little more automated, then maybe the Software Development Kit Manager can help.

INSTALLING WITH THE SOFTWARE DEVELOPMENT KIT MANAGER

The Software Development Kit Manager (SDKMAN; formerly known as GVM) can be used to install and manage multiple versions of Spring Boot CLI installations. In order to use SDKMAN, you'll need to get and install the SDKMAN tool from http://sdkman .io. The easiest way to install SDKMAN is at the command line:

```
$ curl -s get.sdkman.io | bash
```

Follow the instructions given in the output to complete the SDKMAN installation. For my machine, I had to perform the following command at the command line:

```
$ source "/Users/habuma/.sdkman/bin/sdkman-init.sh"
```

Note that this command will be different for different users. In my case, my home directory is at /Users/habuma, so that's the root of the shell script's path. You'll want to adjust accordingly to fit your situation.

Once SDKMAN is installed, you can install Spring Boot's CLI like this:

```
$ sdk install springboot
$ spring --version
```

Assuming all goes well, you'll be shown the current version of Spring Boot.

If you want to upgrade to a newer version of Spring Boot CLI, you just need to install it and start using it. To find out which versions of Spring Boot CLI are available, use SDKMAN's list command:

```
$ sdk list springboot
```

The list command shows all available versions, including which versions are installed and which is currently in use. From this list you can choose to install a version and then use it. For example, to install Spring Boot CLI version 1.3.0.RELEASE, you'd use the install command, specifying the version:

```
$ sdk install springboot 1.3.0.RELEASE
```

This will install the new version and ask if you'd like to make it the default version. If you choose not to make it the default version or if you wish to switch to a different version, you can use the use command:

```
$ sdk use springboot 1.3.0.RELEASE
```

If you'd like that version to be the default for all shells, use the default command:

```
$ sdk default springboot 1.3.0.RELEASE
```

The nice thing about using SDKMAN to manage your Spring Boot CLI installation is that it allows you to easily switch between different versions of Spring Boot. This will enable you to try out snapshot, milestone, and release candidate builds before they're formally released, but still switch back to a stable release for other work.

INSTALLING WITH HOMEBREW

If you'll be developing on an OS X machine, you have the option of using Homebrew to install the Spring Boot CLI. Homebrew is a package manager for OS X that is used to install many different applications and tools. The easiest way to install Homebrew is by running the installation Ruby script:

```
ruby -e "$(curl -fsSL https://raw.githubusercontent.com/Homebrew/install/
    master/install)"
```

You can read more about Homebrew (and find other installation options) at http://brew.sh.

In order to install the Spring Boot CLI using Homebrew, you'll need to "tap" Pivotal's tap:[1]

```
$ brew tap pivotal/tap
```

Now that Homebrew is tapping Pivotal's tap, you can install the Spring Boot CLI like this:

```
$ brew install springboot
```

Homebrew will install the Spring Boot CLI to /usr/local/bin, and it's ready to go. You can verify the installation by checking the version that was installed:

```
$ spring --version
```

It should respond by showing you the version of Spring Boot that was installed. You can also try running the code in listing 1.1.

INSTALLING WITH MACPORTS

Another Spring Boot CLI installation option for OS X users is to use MacPorts, another popular installer for Mac OS X. In order to use MacPorts to install the Spring Boot

---

[1] Tapping is a way to add additional repositories to those that Homebrew works from. Pivotal, the company behind Spring and Spring Boot, has made the Spring Boot CLI available through its tap.

CLI, you must first install MacPorts, which itself requires that you have Xcode installed. Furthermore, the steps for installing MacPorts vary depending on which version of OS X you're using. Therefore, I refer you to https://www.macports.org/install.php for instructions on installing MacPorts.

Once you have MacPorts installed, you can install the Spring Boot CLI at the command line like this:

```
$ sudo port install spring-boot-cli
```

MacPorts will install the Spring Boot CLI to /opt/local/share/java/spring-boot-cli and put a symbolic link to the binary in /opt/local/bin, which should already be in your system path from installing MacPorts. You can verify the installation by checking the version that was installed:

```
$ spring --version
```

It should respond by showing you the version of Spring Boot that was installed. You can also try running the code in listing 1.1.

ENABLING COMMAND-LINE COMPLETION

Spring Boot's CLI offers a handful of commands for running, packaging, and testing your CLI-based application. Moreover, each of those commands has several options. It can be difficult to remember all that the CLI offers. Command-line completion can help you recall how to use the Spring Boot CLI.

If you've installed the Spring Boot CLI with Homebrew, you already have command-line completion installed. But if you installed Spring Boot manually or with SDKMAN, you'll need to source the scripts or install the completion scripts manually. (Command-line completion isn't an option if you've installed the Spring Boot CLI via MacPorts.)

The completion scripts are found in the Spring Boot CLI installation directory under the shell-completion subdirectory. There are two different scripts, one for BASH and one for zsh. To source the completion script for BASH, you can enter the following at the command line (assuming a SDKMAN installation):

```
$ . ~/.sdkman/springboot/current/shell-completion/bash/spring
```

This will give you Spring Boot CLI completion for the current shell, but you'll have to source this script again each time you start a new shell to keep that feature. Optionally, you can copy the script to your personal or system script directory. The location of the script directory varies for different Unix installations, so consult your system documentation (or Google) for details.

With command completion enabled, you should be able to type `spring` at the command line and then hit the Tab key to be offered options for what to type next. Once you've chosen a command, type `--` (double-hyphen) and then hit Tab again to be shown a list of options for that command.

If you're developing on Windows or aren't using BASH or zsh, you can't use these command-line completion scripts. Even so, you can get command completion if you run the Spring Boot CLI shell:

```
$ spring shell
```

Unlike the command-completion scripts for BASH and zsh (which operate within the BASH/zsh shell), the Spring Boot CLI shell opens a new Spring Boot–specific shell. From this shell, you can execute any of the CLI's commands and get command completion with the Tab key.

The Spring Boot CLI offers an easy way to get started with Spring Boot and to prototype simple applications. As we'll discuss later in chapter 8, it can also be used for production-ready applications, given the right production runtime environment.

Even so, Spring Boot CLI's process is rather unconventional in contrast to how most Java projects are developed. Typically, Java projects use tools like Gradle or Maven to build WAR files that are deployed to an application server. If the CLI model feels a little uncomfortable, you can still take advantage of most of the features of Spring Boot in the context of a traditionally built Java project.[2] And the Spring Initializr can help you get started.

1.2.2 *Initializing a Spring Boot project with Spring Initializr*

Sometimes the hardest part of a project is getting started. You need to set up a directory structure for various project artifacts, create a build file, and populate the build file with dependencies. The Spring Boot CLI removes much of this setup work, but if you favor a more traditional Java project structure, you'll want to look at the Spring Initializr.

The Spring Initializr is ultimately a web application that can generate a Spring Boot project structure for you. It doesn't generate any application code, but it will give you a basic project structure and either a Maven or a Gradle build specification to build your code with. All you need to do is write the application code.

Spring Initializr can be used in several ways:

- Through a web-based interface
- Via Spring Tool Suite
- Via IntelliJ IDEA
- Using the Spring Boot CLI

We'll look at how to use each of these interfaces to the Initializr, starting with the web-based interface.

---

[2] You'll only be giving up features that require the flexibility of the Groovy language, such as automatic dependency and import resolution.

USING SPRING INITIALIZR'S WEB INTERFACE

The most straightforward way to use the Spring Initializr is to point your web browser to http://start.spring.io. You should see a form similar to the one in figure 1.1.

The first two things that the form asks is whether you want to build your project with Maven or Gradle and which version of Spring Boot to use. It defaults to a Maven project using the latest release (non-milestone, non-snapshot) version of Spring Boot, but you're welcome to choose a different one.

On the left side of the form, you're asked to specify some project metadata. At minimum, you must provide the project's group and artifact. But if you click the "Switch to the full version" link, you can specify additional metadata such as version and base package name. This metadata is used to populate the generated Maven pom.xml file (or Gradle build.gradle file).

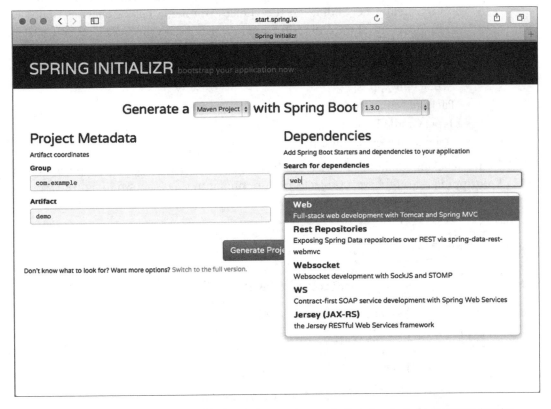

Figure 1.1   Spring Initializr is a web application that generates empty Spring projects as starting points for development.

On the right side of the form, you're asked to specify project dependencies. The easiest way to do that is to type the name of a dependency in the text box. As you type, a list of matching dependencies will appear. Select the one(s) you want and it will be added to the project. If you don't see what you're looking for, click the "Switch to the full version" link to get a complete list of available dependencies.

If you've glanced at appendix B, then you'll recognize that the dependencies offered correspond to Spring Boot starter dependencies. In fact, by selecting any of these dependencies, you're telling the Initializr to add the starters as dependencies to the project's build file. (We'll talk more about Spring Boot starters in chapter 2.)

Once you've filled in the form and made your dependency selections, click the Generate Project button to have Spring Initializr generate a project for you. The project it generates will be presented to you as a zip file (whose name is determined by the value in the Artifact field) that is downloaded by your browser. The contents of the zip file will vary slightly, depending on the choices you made before clicking Generate Project. In any event, the zip file will contain a bare-bones project to get you started developing an application with Spring Boot.

For example, suppose that you were to specify the following to Spring Initializr:

- Artifact: myapp
- Package Name: myapp
- Type: Gradle Project
- Dependencies: Web and JPA

After clicking Generate Project, you'd be given a zip file named myapp.zip. After unzipping it, you'd have a project structure similar to what's shown in figure 1.2.

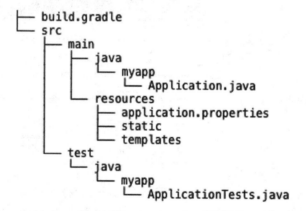

Figure 1.2   Initializr-created projects provide a minimal foundation on which to build Spring Boot applications.

As you can see, there's very little code in this project. Aside from a couple of empty directories, it also includes the following:

- build.gradle—A Gradle build specification. Had you chosen a Maven project, this would be replaced with pom.xml.
- Application.java—A class with a `main()` method to bootstrap the application.
- ApplicationTests.java—An empty JUnit test class instrumented to load a Spring application context using Spring Boot auto-configuration.
- application.properties—An empty properties file for you to add configuration properties to as you see fit.

Even the empty directories have significance in a Spring Boot application. The static directory is where you can put any static content (JavaScript, stylesheets, images, and so on) to be served from the web application. And, as you'll see later, you can put templates that render model data in the templates directory.

You'll probably import the Initializr-created project into your IDE of choice. But if Spring Tool Suite is your IDE of choice, you can create the project directly in the IDE. Let's have a look at Spring Tool Suite's support for creating Spring Boot projects.

CREATING SPRING BOOT PROJECTS IN SPRING TOOL SUITE

Spring Tool Suite[3] has long been a fantastic IDE for developing Spring applications. Since version 3.4.0 it has also been integrated with the Spring Initializr, making it a great way to get started with Spring Boot.

To create a new Spring Boot application in Spring Tool Suite, select the New > Spring Starter Project menu item from the File menu. When you do, Spring Tool Suite will present you with a dialog box similar to the one shown in figure 1.3.

As you can see, this dialog box asks for the same information as the web-based Spring Initializr. In fact, the data you provide here will be fed to Spring Initializr to create a project zip file, just as with the web-based form.

If you'd like to specify where in the filesystem to create the project or whether to add it to a specific working set within the IDE, click the Next button. You'll be presented with a second dialog box like the one shown in figure 1.4.

The Location field specifies where the project will reside on the filesystem. If you take advantage of Eclipse's working sets to organize your projects, you can have the project added to a specific working set by checking the Add Project to Working Sets check box and selecting a working set.

The Site Info section simply describes the URL that will be used to contact the Initializr. For the most part, you can ignore this section. If, however, you were to deploy your own Initializr server (by cloning the code at https://github.com/spring-io/initializr), you could plug in the base URL of your Initializr here.

---

[3] Spring Tool Suite is a distribution of the Eclipse IDE that is outfitted with several features to aid with Spring development. You can download Spring Tool Suite from http://spring.io/tools/sts.

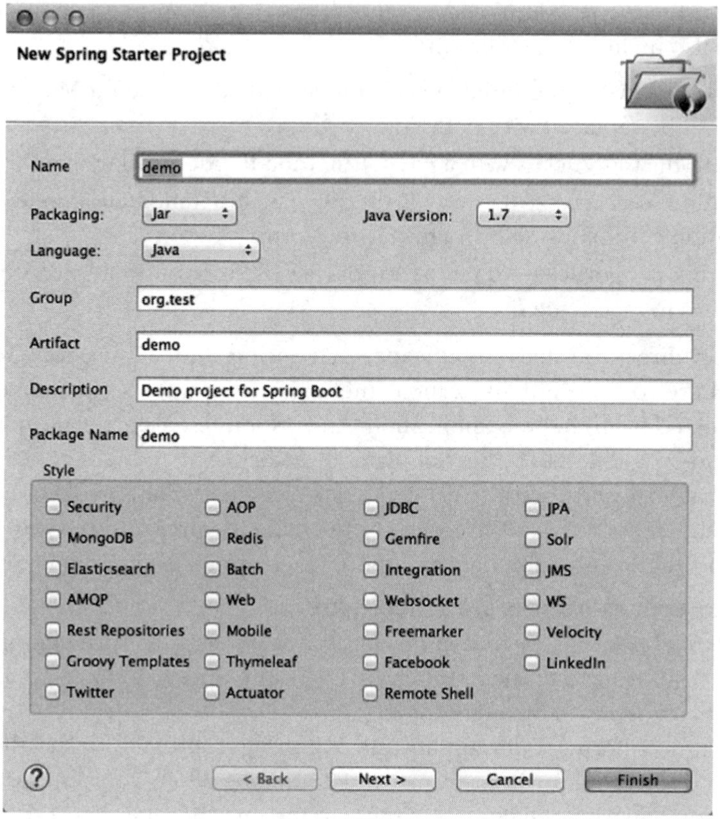

Figure 1.3   Spring Tool Suite integrates with Spring Initializr to create and directly import Spring Boot projects into the IDE.

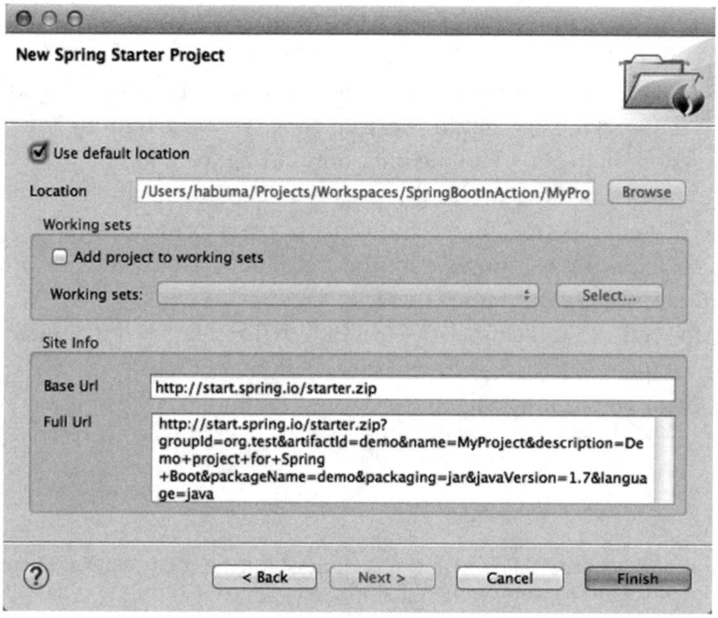

Figure 1.4   The second page of the Spring Starter Project dialog box offers you a chance to specify where the project is created.

Clicking the Finish button kicks off the project generation and import process. It's important to understand that Spring Tool Suite's Spring Starter Project dialog box delegates to the Spring Initializr at http://start.spring.io to produce the project. You must be connected to the internet in order for it to work.

Once the project has been imported into your workspace, you're ready to start developing your application. As you develop the application, you'll find that Spring Tool Suite has a few more Spring Boot-specific tricks up its sleeves. For instance, you can run your application with an embedded server by selecting Run As > Spring Boot Application from the Run menu.

It's important to understand that Spring Tool Suite coordinates with the Initializr via a REST API. Therefore, it will only work if it can connect to the Initializr. If your development machine is offline or Initializr is blocked by a firewall, then using the Spring Start Project wizard in Spring Tool Suite will not work.

CREATING SPRING BOOT PROJECTS IN INTELLIJ IDEA

IntelliJ IDEA is a very popular IDE and, as of IntelliJ IDEA 14.1, it now supports Spring Boot![4]

To get started on a new Spring Boot application in IntelliJ IDEA, select New > Project from the File menu. You'll be presented with the first of a handful of screens (shown in figure 1.5) that ask questions similar to those asked by the Initializr web application and Spring Tool Suite.

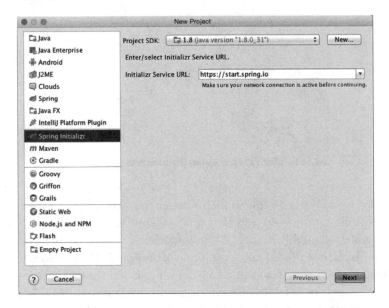

Figure 1.5   The first screen in IntelliJ IDEA's Spring Boot initialization wizard

---

[4] You can get IntelliJ IDEA at https://www.jetbrains.com/idea/. IntelliJ IDEA is a commercial IDE, meaning that you may have to pay for it. You can, however, download a trial of it, and it's freely available for use on open source projects.

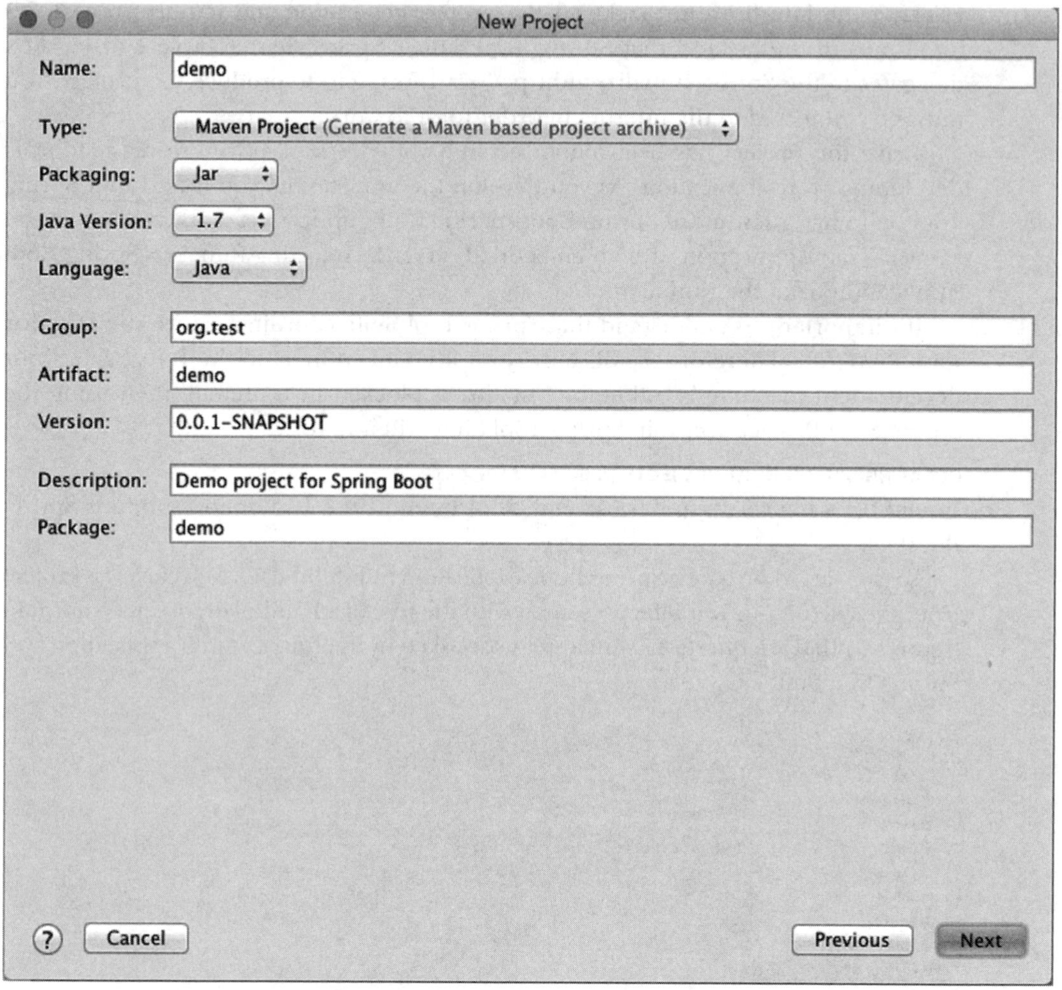

Figure 1.6 Specifying project information in IntelliJ IDEA's Spring Boot initialization wizard

On the initial screen, select Spring Initializr from the project choices on the left. You'll then be prompted to select a Project SDK (essentially, which Java SDK you want to use for the project) and the location of the Initializr web service. Unless you're running your own instance of the Initializr, you'll probably just click the Next button here without making any changes. That will take you to the screen shown in figure 1.6.

The second screen in IntelliJ IDEA's Spring Boot initialization wizard asks some basic questions about the project, such as the project's name, Maven group and artifact, Java version, and whether you want to build it with Maven or Gradle. Once you've described your project, clicking the Next button takes you to the third screen, shown in figure 1.7.

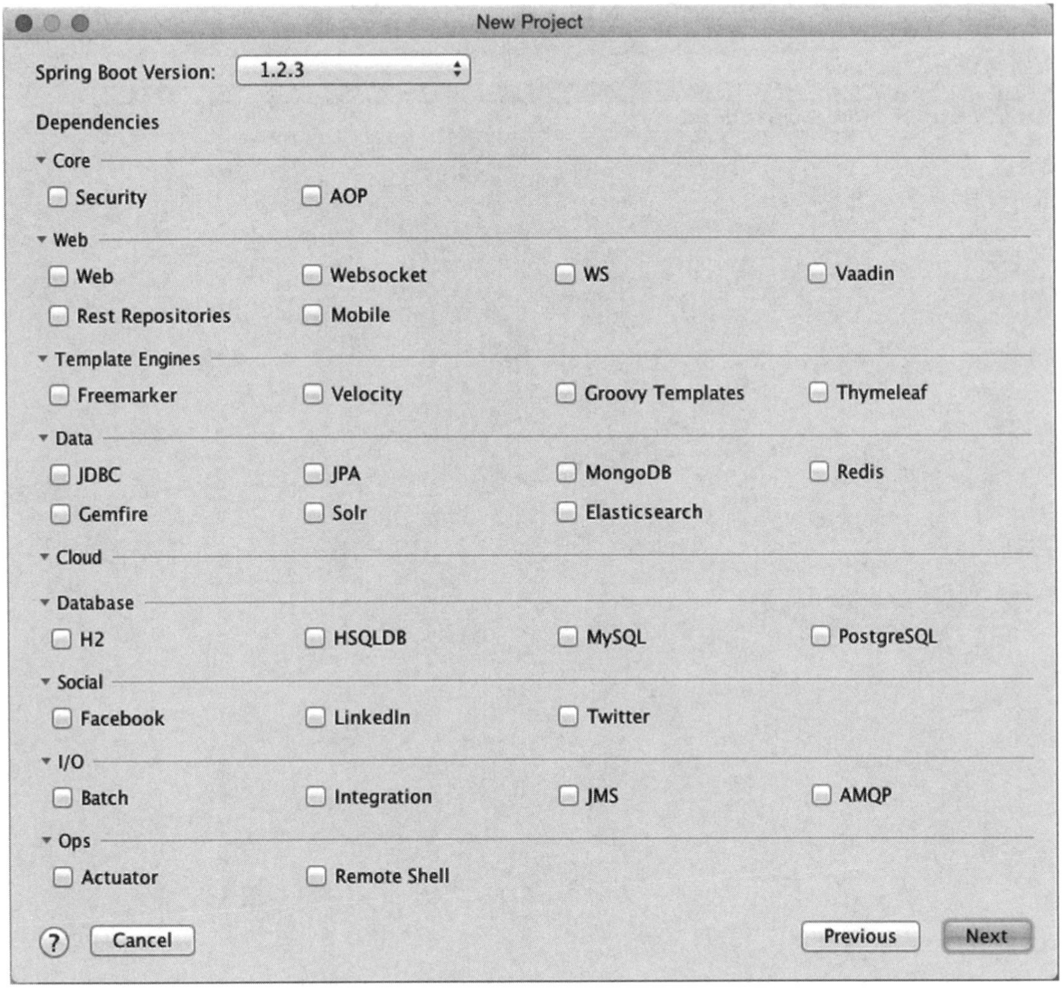

Figure 1.7   Selecting project dependencies in IntelliJ IDEA's Spring Boot initialization wizard

Where the second screen asked you about general project information, the third screen starts by asking you what kind of dependencies you'll need in the project. As before, the check boxes shown on this screen correspond to Spring Boot starter dependencies. After you've made your selections, click Next to be taken to the final screen in the wizard, shown in figure 1.8.

This last screen simply wants you to name the project and tell IntelliJ IDEA where to create it. When you're ready, click the Finish button and you'll have a bare-bones Spring Boot project ready for you in the IDE.

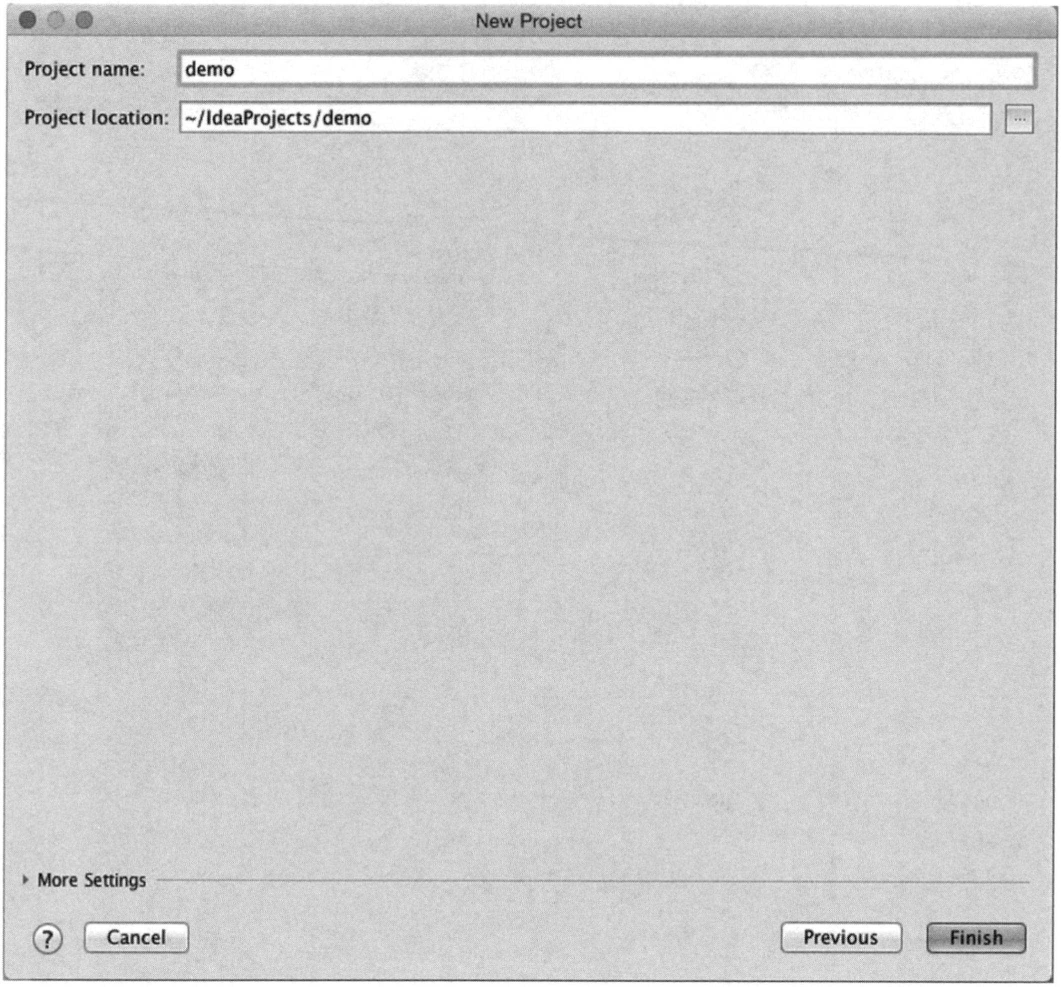

Figure 1.8   The final screen in IntelliJ IDEA's Spring Boot initialization wizard

USING THE INITIALIZR FROM THE SPRING BOOT CLI

As you saw earlier, the Spring Boot CLI is a great way to develop Spring applications by just writing code. However, the Spring Boot CLI also has a few commands that can help you use the Initializr to kick-start development on a more traditional Java project.

The Spring Boot CLI includes an `init` command that acts as a client interface to the Initializr. The simplest use of the `init` command is to create a baseline Spring Boot project:

```
$ spring init
```

After contacting the Initializr web application, the `init` command will conclude by downloading a demo.zip file. If you unzip this project, you'll find a typical project structure with a Maven pom.xml build specification. The Maven build specification is minimal, with only baseline starter dependencies for Spring Boot and testing. You'll probably want a little more than that.

Let's say you want to start out by building a web application that uses JPA for data persistence and that's secured with Spring Security. You can specify those initial dependencies with either - -dependencies or -d:

```
$ spring init -dweb,jpa,security
```

This will give you a demo.zip containing the same project structure as before, but with Spring Boot's web, JPA, and security starters expressed as dependencies in pom.xml. Note that it's important to not type a space between -d and the dependencies. Failing to do so will result in the ZIP file being downloaded with the name web,jpa,security.

Now let's say that you'd rather build this project with Gradle. No problem. Just specify Gradle as the build type with the - -build parameter:

```
$ spring init -dweb,jpa,security --build gradle
```

By default, the build specification for both Maven and Gradle builds will produce an executable JAR file. If you'd rather produce a WAR file, you can specify so with the - -packaging or -p parameter:

```
$ spring init -dweb,jpa,security --build gradle -p war
```

So far, the ways we've used the init command have resulted in a zip file being downloaded. If you'd like for the CLI to crack open that zip file for you, you can specify a directory for the project to be extracted to:

```
$ spring init -dweb,jpa,security --build gradle -p war myapp
```

The last parameter given here indicates that you want the project to be extracted to the myapp directory.

Optionally, if you want the CLI to extract the generated project into the current directory, you can use either the - -extract or the -x parameter:

```
$ spring init -dweb,jpa,security --build gradle -p jar -x
```

The init command has several other parameters, including parameters for building a Groovy-based project, specifying the Java version to compile with, and selecting a version of Spring Boot to build against. You can discover all of the parameters by using the help command:

```
$ spring help init
```

You can also find out what choices are available for those parameters by using the - -list or -l parameter with the init command:

```
$ spring init -l
```

You'll notice that although `spring init -l` lists several parameters that are supported by the Initializr, not all of those parameters are directly supported by the Spring Boot CLI's `init` command. For instance, you can't specify the root package name when initializing a project with the CLI; it will default to "demo". `spring help init` can help you discover what parameters are supported by the CLI's `init` command.

Whether you use Initializr's web-based interface, create your projects from Spring Tool Suite, or use the Spring Boot CLI to initialize a project, projects created using the Spring Boot Initializr have a familiar project layout, not unlike other Java projects you may have developed before.

1.3   *Summary*

Spring Boot is an exciting new way to develop Spring applications with minimal friction from the framework itself. Auto-configuration eliminates much of the boilerplate configuration that infests traditional Spring applications. Spring Boot starters enable you to specify build dependencies by what they offer rather than use explicit library names and version. The Spring Boot CLI takes Spring Boot's frictionless development model to a whole new level by enabling quick and easy development with Groovy from the command line. And the Actuator lets you look inside your running application to see what and how Spring Boot has done.

This chapter has given you a quick overview of what Spring Boot has to offer. You're probably itching to get started on writing a real application with Spring Boot. That's exactly what we'll do in the next chapter. With all that Spring Boot does for you, the hardest part will be turning this page to chapter 2.

Developing your first
Spring Boot application

2

This chapter covers

- Working with Spring Boot starters
- Automatic Spring configuration

When's the last time you went to a supermarket or major retail store and actually had to push the door open? Most large stores have automatic doors that sense your presence and open for you. Any door will enable you to enter a building, but automatic doors don't require that you push or pull them open.

Similarly, many public facilities have restrooms with automatic water faucets and towel dispensers. Although not quite as prevalent as automatic supermarket doors, these devices don't ask much of you and instead are happy to dispense water and towels.

And I honestly don't remember the last time I even saw an ice tray, much less filled it with water or cracked it to get ice for a glass of water. My refrigerator/freezer somehow magically always has ice for me and is at the ready to fill a glass for me.

I bet you can think of countless ways that modern life is automated with devices that work for you, not the other way around. With all of this automation everywhere, you'd think that we'd see more of it in our development tasks. Strangely, that hasn't been so.

Up until recently, creating an application with Spring required you to do a lot of work for the framework. Sure, Spring has long had fantastic features for developing amazing applications. But it was up to you to add all of the library dependencies to the project's build specification. And it was your job to write configuration to tell Spring what to do.

In this chapter, we're going to look at two ways that Spring Boot has added a level of automation to Spring development: starter dependencies and automatic configuration. You'll see how these essential Spring Boot features free you from the tedium and distraction of enabling Spring in your projects and let you focus on actually developing your applications. Along the way, you'll write a small but complete Spring application that puts Spring Boot to work for you.

2.1   *Putting Spring Boot to work*

The fact that you're reading this tells me that you are a reader. Maybe you're quite the bookworm, reading everything you can. Or maybe you only read on an as-needed basis, perhaps picking up this book only because you need to know how to develop applications with Spring.

Whatever the case may be, you're a reader. And readers tend to maintain a reading list of books that they want (or need) to read. Even if it's not a physical list, you probably have a mental list of things you'd like to read.[1]

Throughout this book, we're going to build a simple reading-list application. With it, users can enter information about books they want to read, view the list, and remove books once they've been read. We'll use Spring Boot to help us develop it quickly and with as little ceremony as possible.

To start, we'll need to initialize the project. In chapter 1, we looked at a handful of ways to use the Spring Initializr to kickstart Spring Boot development. Any of those choices will work fine here, so pick the one that suits you best and get ready to put Spring Boot to work.

From a technical standpoint, we're going to use Spring MVC to handle web requests, Thymeleaf to define web views, and Spring Data JPA to persist the reading selections to a database. For now, that database will be an embedded H2 database. Although Groovy is an option, we'll write the application code in Java for now. And we'll use Gradle as our build tool of choice.

If you're using the Initializr, either via its web application or through Spring Tool Suite or IntelliJ IDEA, you'll want to be sure to select the check boxes for Web, Thymeleaf, and JPA. And also remember to check the H2 check box so that you'll have an embedded database to use while developing the application.

As for the project metadata, you're welcome to choose whatever you like. For the purposes of the reading list example, however, I created the project with the information shown in figure 2.1.

---

[1] If you're not a reader, feel free to apply this to movies to watch, restaurants to try, or whatever suits you.

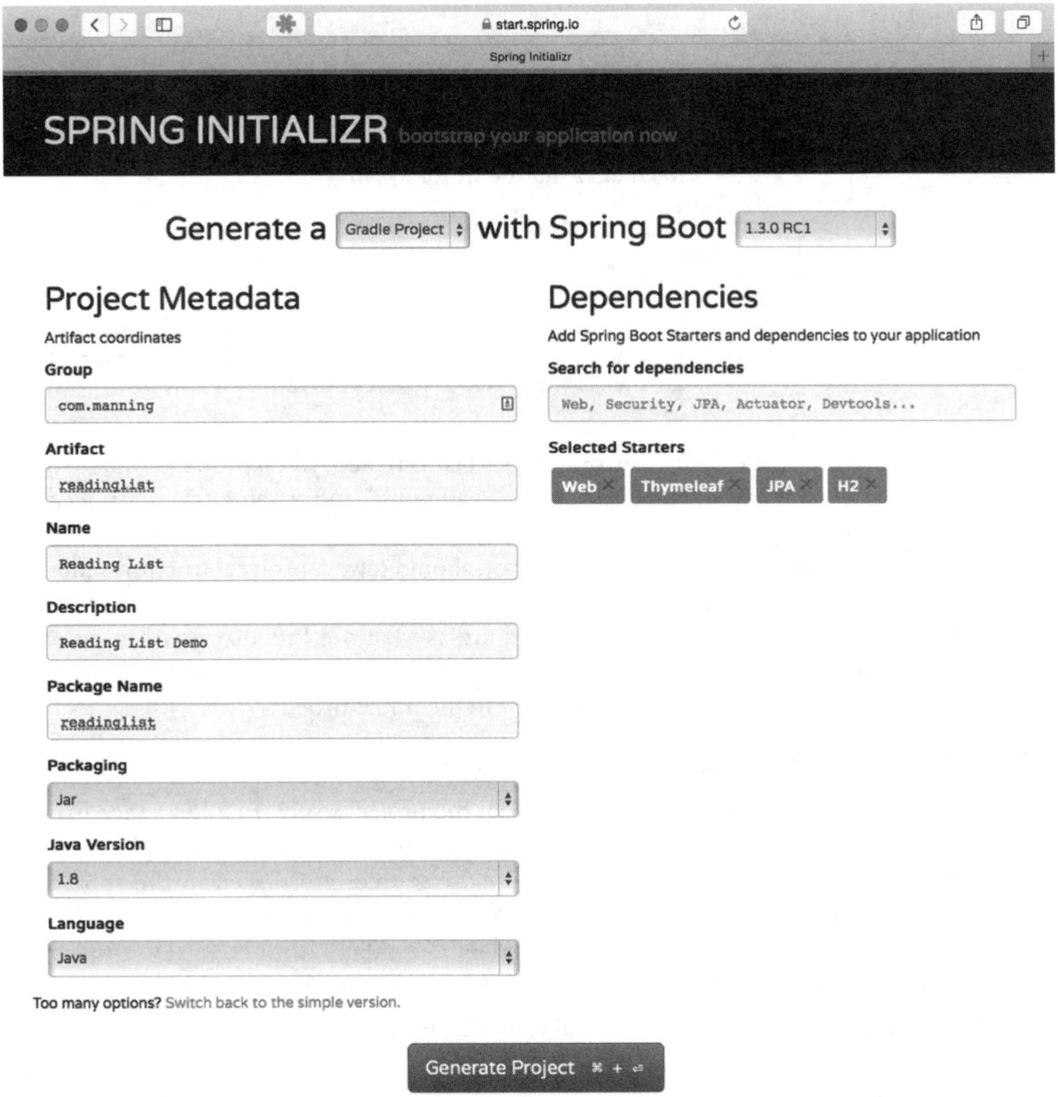

Figure 2.1 Initializing the reading list app via Initializr's web interface

If you're using Spring Tool Suite or IntelliJ IDEA to create the project, adapt the details in figure 2.1 for your IDE of choice.

On the other hand, if you're using the Spring Boot CLI to initialize the application, you can enter the following at the command line:

```
$ spring init -dweb,data-jpa,h2,thymeleaf --build gradle readinglist
```

Remember that the CLI's `init` command doesn't let you specify the project's root package or the project name. The package name will default to "demo" and the project name

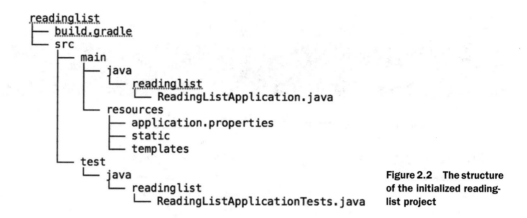

```
readinglist
├── build.gradle
└── src
    ├── main
    │   ├── java
    │   │   └── readinglist
    │   │       └── ReadingListApplication.java
    │   └── resources
    │       ├── application.properties
    │       ├── static
    │       └── templates
    └── test
        └── java
            └── readinglist
                └── ReadingListApplicationTests.java
```

Figure 2.2   The structure of the initialized reading-list project

will default to "Demo". After the project has been created, you'll probably want to open it up and rename the "demo" package to "readinglist" and rename "DemoApplication .java" to "ReadingListApplication.java".

Once the project has been created, you should have a project structure similar to that shown in figure 2.2.

This is essentially the same project structure as what the Initializr gave you in chapter 1. But now that you're going to actually develop an application, let's slow down and take a closer look at what's contained in the initial project.

2.1.1   *Examining a newly initialized Spring Boot project*

The first thing to notice in figure 2.2 is that the project structure follows the layout of a typical Maven or Gradle project. That is, the main application code is placed in the src/main/java branch of the directory tree, resources are placed in the src/main/resources branch, and test code is placed in the src/test/java branch. At this point we don't have any test resources, but if we did we'd put them in src/test/resources.

Digging deeper, you'll see a handful of files sprinkled about the project:

- build.gradle—The Gradle build specification
- ReadingListApplication.java—The application's bootstrap class and primary Spring configuration class
- application.properties—A place to configure application and Spring Boot properties
- ReadingListApplicationTests.java—A basic integration test class

There's a lot of Spring Boot goodness to uncover in the build specification, so I'll save inspection of it until last. Instead, we'll start with ReadingListApplication.java.

BOOTSTRAPPING SPRING

The `ReadingListApplication` class serves two purposes in a Spring Boot application: configuration and bootstrapping. First, it's the central Spring configuration class. Even though Spring Boot auto-configuration eliminates the need for a lot of

Spring configuration, you'll need at least a small amount of Spring configuration to enable auto-configuration. As you can see in listing 2.1, there's only one line of configuration code.

Listing 2.1   ReadingListApplication.java is both a bootstrap class and a configuration class

```
package readinglist;

import org.springframework.boot.SpringApplication;
import org.springframework.boot.autoconfigure.SpringBootApplication;

@SpringBootApplication                                      Enable component-scanning
public class ReadingListApplication {                       and auto-configuration

  public static void main(String[] args) {
    SpringApplication.run(ReadingListApplication.class, args);   Bootstrap the
  }                                                              application

}
```

The `@SpringBootApplication` enables Spring component-scanning and Spring Boot auto-configuration. In fact, `@SpringBootApplication` combines three other useful annotations:

- *Spring's* `@Configuration`—Designates a class as a configuration class using Spring's Java-based configuration. Although we won't be writing a lot of configuration in this book, we'll favor Java-based configuration over XML configuration when we do.
- *Spring's* `@ComponentScan`—Enables component-scanning so that the web controller classes and other components you write will be automatically discovered and registered as beans in the Spring application context. A little later in this chapter, we'll write a simple Spring MVC controller that will be annotated with `@Controller` so that component-scanning can find it.
- *Spring Boot's* `@EnableAutoConfiguration`—This humble little annotation might as well be named `@Abracadabra` because it's the one line of configuration that enables the magic of Spring Boot auto-configuration. This one line keeps you from having to write the pages of configuration that would be required otherwise.

In older versions of Spring Boot, you'd have annotated the `ReadingListApplication` class with all three of these annotations. But since Spring Boot 1.2.0, `@SpringBoot-Application` is all you need.

As I said, `ReadingListApplication` is also a bootstrap class. There are several ways to run Spring Boot applications, including traditional WAR file deployment. But for now the `main()` method here will enable you to run your application as an executable JAR file from the command line. It passes a reference to the `ReadingListApplication` class to `SpringApplication.run()`, along with the command-line arguments, to kick off the application.

In fact, even though you haven't written any application code, you can still build the application at this point and try it out. The easiest way to build and run the application is to use the bootRun task with Gradle:

```
$ gradle bootRun
```

The bootRun task comes from Spring Boot's Gradle plugin, which we'll discuss more in section 2.12. Alternatively, you can build the project with Gradle and run it with java at the command line:

```
$ gradle build
...
$ java -jar build/libs/readinglist-0.0.1-SNAPSHOT.jar
```

The application should start up fine and enable a Tomcat server listening on port 8080. You can point your browser at http://localhost:8080 if you want, but because you haven't written a controller class yet, you'll be met with an HTTP 404 (Not Found) error and an error page. Before this chapter is finished, though, that URL will serve your reading-list application.

You'll almost never need to change ReadingListApplication.java. If your application requires any additional Spring configuration beyond what Spring Boot auto-configuration provides, it's usually best to write it into separate @Configuration-configured classes. (They'll be picked up and used by component-scanning.) In exceptionally simple cases, though, you could add custom configuration to ReadingListApplication.java.

TESTING SPRING BOOT APPLICATIONS

The Initializr also gave you a skeleton test class to help you get started with writing tests for your application. But ReadingListApplicationTests (listing 2.2) is more than just a placeholder for tests—it also serves as an example of how to write tests for Spring Boot applications.

Listing 2.2 @SpringApplicationConfiguration loads a Spring application context

```java
package readinglist;

import org.junit.Test;
import org.junit.runner.RunWith;
import org.springframework.boot.test.SpringApplicationConfiguration;
import org.springframework.test.context.junit4.SpringJUnit4ClassRunner;
import org.springframework.test.context.web.WebAppConfiguration;

import readinglist.ReadingListApplication;

@RunWith(SpringJUnit4ClassRunner.class)
@SpringApplicationConfiguration(                      ⟵  Load context via
        classes = ReadingListApplication.class)           Spring Boot
@WebAppConfiguration
```

```
public class ReadingListApplicationTests {

  @Test                                            Test that the
  public void contextLoads() {        ◁──────      context loads
  }

}
```

In a typical Spring integration test, you'd annotate the test class with `@Context-Configuration` to specify how the test should load the Spring application context. But in order to take full advantage of Spring Boot magic, the `@SpringApplication-Configuration` annotation should be used instead. As you can see from listing 2.2, `ReadingListApplicationTests` is annotated with `@SpringApplicationConfiguration` to load the Spring application context from the `ReadingListApplication` configuration class.

ReadingListApplicationTests also includes one simple test method, `context-Loads()`. It's so simple, in fact, that it's an empty method. But it's sufficient for the purpose of verifying that the application context loads without any problems. If the configuration defined in `ReadingListApplication` is good, the test will pass. If there are any problems, the test will fail.

Of course, you'll add some of your own tests as we flesh out the application. But the `contextLoads()` method is a fine start and verifies every bit of functionality provided by the application at this point. We'll look more at how to test Spring Boot applications in chapter 4.

CONFIGURING APPLICATION PROPERTIES

The application.properties file given to you by the Initializr is initially empty. In fact, this file is completely optional, so you could remove it completely without impacting the application. But there's also no harm in leaving it in place.

We'll definitely find opportunity to add entries to application.properties later. For now, however, if you want to poke around with application.properties, try adding the following line:

```
server.port=8000
```

With this line, you're configuring the embedded Tomcat server to listen on port 8000 instead of the default port 8080. You can confirm this by running the application again.

This demonstrates that the application.properties file comes in handy for fine-grained configuration of the stuff that Spring Boot automatically configures. But you can also use it to specify properties used by application code. We'll look at several examples of both uses of application.properties in chapter 3.

The main thing to notice is that at no point do you explicitly ask Spring Boot to load application.properties for you. By virtue of the fact that application.properties exists, it will be loaded and its properties made available for configuring both Spring and application code.

We're almost finished reviewing the contents of the initialized project. But we have one last artifact to look at. Let's see how a Spring Boot application is built.

2.1.2 *Dissecting a Spring Boot project build*

For the most part, a Spring Boot application isn't much different from any Spring application, which isn't much different from any Java application. Therefore, building a Spring Boot application is much like building any Java application. You have your choice of Gradle or Maven as the build tool, and you express build specifics much the same as you would in an application that doesn't employ Spring Boot. But there are a few small details about working with Spring Boot that benefit from a little extra help in the build.

Spring Boot provides build plugins for both Gradle and Maven to assist in building Spring Boot projects. Listing 2.3 shows the build.gradle file created by Initializr, which applies the Spring Boot Gradle plugin.

Listing 2.3   Using the Spring Boot Gradle plugin

```
buildscript {
  ext {
    springBootVersion = `1.3.0.RELEASE`
  }
  repositories {
    mavenCentral()
  }
  dependencies {
    classpath("org.springframework.boot:spring-boot-gradle-plugin:          ⟵  Depend on Spring Boot plugin
        ➡ ${springBootVersion}")
  }
}

apply plugin: 'java'
apply plugin: 'eclipse'
apply plugin: 'idea'          ⟵  Apply Spring Boot plugin
apply plugin: 'spring-boot'

jar {
  baseName = 'readinglist'
  version = '0.0.1-SNAPSHOT'
}
sourceCompatibility = 1.7
targetCompatibility = 1.7

repositories {
  mavenCentral()
}

dependencies {                                                                ⟵  Starter dependencies
  compile("org.springframework.boot:spring-boot-starter-web")
  compile("org.springframework.boot:spring-boot-starter-data-jpa")
```

```
  compile("org.springframework.boot:spring-boot-starter-thymeleaf")
  runtime("com.h2database:h2")
  testCompile("org.springframework.boot:spring-boot-starter-test")
}

eclipse {
  classpath {
    containers.remove('org.eclipse.jdt.launching.JRE_CONTAINER')
    containers 'org.eclipse.jdt.launching.JRE_CONTAINER/org.eclipse.jdt.internal.
          ➥ debug.ui.launcher.StandardVMType/JavaSE-1.7'
  }
}

task wrapper(type: Wrapper) {
  gradleVersion = '1.12'
}
```

On the other hand, had you chosen to build your project with Maven, the Initializr would have given you a pom.xml file that employs Spring Boot's Maven plugin, as shown in listing 2.4.

Listing 2.4 Using the Spring Boot Maven plugin and parent starter

```
<?xml version="1.0" encoding="UTF-8"?>
<project xmlns="http://maven.apache.org/POM/4.0.0"
  xmlns:xsi="http://www.w3.org/2001/XMLSchema-instance"
  xsi:schemaLocation="http://maven.apache.org/POM/4.0.0
      http://maven.apache.org/xsd/maven-4.0.0.xsd">

  <modelVersion>4.0.0</modelVersion>

  <groupId>com.manning</groupId>
  <artifactId>readinglist</artifactId>
  <version>0.0.1-SNAPSHOT</version>
  <packaging>jar</packaging>

  <name>ReadingList</name>
  <description>Reading List Demo</description>
                                                      Inherit versions
                                                      from starter parent
  <parent>
    <groupId>org.springframework.boot</groupId>
    <artifactId>spring-boot-starter-parent</artifactId>
    <version>{springBootVersion}</version>
    <relativePath/> <!-- lookup parent from repository -->
  </parent>

  <dependencies>                                      Starter
    <dependency>                                      dependencies
      <groupId>org.springframework.boot</groupId>
      <artifactId>spring-boot-starter-web</artifactId>
    </dependency>
    <dependency>
      <groupId>org.springframework.boot</groupId>
```

```
      <artifactId>spring-boot-starter-data-jpa</artifactId>
    </dependency>
    <dependency>
      <groupId>org.springframework.boot</groupId>
      <artifactId>spring-boot-starter-thymeleaf</artifactId>
    </dependency>
    <dependency>
      <groupId>com.h2database</groupId>
      <artifactId>h2</artifactId>
    </dependency>
    <dependency>
      <groupId>org.springframework.boot</groupId>
      <artifactId>spring-boot-starter-test</artifactId>
      <scope>test</scope>
    </dependency>
  </dependencies>

  <properties>
    <project.build.sourceEncoding>
      UTF-8
    </project.build.sourceEncoding>
    <start-class>readinglist.Application</start-class>
    <java.version>1.7</java.version>
  </properties>

  <build>
    <plugins>
      <plugin>                                           ◁──────  Apply Spring
        <groupId>org.springframework.boot</groupId>                Boot plugin
        <artifactId>spring-boot-maven-plugin</artifactId>
      </plugin>
    </plugins>
  </build>

</project>
```

Whether you choose Gradle or Maven, Spring Boot's build plugins contribute to the build in two ways. First, you've already seen how you can use the bootRun task to run the application with Gradle. Similarly, the Spring Boot Maven plugin provides a spring-boot:run goal that achieves the same thing if you're using a Maven build.

The main feature of the build plugins is that they're able to package the project as an executable uber-JAR. This includes packing all of the application's dependencies within the JAR and adding a manifest to the JAR with entries that make it possible to run the application with java -jar.

In addition to the build plugins, notice that the Maven build in listing 2.4 has "spring-boot-starter-parent" as a parent. By rooting the project in the parent starter, the build can take advantage of Maven dependency management to inherit dependency versions for several commonly used libraries so that you don't have to explicitly specify the versions when declaring dependencies. Notice that none of the <dependency> entries in this pom.xml file specify any versions.

Unfortunately, Gradle doesn't provide the same kind of dependency management as Maven. That's why the Spring Boot Gradle plugin offers a third feature; it simulates dependency management for several common Spring and Spring-related dependencies. Consequently, the build.gradle file in listing 2.3 doesn't specify any versions for any of its dependencies.

Speaking of those dependencies, there are only five dependencies expressed in either build specification. And, with the exception of the H2 dependency you added manually, they all have artifact IDs that are curiously prefixed with "spring-boot-starter-". These are Spring Boot starter dependencies, and they offer a bit of build-time magic for Spring Boot applications. Let's see what benefit they provide.

2.2 *Using starter dependencies*

To understand the benefit of Spring Boot starter dependencies, let's pretend for a moment that they don't exist. What kind of dependencies would you add to your build without Spring Boot? Which Spring dependencies do you need to support Spring MVC? Do you remember the group and artifact IDs for Thymeleaf? Which version of Spring Data JPA should you use? Are all of these compatible?

Uh-oh. Without Spring Boot starter dependencies, you've got some homework to do. All you want to do is develop a Spring web application with Thymeleaf views that persists its data via JPA. But before you can even write your first line of code, you have to go figure out what needs to be put into the build specification to support your plan.

After much consideration (and probably a lot of copy and paste from some other application's build that has similar dependencies) you arrive at the following dependencies block in your Gradle build specification:

```
compile("org.springframework:spring-web:4.1.6.RELEASE")
compile("org.thymeleaf:thymeleaf-spring4:2.1.4.RELEASE")
compile("org.springframework.data:spring-data-jpa:1.8.0.RELEASE")
compile("org.hibernate:hibernate-entitymanager:jar:4.3.8.Final")
compile("com.h2database:h2:1.4.187")
```

This dependency list is fine and might even work. But how do you know? What kind of assurance do you have that the versions you chose for those dependencies are even compatible with each other? They might be, but you won't know until you build the application and run it. And how do you know that the list of dependencies is complete? With not a single line of code having been written, you're still a long way from kicking the tires on your build.

Let's take a step back and recall what it is we want to do. We're looking to build an application with these traits:

- It's a web application
- It uses Thymeleaf
- It persists data to a relational database via Spring Data JPA

Wouldn't it be simpler if we could just specify those facts in the build and let the build sort out what we need? That's exactly what Spring Boot starter dependencies do.

2.2.1 *Specifying facet-based dependencies*

Spring Boot addresses project dependency complexity by providing several dozen "starter" dependencies. A starter dependency is essentially a Maven POM that defines transitive dependencies on other libraries that together provide support for some functionality. Many of these starter dependencies are named to indicate the facet or kind of functionality they provide.

For example, the reading-list application is going to be a web application. Rather than add several individually chosen library dependencies to the project build, it's much easier to simply declare that this is a web application. You can do that by adding Spring Boot's web starter to the build.

We also want to use Thymeleaf for web views and persist data with JPA. Therefore, we need the Thymeleaf and Spring Data JPA starter dependencies in the build.

For testing purposes, we also want libraries that will enable us to run integration tests in the context of Spring Boot. Therefore, we also want a test-time dependency on Spring Boot's test starter.

Taken altogether, we have the following five dependencies that the Initializr provided in the Gradle build:

```
dependencies {
  compile "org.springframework.boot:spring-boot-starter-web"
  compile "org.springframework.boot:spring-boot-starter-thymeleaf"
  compile "org.springframework.boot:spring-boot-starter-data-jpa"
  compile "com.h2database:h2"
  testCompile("org.springframework.boot:spring-boot-starter-test")
}
```

As you saw earlier, the easiest way to get these dependencies into your application's build is to select the Web, Thymeleaf, and JPA check boxes in the Initializr. But if you didn't do that when initializing the project, you can certainly go back and add them later by editing the generated build.gradle or pom.xml.

Via transitive dependencies, adding these four dependencies is the equivalent of adding several dozen individual libraries to the build. Some of those transitive dependencies include such things as Spring MVC, Spring Data JPA, Thymeleaf, as well as any transitive dependencies that those dependencies declare.

The most important thing to notice about the four starter dependencies is that they were only as specific as they needed to be. We didn't say that we wanted Spring MVC; we simply said we wanted to build a web application. We didn't specify JUnit or any other testing tools; we just said we wanted to test our code. The Thymeleaf and Spring Data JPA starters are a bit more specific, but only because there's no less-specific way to declare that you want Thymeleaf and Spring Data JPA.

The four starters in this build are only a few of the many starter dependencies that Spring Boot offers. Appendix B lists all of the starters with some detail on what each one transitively brings to a project build.

In no case did we need to specify the version. The versions of the starter dependencies themselves are determined by the version of Spring Boot you're using. The starter dependencies themselves determine the versions of the various transitive dependencies that they pull in.

Not knowing what versions of the various libraries are used may be a little unsettling to you. Be encouraged to know that Spring Boot has been tested to ensure that all of the dependencies pulled in are compatible with each other. It's actually very liberating to just specify a starter dependency and not have to worry about which libraries and which versions of those libraries you need to maintain.

But if you really must know what it is that you're getting, you can always get that from the build tool. In the case of Gradle, the `dependencies` task will give you a dependency tree that includes every library your project is using and their versions:

```
$ gradle dependencies
```

You can get a similar dependency tree from a Maven build with the `tree` goal of the dependency plugin:

```
$ mvn dependency:tree
```

For the most part, you should never concern yourself with the specifics of what each Spring Boot starter dependency provides. Generally, it's enough to know that the web starter enables you to build a web application, the Thymeleaf starter enables you to use Thymeleaf templates, and the Spring Data JPA starter enables data persistence to a database using Spring Data JPA.

But what if, in spite of the testing performed by the Spring Boot team, there's a problem with a starter dependency's choice of libraries? How can you override the starter?

2.2.2 *Overriding starter transitive dependencies*

Ultimately, starter dependencies are just dependencies like any other dependency in your build. That means you can use the facilities of the build tool to selectively override transitive dependency versions, exclude transitive dependencies, and certainly specify dependencies for libraries not covered by Spring Boot starters.

For example, consider Spring Boot's web starter. Among other things, the web starter transitively depends on the Jackson JSON library. This library is handy if you're building a REST service that consumes or produces JSON resource representations. But if you're using Spring Boot to build a more traditional human-facing web application, you may not need Jackson. Even though it shouldn't hurt anything to include it, you can trim the fat off of your build by excluding Jackson as a transitive dependency.

If you're using Gradle, you can exclude transitive dependencies like this:

```
compile("org.springframework.boot:spring-boot-starter-web") {
  exclude group: 'com.fasterxml.jackson.core'
}
```

In Maven, you can exclude transitive dependencies with the <exclusions> element. The following <dependency> for the Spring Boot web starter has <exclusions> to keep Jackson out of the build:

```
<dependency>
  <groupId>org.springframework.boot</groupId>
  <artifactId>spring-boot-starter-web</artifactId>
  <exclusions>
    <exclusion>
      <groupId>com.fasterxml.jackson.core</groupId>
    </exclusion>
  </exclusions>
</dependency>
```

On the other hand, maybe having Jackson in the build is fine, but you want to build against a different version of Jackson than what the web starter references. Suppose that the web starter references Jackson version 2.3.4, but you'd rather user version 2.4.3.[2] Using Maven, you can express the desired dependency directly in your project's pom.xml file like this:

```
<dependency>
  <groupId>com.fasterxml.jackson.core</groupId>
  <artifactId>jackson-databind</artifactId>
  <version>2.4.3</version>
</dependency>
```

Maven always favors the closest dependency, meaning that because you've expressed this dependency in your project's build, it will be favored over the one that's transitively referred to by another dependency.

Similarly, if you're building with Gradle, you can specify the newer version of Jackson in your build.gradle file like this:

```
compile("com.fasterxml.jackson.core:jackson-databind:2.4.3")
```

This dependency works in Gradle because it's newer than the version transitively referred to by Spring Boot's web starter. But suppose that instead of using a newer version of Jackson, you'd like to use an older version. Unlike Maven, Gradle favors the newest version of a dependency. Therefore, if you want to use an older version of

---

[2] The versions mentioned here are for illustration purposes only. The actual version of Jackson referenced by Spring Boot's web starter will be determined by which version of Spring Boot you are using.

Jackson, you'll have to express the older version as a dependency in your build and exclude it from being transitively resolved by the web starter dependency:

```
compile("org.springframework.boot:spring-boot-starter-web") {
  exclude group: 'com.fasterxml.jackson.core'
}
compile("com.fasterxml.jackson.core:jackson-databind:2.3.1")
```

In any case, take caution when overriding the dependencies that are pulled in transitively by Spring Boot starter dependencies. Although different versions may work fine, there's a great amount of comfort that can be taken knowing that the versions chosen by the starters have been tested to play well together. You should only override these transitive dependencies under special circumstances (such as a bug fix in a newer version).

Now that we have an empty project structure and build specification ready, it's time to start developing the application itself. As we do, we'll let Spring Boot handle the configuration details while we focus on writing the code that provides the reading-list functionality.

2.3 *Using automatic configuration*

In a nutshell, Spring Boot auto-configuration is a runtime (more accurately, application startup-time) process that considers several factors to decide what Spring configuration should and should not be applied. To illustrate, here are a few examples of the kinds of things that Spring Boot auto-configuration might consider:

- Is Spring's `JdbcTemplate` available on the classpath? If so and if there is a `DataSource` bean, then auto-configure a `JdbcTemplate` bean.
- Is Thymeleaf on the classpath? If so, then configure a Thymeleaf template resolver, view resolver, and template engine.
- Is Spring Security on the classpath? If so, then configure a very basic web security setup.

There are nearly 200 such decisions that Spring Boot makes with regard to auto-configuration every time an application starts up, covering such areas as security, integration, persistence, and web development. All of this auto-configuration serves to keep you from having to explicitly write configuration unless absolutely necessary.

The funny thing about auto-configuration is that it's difficult to show in the pages of this book. If there's no configuration to write, then what is there to point to and discuss?

2.3.1 *Focusing on application functionality*

One way to gain an appreciation of Spring Boot auto-configuration would be for me to spend the next several pages showing you the configuration that's required in the absence of Spring Boot. But there are already several great books on Spring that show you that, and showing it again wouldn't help us get the reading-list application written any quicker.

Instead of wasting time talking about Spring configuration, knowing that Spring Boot is going to take care of that for us, let's see how taking advantage of Spring Boot auto-configuration keeps us focused on writing application code. I can think of no better way to do that than to start writing the application code for the reading-list application.

DEFINING THE DOMAIN

The central domain concept in our application is a book that's on a reader's reading list. Therefore, we'll need to define an entity class that represents a book. Listing 2.5 shows how the Book type is defined.

Listing 2.5 The Book class represents a book in the reading list

```
package readinglist;

import javax.persistence.Entity;
import javax.persistence.GeneratedValue;
import javax.persistence.GenerationType;
import javax.persistence.Id;

@Entity
public class Book {

  @Id
  @GeneratedValue(strategy=GenerationType.AUTO)
  private Long id;
  private String reader;
  private String isbn;
  private String title;
  private String author;
  private String description;

  public Long getId() {
    return id;
  }

  public void setId(Long id) {
    this.id = id;
  }

  public String getReader() {
    return reader;
  }

  public void setReader(String reader) {
    this.reader = reader;
  }

  public String getIsbn() {
    return isbn;
```

```
  }

  public void setIsbn(String isbn) {
    this.isbn = isbn;
  }

  public String getTitle() {
    return title;
  }

  public void setTitle(String title) {
    this.title = title;
  }

  public String getAuthor() {
    return author;
  }

  public void setAuthor(String author) {
    this.author = author;
  }

  public String getDescription() {
    return description;
  }

  public void setDescription(String description) {
    this.description = description;
  }

}
```

As you can see, the `Book` class is a simple Java object with a handful of properties describing a book and the necessary accessor methods. It's annotated with `@Entity` designating it as a JPA entity. The `id` property is annotated with `@Id` and `@Generated-Value` to indicate that this field is the entity's identity and that its value will be automatically provided.

DEFINING THE REPOSITORY INTERFACE

Next up, we need to define the repository through which the `ReadingList` objects will be persisted to the database. Because we're using Spring Data JPA, that task is a simple matter of creating an interface that extends Spring Data JPA's `JpaRepository` interface:

```
package readinglist;

import java.util.List;
import org.springframework.data.jpa.repository.JpaRepository;

public interface ReadingListRepository extends JpaRepository<Book, Long> {

  List<Book> findByReader(String reader);

}
```

By extending JpaRepository, ReadingListRepository inherits 18 methods for performing common persistence operations. The JpaRepository interface is parameterized with two parameters: the domain type that the repository will work with, and the type of its ID property. In addition, I've added a findByReader() method through which a reading list can be looked up given a reader's username.

If you're wondering about who will implement ReadingListRepository and the 18 methods it inherits, don't worry too much about it. Spring Data provides a special magic of its own, making it possible to define a repository with just an interface. The interface will be implemented automatically at runtime when the application is started.

CREATING THE WEB INTERFACE

Now that we have the application's domain defined and a repository for persisting objects from that domain to the database, all that's left is to create the web front-end. A Spring MVC controller like the one in listing 2.6 will handle HTTP requests for the application.

Listing 2.6   A Spring MVC controller that fronts the reading list application

```java
package readinglist;

import org.springframework.beans.factory.annotation.Autowired;
import org.springframework.stereotype.Controller;
import org.springframework.ui.Model;
import org.springframework.web.bind.annotation.PathVariable;
import org.springframework.web.bind.annotation.RequestMapping;
import org.springframework.web.bind.annotation.RequestMethod;

import java.util.List;

@Controller
@RequestMapping("/")
public class ReadingListController {

  private ReadingListRepository readingListRepository;

  @Autowired
  public ReadingListController(
          ReadingListRepository readingListRepository) {
    this.readingListRepository = readingListRepository;
  }

  @RequestMapping(value="/{reader}", method=RequestMethod.GET)
  public String readersBooks(
      @PathVariable("reader") String reader,
      Model model) {

    List<Book> readingList =
        readingListRepository.findByReader(reader);
    if (readingList != null) {
      model.addAttribute("books", readingList);
    }
    return "readingList";
  }
}
```

```
@RequestMapping(value="/{reader}", method=RequestMethod.POST)
public String addToReadingList(
        @PathVariable("reader") String reader, Book book) {
  book.setReader(reader);
  readingListRepository.save(book);
  return "redirect:/{reader}";
}

}
```

ReadingListController is annotated with @Controller in order to be picked up by component-scanning and automatically be registered as a bean in the Spring application context. It's also annotated with @RequestMapping to map all of its handler methods to a base URL path of "/".

The controller has two methods:

- readersBooks()—Handles HTTP GET requests for /{reader} by retrieving a Book list from the repository (which was injected into the controller's constructor) for the reader specified in the path. It puts the list of Book into the model under the key "books" and returns "readingList" as the logical name of the view to render the model.

- addToReadingList()—Handles HTTP POST requests for /{reader}, binding the data in the body of the request to a Book object. This method sets the Book object's reader property to the reader's name, and then saves the modified Book via the repository's save() method. Finally, it returns by specifying a redirect to /{reader} (which will be handled by the other controller method).

The readersBooks() method concludes by returning "readingList" as the logical view name. Therefore, we must also create that view. I decided at the outset of this project that we'd be using Thymeleaf to define the application views, so the next step is to create a file named readingList.html in src/main/resources/templates with the following content.

Listing 2.7　The Thymeleaf template that presents a reading list

```
<html>
  <head>
    <title>Reading List</title>
    <link rel="stylesheet" th:href="@{/style.css}"></link>
  </head>

  <body>
    <h2>Your Reading List</h2>
    <div th:unless="${#lists.isEmpty(books)}">
      <dl th:each="book : ${books}">
        <dt class="bookHeadline">
          <span th:text="${book.title}">Title</span> by
          <span th:text="${book.author}">Author</span>
          (ISBN: <span th:text="${book.isbn}">ISBN</span>)
```

```
        </dt>
        <dd class="bookDescription">
          <span th:if="${book.description}"
                th:text="${book.description}">Description</span>
          <span th:if="${book.description eq null}">
                No description available</span>
        </dd>
      </dl>
    </div>
    <div th:if="${#lists.isEmpty(books)}">
      <p>You have no books in your book list</p>
    </div>

    <hr/>

    <h3>Add a book</h3>
    <form method="POST">
      <label for="title">Title:</label>
        <input type="text" name="title" size="50"></input><br/>
      <label for="author">Author:</label>
        <input type="text" name="author" size="50"></input><br/>
      <label for="isbn">ISBN:</label>
        <input type="text" name="isbn" size="15"></input><br/>
      <label for="description">Description:</label><br/>
        <textarea name="description" cols="80" rows="5">
        </textarea><br/>
      <input type="submit"></input>
    </form>

  </body>
</html>
```

This template defines an HTML page that is conceptually divided into two parts. At the top of the page is a list of books that are in the reader's reading list. At the bottom is a form the reader can use to add a new book to the reading list.

For aesthetic purposes, the Thymeleaf template references a stylesheet named style.css. That file should be created in src/main/resources/static and look like this:

```
body {
    background-color: #cccccc;
    font-family: arial,helvetica,sans-serif;
}

.bookHeadline {
    font-size: 12pt;
    font-weight: bold;
}

.bookDescription {
    font-size: 10pt;
}

label {
    font-weight: bold;
}
```

This stylesheet is simple and doesn't go overboard to make the application look nice. But it serves our purposes and, as you'll soon see, serves to demonstrate a piece of Spring Boot's auto-configuration.

Believe it or not, that's a complete application. Every single line has been presented to you in this chapter. Take a moment, flip back through the previous pages, and see if you can find any configuration. In fact, aside from the three lines of configuration in listing 2.1 (which essentially turn on auto-configuration), you didn't have to write any Spring configuration.

Despite the lack of Spring configuration, this complete Spring application is ready to run. Let's fire it up and see how it looks.

2.3.2 *Running the application*

There are several ways to run a Spring Boot application. Earlier, in section 2.5, we discussed how to run the application via Maven and Gradle, as well as how to build and run an executable JAR. Later, in chapter 8 you'll also see how to build a WAR file that can be deployed in a traditional manner to a Java web application server such as Tomcat.

If you're developing your application with Spring Tool Suite, you also have the option of running the application within your IDE by selecting the project and choosing Run As > Spring Boot App from the Run menu, as shown in figure 2.3.

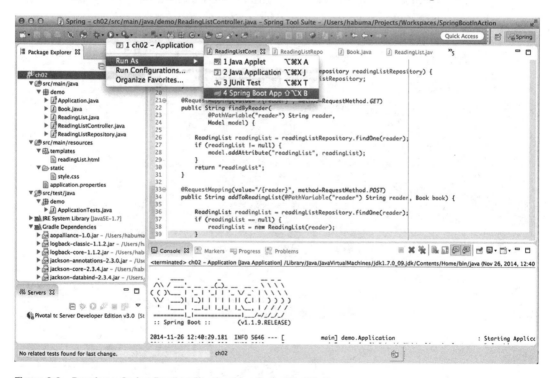

Figure 2.3   Running a Spring Boot application from Spring Tool Suite

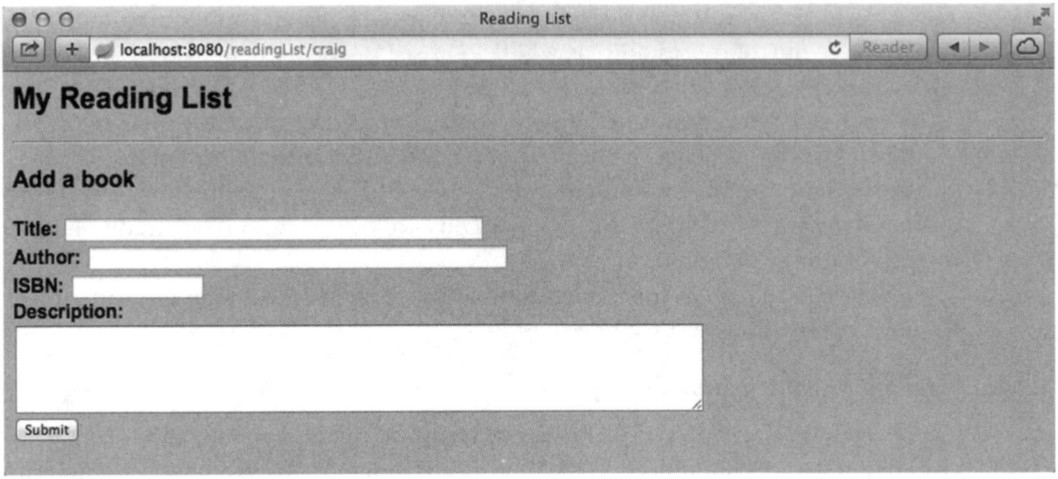

Figure 2.4   An initially empty reading list

Assuming everything works, your browser should show you an empty reading list along with a form for adding a new book to the list. Figure 2.4 shows what it might look like.

Now go ahead and use the form to add a few books to your reading list. After you do, your list might look something like figure 2.5.

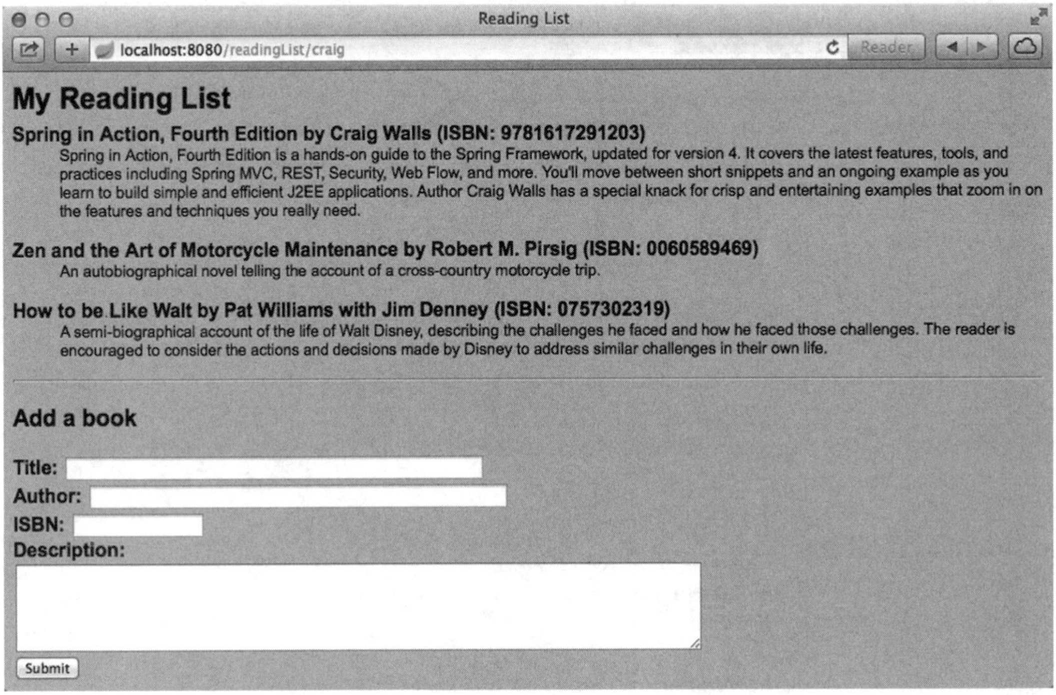

Figure 2.5   The reading list after a few books have been added

Feel free to take a moment to play around with the application. When you're ready, move on and we'll see how Spring Boot made it possible to write an entire Spring application with no Spring configuration code.

2.3.3 *What just happened?*

As I said, it's hard to describe auto-configuration when there's no configuration to point at. So instead of spending time discussing what you don't have to do, this section has focused on what you do need to do—namely, write the application code.

But certainly there is some configuration somewhere, right? Configuration is a central element of the Spring Framework, and there must be something that tells Spring how to run your application.

When you add Spring Boot to your application, there's a JAR file named spring-boot-autoconfigure that contains several configuration classes. Every one of these configuration classes is available on the application's classpath and has the opportunity to contribute to the configuration of your application. There's configuration for Thymeleaf, configuration for Spring Data JPA, configuration for Spring MVC, and configuration for dozens of other things you might or might not want to take advantage of in your Spring application.

What makes all of this configuration special, however, is that it leverages Spring's support for conditional configuration, which was introduced in Spring 4.0. Conditional configuration allows for configuration to be available in an application, but to be ignored unless certain conditions are met.

It's easy enough to write your own conditions in Spring. All you have to do is implement the Condition interface and override its matches() method. For example, the following simple condition class will only pass if JdbcTemplate is available on the classpath:

```
package readinglist;
import org.springframework.context.annotation.Condition;
import org.springframework.context.annotation.ConditionContext;
import org.springframework.core.type.AnnotatedTypeMetadata;

public class JdbcTemplateCondition implements Condition {
  @Override
  public boolean matches(ConditionContext context,
                         AnnotatedTypeMetadata metadata) {
    try {
      context.getClassLoader().loadClass(
          "org.springframework.jdbc.core.JdbcTemplate");
      return true;
    } catch (Exception e) {
      return false;
    }
  }
}
```

You can use this custom condition class when you declare beans in Java:

```
@Conditional(JdbcTemplateCondition.class)
public MyService myService() {
    ...
}
```

In this case, the MyService bean will only be created if the JdbcTemplateCondition passes. That is to say that the MyService bean will only be created if JdbcTemplate is available on the classpath. Otherwise, the bean declaration will be ignored.

Although the condition shown here is rather simple, Spring Boot defines several more interesting conditions and applies them to the configuration classes that make up Spring Boot auto-configuration. Spring Boot applies conditional configuration by defining several special conditional annotations and using them in its configuration classes. Table 2.1 lists the conditional annotations that Spring Boot provides.

Table 2.1   Conditional annotations used in auto-configuration

Conditional annotation	Configuration applied if...?
@ConditionalOnBean	...the specified bean has been configured
@ConditionalOnMissingBean	...the specified bean has not already been configured
@ConditionalOnClass	...the specified class is available on the classpath
@ConditionalOnMissingClass	...the specified class is not available on the classpath
@ConditionalOnExpression	...the given Spring Expression Language (SpEL) expression evaluates to true
@ConditionalOnJava	...the version of Java matches a specific value or range of versions
@ConditionalOnJndi	...there is a JNDI InitialContext available and optionally given JNDI locations exist
@ConditionalOnProperty	...the specified configuration property has a specific value
@ConditionalOnResource	...the specified resource is available on the classpath
@ConditionalOnWebApplication	...the application is a web application
@ConditionalOnNotWebApplication	...the application is not a web application

Generally, you shouldn't ever need to look at the source code for Spring Boot's auto-configuration classes. But as an illustration of how the annotations in table 2.1 are used, consider this excerpt from DataSourceAutoConfiguration (provided as part of Spring Boot's auto-configuration library):

```
@Configuration
@ConditionalOnClass({ DataSource.class, EmbeddedDatabaseType.class })
@EnableConfigurationProperties(DataSourceProperties.class)
```

```
@Import({ Registrar.class, DataSourcePoolMetadataProvidersConfiguration.class
        })
public class DataSourceAutoConfiguration {

  ...

}
```

As you can see, DataSourceAutoConfiguration is a @Configuration-annotated class that (among other things) imports some additional configuration from other configuration classes and defines a few beans of its own. What's most important to notice here is that DataSourceAutoConfiguration is annotated with @ConditionalOnClass to require that both DataSource and EmbeddedDatabaseType be available on the classpath. If they aren't available, then the condition fails and any configuration provided by DataSourceAutoConfiguration will be ignored.

Within DataSourceAutoConfiguration there's a nested JdbcTemplateConfiguration class that provides auto-configuration of a JdbcTemplate bean:

```
@Configuration
@Conditional(DataSourceAutoConfiguration.DataSourceAvailableCondition.class)
protected static class JdbcTemplateConfiguration {

  @Autowired(required = false)
  private DataSource dataSource;

  @Bean
  @ConditionalOnMissingBean(JdbcOperations.class)
  public JdbcTemplate jdbcTemplate() {
    return new JdbcTemplate(this.dataSource);
  }

  ...

}
```

JdbcTemplateConfiguration is an annotation with the low-level @Conditional to require that the DataSourceAvailableCondition pass—essentially requiring that a DataSource bean be available or that one will be created by auto-configuration. Assuming that a DataSource bean will be available, the @Bean-annotated jdbcTemplate() method configures a JdbcTemplate bean. But jdbcTemplate() is annotated with @ConditionalOnMissingBean so that the bean will be configured only if there is not already a bean of type JdbcOperations (the interface that JdbcTemplate implements).

There's a lot more to DataSourceAutoConfiguration and to the other auto-configuration classes provided by Spring Boot than is shown here. But this should give you a taste of how Spring Boot leverages conditional configuration to implement auto-configuration.

As it directly pertains to our example, the following configuration decisions are made by the conditionals in auto-configuration:

- Because H2 is on the classpath, an embedded H2 database bean will be created. This bean is of type `javax.sql.DataSource`, which the JPA implementation (Hibernate) will need to access the database.
- Because Hibernate Entity Manager is on the classpath (transitively via Spring Data JPA), auto-configuration will configure beans needed to support working with Hibernate, including Spring's `LocalContainerEntityManagerFactory-Bean` and `JpaVendorAdapter`.
- Because Spring Data JPA is on the classpath, Spring Data JPA will be configured to automatically create repository implementations from repository interfaces.
- Because Thymeleaf is on the classpath, Thymeleaf will be configured as a view option for Spring MVC, including a Thymeleaf template resolver, template engine, and view resolver. The template resolver is configured to resolve templates from /templates relative to the root of the classpath.
- Because Spring MVC is on the classpath (thanks to the web starter dependency), Spring's `DispatcherServlet` will be configured and Spring MVC will be enabled.
- Because this is a Spring MVC web application, a resource handler will be registered to serve static content from /static relative to the root of the classpath. (The resource handler will also serve static content from /public, /resources, and /META-INF/resources).
- Because Tomcat is on the classpath (transitively referred to by the web starter dependency), an embedded Tomcat container will be started to listen on port 8080.

The main takeaway here, though, is that Spring Boot auto-configuration takes on the burden of configuring Spring so that you can focus on writing your application.

2.4   *Summary*

By taking advantage of Spring Boot starter dependencies and auto-configuration, you can more quickly and easily develop Spring applications. Starter dependencies help you focus on the type of functionality your application needs rather than on the specific libraries and versions that provide that functionality. Meanwhile, auto-configuration frees you from the boilerplate configuration that is common among Spring applications without Spring Boot.

Although auto-configuration is a convenient way to work with Spring, it also represents an opinionated approach to Spring development. What if you want or need to configure Spring differently? In the next chapter, we'll look at how you can override Spring Boot auto-configuration as needed to achieve the goals of your application. You'll also see how to apply some of the same techniques to configure your own application components.

Customizing configuration

Freedom of choice is an awesome thing. If you've ever ordered a pizza (who hasn't?) then you know that you have full control over what toppings are placed on the pie. If you ask for sausage, pepperoni, green peppers, and extra cheese, then you're essentially configuring the pizza to your precise specifications.

On the other hand, most pizza places also offer a form of auto-configuration. You can ask for the meat-lover's pizza, the vegetarian pizza, the spicy Italian pizza, or the ultimate example of pizza auto-configuration, the supreme pizza. When ordering one of these pizzas, you don't have to explicitly specify the toppings. The type of pizza ordered implies what toppings are used.

But what if you like all of the toppings of the supreme pizza, but also want jalapenos and would rather not have mushrooms? Does your taste for spicy food and aversion to fungus mean that auto-configuration isn't applicable and that you must explicitly configure your pizza? Absolutely not. Most pizzerias will let you customize your pizza, even if you started with a preconfigured option from the menu.

Working with traditional Spring configuration is much like ordering a pizza and explicitly specifying all of the toppings. You have full control over what goes into your Spring configuration, but explicitly declaring all of the beans in the application is non-optimal. On the other hand, Spring Boot auto-configuration is like ordering a specialty pizza from the menu. It's easier to let Spring Boot handle the details than to declare each and every bean in the application context.

Fortunately, Spring Boot auto-configuration is flexible. Like the pizzeria that will leave off the mushrooms and add jalapenos to your pizza, Spring Boot will let you step in and influence how it applies auto-configuration.

In this chapter, we're going to look at two ways to influence auto-configuration: explicit configuration overrides and fine-grained configuration with properties. We'll also look at how Spring Boot has provided hooks for you to plug in a custom error page.

3.1   *Overriding Spring Boot auto-configuration*

Generally speaking, if you can get the same results with no configuration as you would with explicit configuration, no configuration is the no-brainer choice. Why would you do extra work, writing and maintaining extra configuration code, if you can get what you need without it?

Most of the time, the auto-configured beans are exactly what you want and there's no need to override them. But there are some cases where the best guess that Spring Boot can make during auto-configuration probably isn't going to be good enough.

A prime example of a case where auto-configuration isn't good enough is when you're applying security to your application. Security is not one-size-fits-all, and there are decisions around application security that Spring Boot has no business making for you. Although Spring Boot provides some basic auto-configuration for security, you'll certainly want to override it to meet your specific security requirements.

To see how to override auto-configuration with explicit configuration, we'll start by adding Spring Security to the reading-list example. After seeing what you get for free with auto-configuration, we'll then override the basic security configuration to fit a particular situation.

3.1.1   *Securing the application*

Spring Boot auto-configuration makes securing an application a piece of cake. All you need to do is add the security starter to the build. For Gradle, the following dependency will do:

```
compile("org.springframework.boot:spring-boot-starter-security")
```

Or, if you're using Maven, add this <dependency> to your build's <dependencies> block:

```
<dependency>
  <groupId>org.springframework.boot</groupId>
  <artifactId>spring-boot-starter-security</artifactId>
</dependency>
```

That's it! Rebuild your application and run it. It's now a secure web application! The security starter adds Spring Security (among other things) to the application's classpath. With Spring Security on the classpath, auto-configuration kicks in and a very basic Spring Security setup is created.

If you try to open the application in your browser, you'll be immediately met with an HTTP Basic authentication dialog box. The username you'll need to enter is "user". As for the password, it's a bit trickier. The password is randomly generated and written to the logs each time the application is run. You'll need to look through the logging messages (written to `stdout` by default) and look for a line that looks something like this:

```
Using default security password: d9d8abe5-42b5-4f20-a32a-76ee3df658d9
```

I can't say for certain, but I'm guessing that this particular security setup probably isn't ideal for you. First, HTTP Basic dialog boxes are clunky and not very user-friendly. And I'll bet that you don't develop too many applications that have only one user who doesn't mind looking up their password from a log file. Therefore, you'll probably want to make a few changes to how Spring Security is configured. At very least, you'll want to provide a nice-looking login page and specify an authentication service that operates against a database or LDAP-based user store.

Let's see how to do that by writing some explicit Spring Security configuration to override the auto-configured security scheme.

3.1.2   Creating a custom security configuration

Overriding auto-configuration is a simple matter of explicitly writing the configuration as if auto-configuration didn't exist. This explicit configuration can take any form that Spring supports, including XML configuration and Groovy-based configuration.

For our purposes, we're going to focus on Java configuration when writing explicit configuration. In the case of Spring Security, this means writing a configuration class that extends `WebSecurityConfigurerAdapter`. `SecurityConfig` in listing 3.1 is the configuration class we'll use.

Listing 3.1   Explicit configuration to override auto-configured security

```
package readinglist;

import org.springframework.beans.factory.annotation.Autowired;
import org.springframework.context.annotation.Configuration;
import org.springframework.security.config.annotation.authentication.
                        builders.AuthenticationManagerBuilder;
import org.springframework.security.config.annotation.web.builders.
                        HttpSecurity;
```

```
import org.springframework.security.config.annotation.web.configuration.
                                      EnableWebSecurity;
import org.springframework.security.config.annotation.web.configuration.
                                      WebSecurityConfigurerAdapter;
import org.springframework.security.core.userdetails.UserDetails;
import org.springframework.security.core.userdetails.UserDetailsService;
import org.springframework.security.core.userdetails.
                                      UsernameNotFoundException;


@Configuration
@EnableWebSecurity
public class SecurityConfig extends WebSecurityConfigurerAdapter {

  @Autowired
  private ReaderRepository readerRepository;

  @Override
  protected void configure(HttpSecurity http) throws Exception {
    http
      .authorizeRequests()
        .antMatchers("/").access("hasRole('READER')")      Require READER
        .antMatchers("/**").permitAll()                    access

      .and()

      .formLogin()                          Set login
        .loginPage("/login")                form path
        .failureUrl("/login?error=true");
  }

  @Override
  protected void configure(
            AuthenticationManagerBuilder auth) throws Exception {
    auth
      .userDetailsService(new UserDetailsService() {        Define custom
        @Override                                           UserDetailsService
        public UserDetails loadUserByUsername(String username)
            throws UsernameNotFoundException {
          return readerRepository.findOne(username);
        }
      });
  }

}
```

SecurityConfig is a very basic Spring Security configuration. Even so, it does a lot of what we need to customize security of the reading-list application. By providing this custom security configuration class, we're asking Spring Boot to skip security auto-configuration and to use our security configuration instead.

Configuration classes that extend WebSecurityConfigurerAdapter can override two different configure() methods. In SecurityConfig, the first configure() method specifies that requests for "/" (which ReadingListController's methods are mapped to) require an authenticated user with the READER role. All other request paths are configured for open access to all users. It also designates /login as the path for the login page as well as the login failure page (along with an error attribute).

Spring Security offers several options for authentication, including authentication against JDBC-backed user stores, LDAP-backed user stores, and in-memory user stores. For our application, we're going to authenticate users against the database via JPA. The second configure() method sets this up by setting a custom user details service. This service can be any class that implements UsersDetailsService and is used to look up user details given a username. The following listing has given it an anonymous inner-class implementation that simply calls the findOne() method on an injected ReaderRepository (which is a Spring Data JPA repository interface).

Listing 3.2 A repository interface for persisting readers

```
package readinglist;
import org.springframework.data.jpa.repository.JpaRepository;

public interface ReaderRepository                              Persist readers
        extends JpaRepository<Reader, String> {   ◁───┘  via JPA
}
```

As with BookRepository, there's no need to write an implementation of Reader-Repository. Because it extends JpaRepository, Spring Data JPA will automatically create an implementation of it at runtime. This affords you 18 methods for working with Reader entities.

Speaking of Reader entities, the Reader class (shown in listing 3.3) is the final piece of the puzzle. It's a simple JPA entity type with a few fields to capture the username, password, and full name of the user.

Listing 3.3 A JPA entity that defines a Reader

```
package readinglist;
import java.util.Arrays;
import java.util.Collection;
import javax.persistence.Entity;
import javax.persistence.Id;
import org.springframework.security.core.GrantedAuthority;
import org.springframework.security.core.authority.SimpleGrantedAuthority;
import org.springframework.security.core.userdetails.UserDetails;

@Entity
public class Reader implements UserDetails {

  private static final long serialVersionUID = 1L;

  @Id
  private String username;
  private String fullname;        Reader fields
  private String password;
```

```
    public String getUsername() {
      return username;
    }

    public void setUsername(String username) {
      this.username = username;
    }

    public String getFullname() {
      return fullname;
    }

    public void setFullname(String fullname) {
      this.fullname = fullname;
    }

    public String getPassword() {
      return password;
    }

    public void setPassword(String password) {
      this.password = password;
    }

    // UserDetails methods

    @Override                                                           Grant
    public Collection<? extends GrantedAuthority> getAuthorities() {  ⟵ READER
      return Arrays.asList(new SimpleGrantedAuthority("READER"));        privilege
    }

    @Override
    public boolean isAccountNonExpired() {    ⟵
      return true;
    }

    @Override
    public boolean isAccountNonLocked() {     ⟵
      return true;
    }                                                        Do not expire,
                                                             lock, or disable
    @Override
    public boolean isCredentialsNonExpired() {  ⟵
      return true;
    }

    @Override
    public boolean isEnabled() {    ⟵
      return true;
    }

}
```

As you can see, Reader is annotated with @Entity to make it a JPA entity. In addition, its username field is annotated with @Id to designate it as the entity's ID. This seemed like a natural choice, as the username should uniquely identify the Reader.

You'll also notice that `Reader` implements the `UserDetails` interface and several of its methods. This makes it possible to use a `Reader` object to represent a user in Spring Security. The `getAuthorities()` method is overridden to always grant users READER authority. The `isAccountNonExpired()`, `isAccountNonLocked()`, `isCredentials-NonExpired()`, and `isEnabled()` methods are all implemented to return true so that the reader account is never expired, locked, or revoked.

Rebuild and restart the application and you should be able to log in to the application as one of the readers.

> **KEEPING IT SIMPLE** In a larger application, the authorities granted to a user might themselves be entities and be maintained in a separate database table. Likewise, the `boolean` values indicating whether an account is non-expired, non-locked, and enabled might be fields drawn from the database. For our purposes, however, I've decided to keep these details simple so as not to distract from what it is we're really discussing ... namely, overriding Spring Boot auto-configuration.

There's a lot more we could do with regard to security configuration,[1] but this is all we need here, and it does demonstrate how to override the security auto-configuration provided by Spring Boot.

Again, all you need to do to override Spring Boot auto-configuration is to write explicit configuration. Spring Boot will see your configuration, step back, and let your configuration take precedence. To understand how this works, let's take a look under the covers of Spring Boot auto-configuration to see how it works and how it allows itself to be overridden.

3.1.3   *Taking another peek under the covers of auto-configuration*

As we discussed in section 2.3.3, Spring Boot auto-configuration comes with several configuration classes, any of which can be applied in your application. All of this configuration uses Spring 4.0's conditional configuration support to make runtime decisions as to whether or not Spring Boot's configuration should be used or ignored.

For the most part, the `@ConditionalOnMissingBean` annotation described in table 2.1 is what makes it possible to override auto-configuration. The `JdbcTemplate` bean defined in Spring Boot's `DataSourceAutoConfiguration` is a very simple example of how `@ConditionalOnMissingBean` works:

```
@Bean
@ConditionalOnMissingBean(JdbcOperations.class)
public JdbcTemplate jdbcTemplate() {
  return new JdbcTemplate(this.dataSource);
}
```

---

[1] For a deeper dive into Spring Security, have a look at chapters 9 and 14 of my *Spring in Action, Fourth Edition* (Manning, 2014).

The jdbcTemplate() method is annotated with @Bean and is ready to configure a JdbcTemplate bean if needed. But it's also annotated with @ConditionalOnMissing-Bean, which requires that there not already be a bean of type JdbcOperations (the interface that JdbcTemplate implements). If there's already a JdbcOperations bean, then the condition will fail and the jdbcTemplate() bean method will not be used.

What circumstances would result in there already being a JdbcOperation bean? Spring Boot is designed to load application-level configuration before considering its auto-configuration classes. Therefore, if you've already configured a JdbcTemplate bean, then there will be a bean of type JdbcOperations by the time that auto-configuration takes place, and the auto-configured JdbcTemplate bean will be ignored.

As it pertains to Spring Security, there are several configuration classes considered during auto-configuration. It would be impractical to go over each of them in detail here, but the one that's most significant in allowing us to override Spring Boot's auto-configured security configuration is SpringBootWebSecurityConfiguration. Here's an excerpt from that configuration class:

```
@Configuration
@EnableConfigurationProperties
@ConditionalOnClass({ EnableWebSecurity.class })
@ConditionalOnMissingBean(WebSecurityConfiguration.class)
@ConditionalOnWebApplication
public class SpringBootWebSecurityConfiguration {

    ...

}
```

As you can see, SpringBootWebSecurityConfiguration is annotated with a few conditional annotations. Per the @ConditionalOnClass annotation, the @Enable-WebSecurity annotation must be available on the classpath. And per @ConditionalOnWebApplication, the application must be a web application. But it's the @ConditionalOnMissingBean annotation that makes it possible for our security configuration class to be used instead of SpringBootWebSecurityConfiguration.

The @ConditionalOnMissingBean requires that there not already be a bean of type WebSecurityConfiguration. Although it may not be apparent on the surface, by annotating our SecurityConfig class with @EnableWebSecurity, we're indirectly creating a bean of type WebSecurityConfiguration. Therefore, by the time auto-configuration takes place, there will already be a bean of type WebSecurityConfiguration, the @ConditionalOnMissingBean condition will fail, and any configuration offered by SpringBootWebSecurityConfiguration will be skipped over.

Although Spring Boot's auto-configuration and @ConditionalOnMissingBean make it possible for you to explicitly override any of the beans that would otherwise be auto-configured, it's not always necessary to go to that extreme. Let's see how you can set a few simple configuration properties to tweak the auto-configured components.

3.2 *Externalizing configuration with properties*

When dealing with application security, you'll almost certainly want to take full charge of the configuration. But it would be a shame to give up on auto-configuration just to tweak a small detail such as a server port number or a logging level. If you need to set a database URL, wouldn't it be easier to set a property somewhere than to completely declare a data source bean?

As it turns out, the beans that are automatically configured by Spring Boot offer well over 300 properties for fine-tuning. When you need to adjust the settings, you can specify these properties via environment variables, Java system properties, JNDI, command-line arguments, or property files.

To get started with these properties, let's look at a very simple example. You may have noticed that Spring Boot emits an ascii-art banner when you run the reading-list application from the command line. If you'd like to disable the banner, you can do so by setting a property named `spring.main.show-banner` to `false`. One way of doing that is to specify the property as a command-line parameter when you run the app:

```
$ java -jar readinglist-0.0.1-SNAPSHOT.jar --spring.main.show-banner=false
```

Another way is to create a file named application.properties that includes the following line:

```
spring.main.show-banner=false
```

Or, if you'd prefer, create a YAML file named application.yml that looks like this:

```
spring:
  main:
    show-banner: false
```

You could also set the property as an environment variable. For example, if you're using the bash or zsh shell, you can set it with the `export` command:

```
$ export spring_main_show_banner=false
```

Note the use of underscores instead of periods and dashes, as required for environment variable names.

There are, in fact, several ways to set properties for a Spring Boot application. Spring Boot will draw properties from several property sources, including the following:

1 Command-line arguments
2 JNDI attributes from java:comp/env
3 JVM system properties
4 Operating system environment variables
5 Randomly generated values for properties prefixed with `random.*` (referenced when setting other properties, such as `` `${random.long}``)
6 An application.properties or application.yml file outside of the application

7 An application.properties or application.yml file packaged inside of the application

8 Property sources specified by `@PropertySource`

9 Default properties

This list is in order of precedence. That is, any property set from a source higher in the list will override the same property set on a source lower in the list. Command-line arguments, for instance, override properties from any other property source.

As for the application.properties and application.yml files, they can reside in any of four locations:

1 Externally, in a /config subdirectory of the directory from which the application is run

2 Externally, in the directory from which the application is run

3 Internally, in a package named "config"

4 Internally, at the root of the classpath

Again, this list is in order of precedence. That is, an application.properties file in a /config subdirectory will override the same properties set in an application.properties file in the application's classpath.

Also, I've found that if you have both application.properties and application.yml side by side at the same level of precedence, properties in application.yml will override those in application.properties.

Disabling an ascii-art banner is just a small example of how to use properties. Let's look at a few more common ways to tweak the auto-configured beans.

3.2.1 *Fine-tuning auto-configuration*

As I said, there are well over 300 properties that you can set to tweak and adjust the beans in a Spring Boot application. Appendix C gives an exhaustive list of these properties, but it'd be impossible to go over each and every one of them here. Instead, let's examine a few of the more commonly useful properties exposed by Spring Boot.

DISABLING TEMPLATE CACHING

If you've been tinkering around much with the reading-list application, you may have noticed that changes to any of the Thymeleaf templates aren't applied unless you restart the application. That's because Thymeleaf templates are cached by default. This improves application performance because you only compile the templates once, but it's difficult to make changes on the fly during development.

You can disable Thymeleaf template caching by setting `spring.thymeleaf.cache` to `false`. You can do this when you run the application from the command line by setting it as a command-line argument:

```
$ java -jar readinglist-0.0.1-SNAPSHOT.jar --spring.thymeleaf.cache=false
```

Or, if you'd rather have caching turned off every time you run the application, you might create an application.yml file with the following lines:

```
spring:
  thymeleaf:
    cache: false
```

You'll want to make sure that this application.yml file doesn't follow the application into production, or else your production application won't realize the performance benefits of template caching.

As a developer, you may find it convenient to have template caching turned off all of the time while you make changes to the templates. In that case, you can turn off Thymeleaf caching via an environment variable:

```
$ export spring_thymeleaf_cache=false
```

Even though we're using Thymeleaf for our application's views, template caching can be turned off for Spring Boot's other supported template options by setting these properties:

- `spring.freemarker.cache` (Freemarker)
- `spring.groovy.template.cache` (Groovy templates)
- `spring.velocity.cache` (Velocity)

By default, all of these properties are `true`, meaning that the templates are cached. Setting them to `false` disables caching.

CONFIGURING THE EMBEDDED SERVER

When you run a Spring Boot application from the command line (or via Spring Tool Suite), the application starts an embedded server (Tomcat, by default) listening on port 8080. This is fine for most cases, but it can become problematic if you find yourself needing to run multiple applications simultaneously. If all of the applications try to start a Tomcat server on the same port, there'll be port collisions starting with the second application.

If, for any reason, you'd rather the server listen on a different port, then all you need to do is set the `server.port` property. If this is a one-time change, it's easy enough to do this as a command-line argument:

```
$ java -jar readinglist-0.0.1-SNAPSHOT.jar --server.port=8000
```

But if you want the port change to be more permanent, you could set `server.port` in one of the other supported locations. For instance, you might set it in an application.yml file at the root of the application's classpath:

```
server:
  port: 8000
```

Aside from adjusting the server's port, you might also need to enable the server to serve securely over HTTPS. The first thing you'll need to do is create a keystore using the JDK's `keytool` utility:

```
$ keytool -keystore mykeys.jks -genkey -alias tomcat -keyalg RSA
```

You'll be asked several questions about your name and organization, most of which are irrelevant. But when asked for a password, be sure to remember what you choose. For the sake of this example, I chose "letmein" as the password.

Now you just need to set a few properties to enable HTTPS in the embedded server. You could specify them all at the command line, but that would be terribly inconvenient. Instead, you'll probably set them in application.properties or application.yml. In application.yml, they might look like this:

```
server:
  port: 8443
  ssl:
    key-store: file:///path/to/mykeys.jks
    key-store-password: letmein
    key-password: letmein
```

Here the `server.port` property is being set to 8443, a common choice for development HTTPS servers. The `server.ssl.key-store` property should be set to the path where the keystore file was created. Here it's shown with a file:// URL to load it from the filesystem, but if you package it within the application JAR file, you should use a classpath: URL to reference it. And both the `server.ssl.key-store-password` and `server.ssl.key-password` properties are set to the password that was given when creating the keystore.

With these properties in place, your application should be listening for HTTPS requests on port 8443. (Depending on which browser you're using, you may encounter a warning about the server not being able to verify its identity. This is nothing to worry about when serving from localhost during development.)

CONFIGURING LOGGING

Most applications provide some form of logging. And even if your application doesn't log anything directly, the libraries that your application uses will certainly log their activity.

By default, Spring Boot configures logging via Logback (http://logback.qos.ch) to log to the console at INFO level. You've probably already seen plenty of INFO-level logging as you've run the application and other examples.

Swapping out Logback for another logging implementation

Generally speaking, you should never need to switch logging implementations; Logback should suit you fine. However, if you decide that you'd rather use Log4j or Log4j2, you'll need to change your dependencies to include the appropriate starter for the logging implementation you want to use and to exclude Logback.

(continued)

For Maven builds, you can exclude Logback by excluding the default logging starter transitively resolved by the root starter dependency:

```
<dependency>
  <groupId>org.springframework.boot</groupId>
  <artifactId>spring-boot-starter</artifactId>
  <exclusions>
    <exclusion>
      <groupId>org.springframework.boot</groupId>
      <artifactId>spring-boot-starter-logging</artifactId>
    </exclusion>
  </exclusions>
</dependency>
```

In Gradle, it's easiest to place the exclusion under the `configurations` section:

```
configurations {
  all*.exclude group:'org.springframework.boot',
               module:'spring-boot-starter-logging'
}
```

With the default logging starter excluded, you can now include the starter for the logging implementation you'd rather use. With a Maven build you can add Log4j like this:

```
<dependency>
  <groupId>org.springframework.boot</groupId>
  <artifactId>spring-boot-starter-log4j</artifactId>
</dependency>
```

In a Gradle build you can add Log4j like this:

```
compile("org.springframework.boot:spring-boot-starter-log4j")
```

If you'd rather use Log4j2, change the artifact from "spring-boot-starter-log4j" to "spring-boot-starter-log4j2".

For full control over the logging configuration, you can create a logback.xml file at the root of the classpath (in src/main/resources). Here's an example of a simple logback.xml file you might use:

```
<configuration>
  <appender name="STDOUT" class="ch.qos.logback.core.ConsoleAppender">
    <encoder>
      <pattern>
        %d{HH:mm:ss.SSS} [%thread] %-5level %logger{36} - %msg%n
      </pattern>
    </encoder>
  </appender>

  <logger name="root" level="INFO"/>
```

```
    <root level="INFO">
      <appender-ref ref="STDOUT" />
    </root>
</configuration>
```

Aside from the pattern used for logging, this Logback configuration is more or less equivalent to the default you'll get if you have no logback.xml file. But by editing logback.xml you can gain full control over your application's log files. The specifics of what can go into logback.xml are outside the scope of this book, so refer to Logback's documentation for more information.

Even so, the most common changes you'll make to a logging configuration are to change the logging levels and perhaps to specify a file where the logs should be written. With Spring Boot configuration properties, you can make those changes without having to create a logback.xml file.

To set the logging levels, you create properties that are prefixed with `logging.level`, followed by the name of the logger for which you want to set the logging level. For instance, suppose you'd like to set the root logging level to WARN, but log Spring Security logs at DEBUG level. The following entries in application.yml will take care of it for you:

```
logging:
  level:
    root: WARN
    org:
      springframework:
        security: DEBUG
```

Optionally, you can collapse the Spring Security package name to a single line:

```
logging:
  level:
    root: WARN
    org.springframework.security: DEBUG
```

Now suppose that you want to write the log entries to a file named BookWorm.log at /var/logs/. The `logging.path` and `logging.file` properties can help with that:

```
logging:
  path: /var/logs/
  file: BookWorm.log
  level:
    root: WARN
    org:
      springframework:
        security: DEBUG
```

Assuming that the application has write permissions to /var/logs/, the log entries will be written to /var/logs/BookWorm.log. By default, the log files will rotate once they hit 10 megabytes in size.

Similarly, all of these properties can be set in application.properties like this:

```
logging.path=/var/logs/
logging.file=BookWorm.log
logging.level.root=WARN
logging.level.root.org.springframework.security=DEBUG
```

If you still need full control of the logging configuration, but would rather name the Logback configuration file something other than logback.xml, you can specify a custom name by setting the `logging.config` property:

```
logging:
  config:
    classpath:logging-config.xml
```

Although you usually won't need to change the configuration file's name, it can come in handy if you want to use two different logging configurations for different runtime profiles (see section 3.2.3).

CONFIGURING A DATA SOURCE

At this point, we're still developing our reading-list application. As such, the embedded H2 database we're using is perfect for our needs. But once we take the application into production, we may want to consider a more permanent database solution.

Although you could explicitly configure your own `DataSource` bean, it's usually not necessary. Instead, simply configure the URL and credentials for your database via properties. For example, if you're using a MySQL database, your application.yml file might look like this:

```
spring:
  datasource:
    url: jdbc:mysql://localhost/readinglist
    username: dbuser
    password: dbpass
```

You usually won't need to specify the JDBC driver; Spring Boot can figure it out from the database URL. But if there is a problem, you can try setting the `spring.datasource .driver-class-name` property:

```
spring:
  datasource:
    url: jdbc:mysql://localhost/readinglist
    username: dbuser
    password: dbpass
    driver-class-name: com.mysql.jdbc.Driver
```

Spring Boot will use this connection data when auto-configuring the `DataSource` bean. The `DataSource` bean will be pooled, using Tomcat's pooling `DataSource` if it's available on the classpath. If not, it will look for and use one of these other connection pool implementations on the classpath:

- HikariCP
- Commons DBCP
- Commons DBCP 2

Although these are the only connection pool options available through auto-configuration, you are always welcome to explicitly configure a `DataSource` bean to use whatever connection pool implementation you'd like.

You may also choose to look up the `DataSource` from JNDI by setting the `spring.datasource.jndi-name` property:

```
spring:
  datasource:
    jndi-name: java:/comp/env/jdbc/readingListDS
```

If you set the `spring.datasource.jndi-name` property, the other datasource connection properties (if set) will be ignored.

There are many ways to influence the components that Spring Boot auto-configures by just setting a property or two. But this style of externalized configuration is not limited to the beans configured by Spring Boot. Let's look at how you can use the very same property configuration mechanism to fine-tune your own application components.

3.2.2 *Externally configuring application beans*

Suppose that we wanted to show not just the title of a book on someone's reading list, but also provide a link to the book on Amazon.com. And, not only do we want to provide a link to the book, but we also want to tag the book to take advantage of Amazon's associate program so that if anyone purchases a book through one of the links in our application, we'd receive a small payment for the referral.

This is simple enough to do by changing the Thymeleaf template to render the title of each book as a link:

```
<a th:href="''http://www.amazon.com/gp/product/'
          + ${book.isbn}
          + '/tag=habuma-20'"
   th:text="${book.title}">Title</a>
```

This will work perfectly. Now if anyone clicks on the link and buys the book, *I* will get credit for the referral. That's because "habuma-20" is *my* Amazon Associate ID. If you'd rather receive credit, you can easily change the value of the `tag` attribute to your Amazon Associate ID in the Thymeleaf template.

Even though it's easy enough to change the Amazon Associate ID in the template, it's still hard-coded. We're only linking to Amazon from this one template, but we may later add features to the application where we link to Amazon from several pages. In that case, changes to the Amazon Associate ID would require changes to several places in the application code. That's why details like this are often better kept out of the code so that they can be managed in a single place.

Rather than hard-code the Amazon Associate ID in the template, we can refer to it as a value in the model:

```
<a th:href="''http://www.amazon.com/gp/product/'
          + ${book.isbn}
          + '/tag=' + ${amazonID}"
   th:text="${book.title}">Title</a>
```

In addition, `ReadingListController` will need to populate the model at the key "amazonID" to contain the Amazon Associate ID. Again, we shouldn't hard-code it, but instead refer to an instance variable. And that instance variable should be populated from the property configuration. Listing 3.4 shows the new `ReadingListController`, which populates the model from an injected Amazon Associate ID.

> **Listing 3.4   `ReadingListController` modified to accept an Amazon ID**

```
package readinglist;

import java.util.List;

import org.springframework.beans.factory.annotation.Autowired;
import org.springframework.boot.context.properties.ConfigurationProperties;
import org.springframework.stereotype.Controller;
import org.springframework.ui.Model;
import org.springframework.web.bind.annotation.RequestMapping;
import org.springframework.web.bind.annotation.RequestMethod;

@Controller
@RequestMapping("/")
@ConfigurationProperties(prefix="amazon")          Inject with
public class ReadingListController {               properties

  private String associateId;

  private ReadingListRepository readingListRepository;

  @Autowired
  public ReadingListController(
      ReadingListRepository readingListRepository) {
    this.readingListRepository = readingListRepository;
  }
                                                   Setter method
                                                   for associateId
  public void setAssociateId(String associateId) {
    this.associateId = associateId;
  }

  @RequestMapping(method=RequestMethod.GET)
  public String readersBooks(Reader reader, Model model) {
    List<Book> readingList =
```

```
            readingListRepository.findByReader(reader);
   if (readingList != null) {
     model.addAttribute("books", readingList);
     model.addAttribute("reader", reader);
     model.addAttribute("amazonID", associateId);
   }
   return "readingList";
 }

 @RequestMapping(method=RequestMethod.POST)
 public String addToReadingList(Reader reader, Book book) {
   book.setReader(reader);
   readingListRepository.save(book);
   return "redirect:/";
 }

}
```

Put associateId into model

As you can see, the `ReadingListController` now has an `associateId` property and a corresponding `setAssociateId()` method through which the property can be set. And `readersBooks()` now adds the value of `associateId` to the model under the key "amazonID".

Perfect! Now the only question is where `associateId` gets its value.

Notice that `ReadingListController` is now annotated with `@Configuration-Properties`. This specifies that this bean should have its properties injected (via setter methods) with values from configuration properties. More specifically, the `prefix` attribute specifies that the `ReadingListController` bean will be injected with properties with an "amazon" prefix.

Putting this all together, we've specified that `ReadingListController` should have its properties injected from "amazon"-prefixed configuration properties. `Reading-ListController` has only one property with a setter method—the `associateId` property. Therefore, all we need to do to specify the Amazon Associate ID is to add an `amazon.associateId` property in one of the supported property source locations.

For example, we could set that property in application.properties:

```
amazon.associateId=habuma-20
```

Or in application.yml:

```
amazon:
  associateId: habuma-20
```

Or we could set it as an environment variable, specify it as a command-line argument, or add it in any of the other places where configuration properties can be set.

ENABLING CONFIGURATION PROPERTIES Technically, the `@Configuration-Properties` annotation won't work unless you've enabled it by adding `@EnableConfigurationProperties` in one of your Spring configuration classes. This is often unnecessary, however, because all of the configuration classes behind Spring Boot auto-configuration are already annotated with `@EnableConfigurationProperties`. Therefore, unless you aren't taking advantage of auto-configuration at all (and why would that ever happen?), you shouldn't need to explicitly use `@EnableConfigurationProperties`.

It's also worth noting that Spring Boot's property resolver is clever enough to treat camel-cased properties as interchangeable with similarly named properties with hyphens or underscores. In other words, a property named `amazon.associateId` is equivalent to both `amazon.associate_id` and `amazon.associate-id`. Feel free to use the naming convention that suits you best.

COLLECTING PROPERTIES IN ONE CLASS

Although annotating `ReadingListController` with `@ConfigurationProperties` works fine, it may not be ideal. Doesn't it seem a little odd that the property prefix is "amazon" when, in fact, `ReadingListController` has little to do with Amazon? Moreover, future enhancements might present the need to configure properties unrelated to Amazon in `ReadingListController`.

Instead of capturing the configuration properties in `ReadingListController`, it may be better to annotate a separate bean with `@ConfigurationProperties` and let that bean collect all of the configuration properties. `AmazonProperties` in listing 3.5, for example, captures the Amazon-specific configuration properties.

Listing 3.5 Capturing configuration properties in a bean

```java
package readinglist;

import org.springframework.boot.context.properties.
                                        ConfigurationProperties;
import org.springframework.stereotype.Component;

@Component
@ConfigurationProperties("amazon")          ⟵ Inject with "amazon"-prefixed properties
public class AmazonProperties {

  private String associateId;

  public void setAssociateId(String associateId) {   ⟵ associateId setter method
    this.associateId = associateId;
  }

  public String getAssociateId() {
    return associateId;
  }

}
```

With `AmazonProperties` capturing the `amazon.associateId` configuration property, we can change `ReadingListController` (as shown in listing 3.6) to pull the Amazon Associate ID from an injected `AmazonProperties`.

Listing 3.6 ReadingListController injected with AmazonProperties

```
package readinglist;

import java.util.List;

import org.springframework.beans.factory.annotation.Autowired;
import org.springframework.stereotype.Controller;
import org.springframework.ui.Model;
import org.springframework.web.bind.annotation.RequestMapping;
import org.springframework.web.bind.annotation.RequestMethod;

@Controller
@RequestMapping("/")
public class ReadingListController {

  private ReadingListRepository readingListRepository;
  private AmazonProperties amazonProperties;

  @Autowired
  public ReadingListController(
      ReadingListRepository readingListRepository,            Inject
      AmazonProperties amazonProperties) {         ◁────── AmazonProperties
    this.readingListRepository = readingListRepository;
    this.amazonProperties = amazonProperties;
  }

  @RequestMapping(method=RequestMethod.GET)
  public String readersBooks(Reader reader, Model model) {
    List<Book> readingList =
        readingListRepository.findByReader(reader);
    if (readingList != null) {                                  Add Associate ID
      model.addAttribute("books", readingList);                        to model
      model.addAttribute("reader", reader);
      model.addAttribute("amazonID", amazonProperties.getAssociateId());   ◁──┘
    }
    return "readingList";
  }

  @RequestMapping(method=RequestMethod.POST)
  public String addToReadingList(Reader reader, Book book) {
    book.setReader(reader);
    readingListRepository.save(book);
    return "redirect:/";
  }

}
```

ReadingListController is no longer the direct recipient of configuration properties. Instead, it obtains the information it needs from the injected AmazonProperties bean.

As we've seen, configuration properties are useful for tweaking both auto-configured components as well as the details injected into our own application beans. But what if we need to configure different properties for different deployment environments? Let's take a look at how to use Spring profiles to set up environment-specific configuration.

3.2.3   *Configuring with profiles*

When applications are deployed to different runtime environments, there are usually some configuration details that will differ. The details of a database connection, for instance, are likely different in a development environment than in a quality assurance environment, and different still in a production environment. The Spring Framework introduced support for profile-based configuration in Spring 3.1. Profiles are a type of conditional configuration where different beans or configuration classes are used or ignored based on what profiles are active at runtime.

For instance, suppose that the security configuration we created in listing 3.1 is for production purposes, but the auto-configured security configuration is fine for development. In that case, we can annotate `SecurityConfig` with `@Profile` like this:

```
@Profile("production")
@Configuration
@EnableWebSecurity
public class SecurityConfig extends WebSecurityConfigurerAdapter {

    ...

}
```

The `@Profile` annotation used here requires that the "production" profile be active at runtime for this configuration to be applied. If the "production" profile isn't active, this configuration will be ignored and, for lack of another overriding security configuration, the auto-configured security configuration will be applied.

Profiles can be activated by setting the `spring.profiles.active` property using any of the means available for setting any other configuration property. For example, you could activate the "production" profile by running the application at the command line like this:

```
$ java -jar readinglist-0.0.1-SNAPSHOT.jar --
    spring.profiles.active=production
```

Or you can add the `spring.profiles.active` property to application.yml:

```
spring:
  profiles:
    active: production
```

Or you could set an environment variable and put it in application.properties or use any of the other options mentioned at the beginning of section 3.2.

But because Spring Boot auto-configures so much for you, it would be very inconvenient to write explicit configuration just so that you can have a place to put `@Profile`.

Fortunately, Spring Boot supports profiles for properties set in application.properties and application.yml.

To demonstrate profiled properties, suppose that you want a different logging configuration in production than in development. In production, you're only interested in log entries at WARN level or higher, and you want to write the log entries to a log file. In development, however, you only want things logged to the console and at DEBUG level or higher.

All you need to do is create separate configurations for each environment. How you do that, however, depends on whether you're using a properties file configuration or YAML configuration.

WORKING WITH PROFILE-SPECIFIC PROPERTIES FILES

If you're using application.properties to express configuration properties, you can provide profile-specific properties by creating additional properties files named with the pattern "application-{profile}.properties".

For the logging scenario, the development configuration would be in a file named application-development.properties and contain properties for verbose, console-written logging:

```
logging.level.root=DEBUG
```

But for production, application-production.properties would configure logging to be at WARN level and higher and to write to a log file:

```
logging.path=/var/logs/
logging.file=BookWorm.log
logging.level.root=WARN
```

Meanwhile, any properties that aren't specific to any profile or that serve as defaults (in case a profile-specific configuration doesn't specify otherwise) can continue to be expressed in application.properties:

```
amazon.associateId=habuma-20
logging.level.root=INFO
```

CONFIGURING WITH MULTI-PROFILE YAML FILES

If you're using YAML for configuration properties, you can follow a similar naming convention as for properties files. That is, you can create YAML files whose names follow a pattern of "application-{profile}.yml" and continue to put non-profiled properties in application.yml.

But with YAML, you also have the option of expressing configuration properties for all profiles in a single application.yml file. For example, the logging configuration we want can be declared in application.yml like this:

```
logging:
  level:
    root: INFO
```

```
---

spring:
  profiles: development

logging:
  level:
    root: DEBUG


---

spring:
  profiles: production

logging:
  path: /tmp/
  file: BookWorm.log
  level:
    root: WARN
```

As you can see, this application.yml file is divided into three sections by a set of triple hyphens (`---`). The second and third sections each specify a value for `spring` `.profiles`. This property indicates which profile each section's properties apply to. The properties defined in the middle section apply to development because it sets `spring.profiles` to "development". Similarly, the last section has `spring.profiles` set to "production", making it applicable when the "production" profile is active.

The first section, on the other hand, doesn't specify a value for `spring.profiles`. Therefore, its properties are common to all profiles or are defaults if the active profile doesn't otherwise have the properties set.

Aside from auto-configuration and external configuration properties, Spring Boot has one other trick up its sleeve to simplify a common development task: it automatically configures a page to be displayed when an application encounters any errors. To wrap up this chapter, we'll take a look at Spring Boot's error page and see how to customize it to fit our application.

3.3 *Customizing application error pages*

Errors happen. Even some of the most robust applications running in production occasionally run into trouble. Although it's important to reduce the chance that a user will encounter an error, it's also important that your application still present itself well when displaying an error page.

In recent years, creative error pages have become an art form. If you've ever seen the Star Wars–inspired error page at GitHub.com or DropBox.com's Escher-like error page, you have an idea of what I'm talking about.

I don't know if you've encountered any errors while trying out the reading-list application, but if so you've probably seen an error page much like the one in figure 3.1.

Figure 3.1   Spring Boot's default whitelabel error page.

Spring Boot offers this "whitelabel" error page by default as part of auto-configuration. Even though it's slightly more attractive than a stack trace, it doesn't compare with some of the great works of error art available on the internet. In the interest of presenting your application failures as masterpieces, you'll probably want to create a custom error page for your applications.

The default error handler that's auto-configured by Spring Boot looks for a view whose name is "error". If it can't find one, it uses its default whitelabel error view shown in figure 3.1. Therefore, the easiest way to customize the error page is to create a custom view that will resolve for a view named "error".

Ultimately this depends on the view resolvers in place when the error view is being resolved. This includes

- Any bean that implements Spring's `View` interface and has a bean ID of "error" (resolved by Spring's `BeanNameViewResolver`)
- A Thymeleaf template named "error.html" if Thymeleaf is configured
- A FreeMarker template named "error.ftl" if FreeMarker is configured
- A Velocity template named "error.vm" if Velocity is configured
- A JSP template named "error.jsp" if using JSP views

Because we're using Thymeleaf for the reading-list application, all we must do to customize the error page is create a file named "error.html" and place it in the templates folder along with our other application templates. Listing 3.7 shows a simple, yet effective replacement for the default whitelabel error page.

Listing 3.7 Custom error page for the reading-list application

```html
<html>
  <head>
    <title>Oops!</title>
    <link rel="stylesheet" th:href="@{/style.css}"></link>
  </head>

  <html>
    <div class="errorPage">
      <span class="oops">Oops!</span><br/>
      <img th:src="@{/MissingPage.png}"></img>
      <p>There seems to be a problem with the page you requested
        (<span th:text="${path}"></span>).</p>

      <p th:text="${'Details: ' + message}"></p>
    </div>
  </html>

</html>
```

Show requested path

Show error details

This custom error template should be named "error.html" and placed in the templates directory for the Thymeleaf template resolver to find. For a typical Maven or Gradle build, that means putting it in src/main/resources/templates so that it's at the root of the classpath during runtime.

For the most part, this is a simple Thymeleaf template that displays an image and some error text. There are two specific pieces of information that it also renders: the request path of the error and the exception message. These aren't the only details available to an error page, however. By default, Spring Boot makes the following error attributes available to the error view:

- timestamp—The time that the error occurred
- status—The HTTP status code
- error—The error reason
- exception—The class name of the exception
- message—The exception message (if the error was caused by an exception)
- errors—Any errors from a BindingResult exception (if the error was caused by an exception)
- trace—The exception stack trace (if the error was caused by an exception)
- path—The URL path requested when the error occurred

Some of these attributes, such as path, are useful when communicating the problem to the user. Others, such as trace, should be used sparingly, be hidden, or be used cleverly on the error page to keep the error page as user-friendly as possible.

You'll also notice that the template references an image named MissingPage.png. The actual content of the image is unimportant, so feel free to flex your graphic design muscles and come up with an image that suits you. But be sure to put it in src/main/resources/static or src/main/resources/public so that it can be served when the application is running.

Figure 3.2   A custom error page exhibits style in the face of failure

Figure 3.2 shows what the user will see when an error occurs. It may not quite be a work of art, but I think it raises the aesthetics of the application's error page a notch or two.

3.4   Summary

Spring Boot eliminates much of the boilerplate configuration that's often required in Spring applications. But by letting Spring Boot do all of the configuration, you're relying on it to configure components in ways that suit your application. When auto-configuration doesn't fit your needs, Spring Boot allows you to override and fine-tune the configuration it provides.

   Overriding auto-configuration is a simple matter of writing explicit Spring configuration as you would in the absence of Spring Boot. Spring Boot's auto-configuration is designed to favor application-provided configuration over its own auto-configuration.

Even when auto-configuration is suitable, you may need to adjust a few details. Spring Boot enables several property resolvers that let you tweak configuration by setting properties as environment variables, in properties files, in YAML files, and in several other ways. This same property-based configuration model can even be applied to application-defined components, enabling value-injection into bean properties from external configuration sources.

Spring Boot also auto-configures a simple whitelabel error page. Although it's more user-friendly than an exception and stack trace, the whitelabel error page still leaves a lot to be desired aesthetically. Fortunately, Spring Boot offers several options for customizing or completely replacing the whitelabel error page to suit an application's specific style.

Now that we've written a complete application with Spring Boot, we should verify that it actually does what we expect it to do. That is, instead of poking at it in the web browser manually, we should write some automated and repeatable tests that exercise the application and prove that it's working correctly. That's exactly what we'll do in the next chapter.

Testing with Spring Boot

It's been said that if you don't know where you're going, any road will get you there. But with software development, if you don't know where you're going, you'll likely end up with a buggy application that nobody can use.

The best way to know for sure where you're going when writing applications is to write tests that assert the desired behavior of an application. If those tests fail, you know you have some work to do. If they pass, then you've arrived (at least until you think of some more tests that you can write).

Whether you write tests first or after the code has already been written, it's important that you write tests to not only verify the accuracy of your code, but to also to make sure it does everything you expect it to. Tests are also a great safeguard to make sure that things don't break as your application continues to evolve.

When it comes to writing unit tests, Spring is generally out of the picture. Loose coupling and interface-driven design, which Spring encourages, makes it really easy to write unit tests. But Spring isn't necessarily involved in those unit tests.

Integration tests, on the other hand, require some help from Spring. If Spring is responsible for configuring and wiring up the components in your production application, then Spring should also be responsible for configuring and wiring up those components in your tests.

Spring's `SpringJUnit4ClassRunner` helps load a Spring application context in JUnit-based application tests. Spring Boot builds on Spring's integration testing support by enabling auto-configuration and web server startup when testing Spring Boot applications. It also offers a handful of useful testing utilities.

In this chapter, we'll look at all of the ways that Spring Boot supports integration testing. We'll start by looking at how to test with a fully Spring Boot-enabled application context.

4.1 Integration testing auto-configuration

At the core of everything that the Spring Framework does, its most essential task is to wire together all of the components that make up an application. It does this by reading a wiring specification (whether it be XML, Java-based, Groovy-based, or otherwise), instantiating beans in an application context, and injecting beans into other beans that depend on them.

When integration testing a Spring application, it's important to let Spring wire up the beans that are the target of the test the same way it wires up those beans when the application is running in production. Sure, you might be able to manually instantiate the components and inject them into each other, but for any substantially big application, that can be an arduous task. Moreover, Spring offers additional facilities such as component-scanning, autowiring, and declarative aspects such as caching, transactions, and security. Given all that would be required to recreate what Spring does, it's generally best to let Spring do the heavy lifting, even in an integration test.

Spring has offered excellent support for integration testing since version 1.1.1. Since Spring 2.5, integration testing support has been offered in the form of `SpringJUnit4ClassRunner`, a JUnit class runner that loads a Spring application context for use in a JUnit test and enables autowiring of beans into the test class.

For example, consider the following listing, which shows a very basic Spring integration test.

Listing 4.1 Integration testing Spring with `SpringJUnit4ClassRunner`

```
@RunWith(SpringJUnit4ClassRunner.class)
@ContextConfiguration(                          ← Loads application
      classes=AddressBookConfiguration.class)       context
public class AddressServiceTests {

  @Autowired                                    ← Injects address
  private AddressService addressService;            service

  @Test
```

```
  public void testService() {                                          Tests address
    Address address = addressService.findByLastName("Sheman");         service
    assertEquals("P", address.getFirstName());
    assertEquals("Sherman", address.getLastName());
    assertEquals("42 Wallaby Way", address.getAddressLine1());
    assertEquals("Sydney", address.getCity());
    assertEquals("New South Wales", address.getState());
    assertEquals("2000", address.getPostCode());
  }

}
```

As you can see, `AddressServiceTests` is annotated with both `@RunWith` and `@Context-Configuration`. `@RunWith` is given `SpringJUnit4ClassRunner.class` to enable Spring integration testing.[1] Meanwhile, `@ContextConfiguration` specifies how to load the application context. Here we're asking it to load the Spring application context given the specification defined in `AddressBookConfiguration`.

In addition to loading the application context, `SpringJUnit4ClassRunner` also makes it possible to inject beans from the application context into the test itself via autowiring. Because this test is targeting an `AddressService` bean, it is autowired into the test. Finally, the `testService()` method makes calls to the address service and verifies the results.

Although `@ContextConfiguration` does a great job of loading the Spring application context, it doesn't load it with the full Spring Boot treatment. Spring Boot applications are ultimately loaded by `SpringApplication`, either explicitly (as in listing 2.1) or using `SpringBootServletInitializer` (which we'll look at in chapter 8). `SpringApplication` not only loads the application context, but also enables logging, the loading of external properties (application.properties or application.yml), and other features of Spring Boot. If you're using `@ContextConfiguration`, you won't get those features.

To get those features back in your integration tests, you can swap out `@Context-Configuration` for Spring Boot's `@SpringApplicationConfiguration`:

```
@RunWith(SpringJUnit4ClassRunner.class)
@SpringApplicationConfiguration(
      classes=AddressBookConfiguration.class)
public class AddressServiceTests {
  ...
}
```

The use of `@SpringApplicationConfiguration` is largely identical to `@Context-Configuration`. But unlike `@ContextConfiguration`, `@SpringApplicationConfigu-ration` loads the Spring application context using `SpringApplication` the same way and with the same treatment it would get if it was being loaded in a production application. This includes the loading of external properties and Spring Boot logging.

---

[1] As of Spring 4.2, you can optionally use `SpringClassRule` and `SpringMethodRule` as JUnit rule-based alternatives to `SpringJUnit4ClassRunner`.

Suffice it to say that, for the most part, @SpringApplicationConfiguration replaces @ContextConfiguration when writing tests for Spring Boot applications. We'll certainly use @SpringApplicationConfiguration throughout this chapter as we write tests for our Spring Boot application, including tests that target the web front end of the application.

Speaking of web testing, that's what we're going to do next.

4.2 Testing web applications

One of the nice things about Spring MVC is that it promotes a programming model around plain old Java objects (POJOs) that are annotated to declare how they should process web requests. This programming model is not only simple, it enables you to treat controllers just as you would any other component in your application. You might even be tempted to write tests against your controller that test them as POJOs.

For instance, consider the addToReadingList() method from ReadingList-Controller:

```
@RequestMapping(method=RequestMethod.POST)
public String addToReadingList(Book book) {
  book.setReader(reader);
  readingListRepository.save(book);
  return "redirect:/readingList";
}
```

If you were to disregard the @RequestMapping method, you'd be left with a rather basic Java method. It wouldn't take much to imagine a test that provides a mock implementation of ReadingListRepository, calls addToReadingList() directly, and asserts the return value and verifies the call to the repository's save() method.

The problem with such a test is that it only tests the method itself. While that's better than no test at all, it fails to test that the method handles a POST request to /readingList. It also fails to test that form fields are properly bound to the Book parameter. And although you could assert that the returned String contains a certain value, it would be impossible to test definitively that the request is, in fact, redirected to /readingList after the method is finished.

To properly test a web application, you need a way to throw actual HTTP requests at it and assert that it processes those requests correctly. Fortunately, there are two options available to Spring Boot application developers that make those kinds of tests possible:

- *Spring Mock MVC*—Enables controllers to be tested in a mocked approximation of a servlet container without actually starting an application server
- *Web integration tests*—Actually starts the application in an embedded servlet container (such as Tomcat or Jetty), enabling tests that exercise the application in a real application server

Each of these kinds of tests has its share of pros and cons. Obviously, starting a server will result in a slower test than mocking a servlet container. But there's no doubt that server-based tests are closer to the real-world environment that they'll be running in when deployed to production.

We're going to start by looking at how you can test a web application using Spring's Mock MVC test framework. Then, in section 4.3, you'll see how to write tests against an application that's actually running in an application server.

4.2.1   *Mocking Spring MVC*

Since Spring 3.2, the Spring Framework has had a very useful facility for testing web applications by mocking Spring MVC. This makes it possible to perform HTTP requests against a controller without running the controller within an actual servlet container. Instead, Spring's Mock MVC framework mocks enough of Spring MVC to make it almost as though the application is running within a servlet container ... but it's not.

To set up a Mock MVC in your test, you can use `MockMvcBuilders`. This class offers two static methods:

- `standaloneSetup()`—Builds a Mock MVC to serve one or more manually created and configured controllers
- `webAppContextSetup()`—Builds a Mock MVC using a Spring application context, which presumably includes one or more configured controllers

The primary difference between these two options is that `standaloneSetup()` expects you to manually instantiate and inject the controllers you want to test, whereas `webAppContextSetup()` works from an instance of `WebApplicationContext`, which itself was probably loaded by Spring. The former is slightly more akin to a unit test in that you'll likely only use it for very focused tests around a single controller. The latter, however, lets Spring load your controllers as well as their dependencies for a full-blown integration test.

For our purposes, we're going to use `webAppContextSetup()` so that we can test the `ReadingListController` as it has been instantiated and injected from the application context that Spring Boot has auto-configured.

The `webAppContextSetup()` takes a `WebApplicationContext` as an argument. Therefore, we'll need to annotate the test class with `@WebAppConfiguration` and use `@Autowired` to inject the `WebApplicationContext` into the test as an instance variable. The following listing shows the starting point for our Mock MVC tests.

Listing 4.2   Creating a Mock MVC for integration testing controllers

```
@RunWith(SpringJUnit4ClassRunner.class)
@SpringApplicationConfiguration(
      classes = ReadingListApplication.class)
@WebAppConfiguration                              ◁——— Enables web
public class MockMvcWebTests {                          context testing
```

```
   @Autowired
   private WebApplicationContext webContext;          ⊲──┐  Injects
                                                          │  WebApplicationContext
   private MockMvc mockMvc;

   @Before
   public void setupMockMvc() {
     mockMvc = MockMvcBuilders                        ⊲──┐  Sets up
         .webAppContextSetup(webContext)                 │  MockMvc
         .build();
   }

}
```

The `@WebAppConfiguration` annotation declares that the application context created by `SpringJUnit4ClassRunner` should be a `WebApplicationContext` (as opposed to a basic non-web `ApplicationContext`).

The `setupMockMvc()` method is annotated with JUnit's `@Before`, indicating that it should be executed before any test methods. It passes the injected `WebApplication-Context` into the `webAppContextSetup()` method and then calls `build()` to produce a `MockMvc` instance, which is assigned to an instance variable for test methods to use.

Now that we have a `MockMvc`, we're ready to write some test methods. Let's start with a simple test method that performs an HTTP GET request against /readingList and asserts that the model and view meet our expectations. The following `homePage()` test method does what we need:

```
@Test
public void homePage() throws Exception {
  mockMvc.perform(MockMvcRequestBuilders.get("/readingList"))
      .andExpect(MockMvcResultMatchers.status().isOk())
      .andExpect(MockMvcResultMatchers.view().name("readingList"))
      .andExpect(MockMvcResultMatchers.model().attributeExists("books"))
      .andExpect(MockMvcResultMatchers.model().attribute("books",
          Matchers.is(Matchers.empty())));
}
```

As you can see, a lot of static methods are being used in this test method, including static methods from Spring's `MockMvcRequestBuilders` and `MockMvcResultMatchers`, as well as from the Hamcrest library's `Matchers`. Before we dive into the details of this test method, let's add a few static imports so that the code is easier to read:

```
import static org.hamcrest.Matchers.*;
import static org.springframework.test.web.servlet.request.
    ➥ MockMvcRequestBuilders.*;
import static org.springframework.test.web.servlet.result.
    ➥ MockMvcResultMatchers.*;
```

With those static imports in place, the test method can be rewritten like this:

```
@Test
public void homePage() throws Exception {
  mockMvc.perform(get("/readingList"))
      .andExpect(status().isOk())
      .andExpect(view().name("readingList"))
      .andExpect(model().attributeExists("books"))
      .andExpect(model().attribute("books", is(empty())));
}
```

Now the test method almost reads naturally. First it performs a GET request against /readingList. Then it expects that the request is successful (isOk() asserts an HTTP 200 response code) and that the view has a logical name of readingList. It also asserts that the model contains an attribute named books, but that attribute is an empty collection. It's all very straightforward.

The main thing to note here is that at no time is the application deployed to a web server. Instead it's run within a mocked out Spring MVC, just capable enough to handle the HTTP requests we throw at it via the MockMvc instance.

Pretty cool, huh?

Let's try one more test method. This time we'll make it a bit more interesting by actually sending an HTTP POST request to post a new book. We should expect that after the POST request is handled, the request will be redirected back to /readingList and that the books attribute in the model will contain the newly added book. The following listing shows how we can use Spring's Mock MVC to do this kind of test.

Listing 4.3   Testing the post of a new book

```
@Test
public void postBook() throws Exception {
mockMvc.perform(post("/readingList")                          ◁─── Performs
        .contentType(MediaType.APPLICATION_FORM_URLENCODED)        POST request
        .param("title", "BOOK TITLE")
        .param("author", "BOOK AUTHOR")
        .param("isbn", "1234567890")
        .param("description", "DESCRIPTION"))
        .andExpect(status().is3xxRedirection())
        .andExpect(header().string("Location", "/readingList"));

Book expectedBook = new Book();               ◁─── Sets up
expectedBook.setId(1L);                            expected book
expectedBook.setReader("craig");
expectedBook.setTitle("BOOK TITLE");
expectedBook.setAuthor("BOOK AUTHOR");
expectedBook.setIsbn("1234567890");
expectedBook.setDescription("DESCRIPTION");

mockMvc.perform(get("/readingList"))          ◁─── Performs GET
        .andExpect(status().isOk())                request
        .andExpect(view().name("readingList"))
```

```
.andExpect(model().attributeExists("books"))
.andExpect(model().attribute("books", hasSize(1)))
.andExpect(model().attribute("books",
            contains(samePropertyValuesAs(expectedBook))));
}
```

Obviously, the test in listing 4.3 is a bit more involved. It's actually two tests in one method. The first part posts the book and asserts the results from that request. The second part performs a fresh GET request against the home page and asserts that the newly created book is in the model.

When posting the book, we must make sure we set the content type to "application/ x-www-form-urlencoded" (with MediaType.APPLICATION_FORM_URLENCODED) as that will be the content type that a browser will send when the book is posted in the running application. We then use the MockMvcRequestBuilders's param() method to set the fields that simulate the form being submitted. Once the request has been performed, we assert that the response is a redirect to /readingList.

Assuming that much of the test method passes, we move on to part two. First, we set up a Book object that contains the expected values. We'll use this to compare with the value that's in the model after fetching the home page.

Then we perform a GET request for /readingList. For the most part, this is no different than how we tested the home page before, except that instead of an empty collection in the model, we're checking that it has one item, and that the item is the same as the expected Book we created. If so, then our controller seems to be doing its job of saving a book when one is posted to it.

So far, these tests have assumed an unsecured application, much like the one we wrote in chapter 2. But what if we want to test a secured application, such as the one from chapter 3?

4.2.2 Testing web security

Spring Security offers support for testing secured web applications easily. In order to take advantage of it, you must add Spring Security's test module to your build. The following testCompile dependency in Gradle is all you need:

```
testCompile("org.springframework.security:spring-security-test")
```

Or if you're using Maven, add the following <dependency> to your build:

```
<dependency>
  <groupId>org.springframework.security</groupId>
  <artifactId>spring-security-test</artifactId>
  <scope>test</scope>
</dependency>
```

With Spring Security's test module in your application's classpath, you just need to apply the Spring Security configurer when creating the MockMvc instance:

```
@Before
public void setupMockMvc() {
mockMvc = MockMvcBuilders
    .webAppContextSetup(webContext)
    .apply(springSecurity())
    .build();
}
```

The `springSecurity()` method returns a Mock MVC configurer that enables Spring Security for Mock MVC. By simply applying it as shown here, Spring Security will be in play on all requests performed through `MockMvc`. The specific security configuration will depend on how you've configured Spring Security (or how Spring Boot has auto-configured Spring Security). In the case of the reading-list application, it's the same security configuration we created in `SecurityConfig.java` in chapter 3.

> **THE SPRINGSECURITY() METHOD**   `springSecurity()` is a static method of `SecurityMockMvcConfigurers`, which I've statically imported for readability's sake.

With Spring Security enabled, we can no longer simply request the home page and expect an HTTP 200 response. If the request isn't authenticated, we should expect a redirect to the login page:

```
@Test
public void homePage_unauthenticatedUser() throws Exception {
mockMvc.perform(get("/"))
    .andExpect(status().is3xxRedirection())
    .andExpect(header().string("Location",
                              "http://localhost/login"));
}
```

But how can we perform an authenticated request? Spring Security offers two annotations that can help:

- `@WithMockUser`—Loads the security context with a `UserDetails` using the given username, password, and authorization
- `@WithUserDetails`—Loads the security context by looking up a `UserDetails` object for the given username

In both cases, Spring Security's security context is loaded with a `UserDetails` object that is to be used for the duration of the annotated test method. The `@WithMockUser` annotation is the most basic of the two. It allows you to explicitly declare a `UserDetails` to be loaded into the security context:

```
@Test
@WithMockUser(username="craig",
              password="password",
              roles="READER")
public void homePage_authenticatedUser() throws Exception {
  ...
}
```

As you can see, `@WithMockUser` bypasses the normal lookup of a `UserDetails` object and instead creates one with the values specified. For simple tests, this may be fine. But for our test, we need a `Reader` (which implements `UserDetails`) instead of the generic `UserDetails` that `@WithMockUser` creates. For that, we'll need `@WithUserDetails`.

The `@WithUserDetails` annotation uses the configured `UserDetailsService` to load the `UserDetails` object. As you'll recall from chapter 3, we configured a `UserDetailsService` bean that looks up and returns a `Reader` object for a given username. That's perfect! So we'll annotate our test method with `@WithUserDetails`, as shown in the following listing.

Listing 4.4 Testing a secured method with user authentication

```
@Test
@WithUserDetails("craig")                                          Uses "craig"
public void homePage_authenticatedUser() throws Exception {        user

    Reader expectedReader = new Reader();
    expectedReader.setUsername("craig");                           Sets up expected
    expectedReader.setPassword("password");                        Reader
    expectedReader.setFullname("Craig Walls");

    mockMvc.perform(get("/"))                                      Performs GET
        .andExpect(status().isOk())                                request
        .andExpect(view().name("readingList"))
        .andExpect(model().attribute("reader",
                        samePropertyValuesAs(expectedReader)))
        .andExpect(model().attribute("books", hasSize(0)))

}
```

In listing 4.4, we use `@WithUserDetails` to declare that the "craig" user should be loaded into the security context for the duration of this test method. Knowing that the `Reader` will be placed into the model, the method starts by creating an expected `Reader` object that it can compare with the model later in the test. Then it performs the GET request and asserts the view name and model contents, including the model attribute with the name "reader".

Once again, no servlet container is started up to run these tests. Spring's Mock MVC takes the place of an actual servlet container. The benefit of this approach is that the test methods run faster because they don't have to wait for the server to start. Moreover, there's no need to fire up a web browser to post the form, so the test is simpler and faster.

On the other hand, it's not a complete test. It's better than simply calling the controller methods directly, but it doesn't truly exercise the application in a web browser and verify the rendered view. To do that, we'll need to start a real web server and hit it with a real web browser. Let's see how Spring Boot can help us start a real web server for our tests.

4.3   *Testing a running application*

When it comes to testing web applications, nothing beats the real thing. Firing up the application in a real server and hitting it with a real web browser is far more indicative of how it will behave in the hands of users than poking at it with a mock testing engine.

But real tests in real servers with real web browsers can be tricky. Although there are build-time plugins for deploying applications in Tomcat or Jetty, they are clunky to set up. Moreover, it's nearly impossible to run any one of a suite of many such tests in isolation or without starting up your build tool.

Spring Boot, however, has a solution. Because Spring Boot already supports running embedded servlet containers such as Tomcat or Jetty as part of the running application, it stands to reason that the same mechanism could be used to start up the application along with its embedded servlet container for the duration of a test.

That's exactly what Spring Boot's @WebIntegrationTest annotation does. By annotating a test class with @WebIntegrationTest, you declare that you want Spring Boot to not only create an application context for your test, but also to start an embedded servlet container. Once the application is running along with the embedded container, you can issue real HTTP requests against it and make assertions against the results.

For example, consider the simple web test in listing 4.5, which uses @WebIntegrationTest to start the application along with a server and uses Spring's RestTemplate to perform HTTP requests against the application.

Listing 4.5   Testing a web application in-server

```java
@RunWith(SpringJUnit4ClassRunner.class)
@SpringApplicationConfiguration(
      classes=ReadingListApplication.class)        │ Runs test
@WebIntegrationTest                            ◁───┘ in server
public class SimpleWebTest {

  @Test(expected=HttpClientErrorException.class)
  public void pageNotFound() {
    try {
      RestTemplate rest = new RestTemplate();              │ Performs GET
      rest.getForObject(                                   │ request
          "http://localhost:8080/bogusPage", String.class);  ◁─┘
      fail("Should result in HTTP 404");
    } catch (HttpClientErrorException e) {
      assertEquals(HttpStatus.NOT_FOUND, e.getStatusCode());  ◁── Asserts HTTP
      throw e;                                                    404 (not found)
    }                                                             response
  }

}
```

Although this is a very simple test, it sufficiently demonstrates how to use the @WebIntegrationTest to start the application with a server. The actual server that's started will be determined in the same way it would be if we were running the application at the command line. By default, it starts Tomcat listening on port 8080. Optionally, however, it could start Jetty or Undertow if either of those is in the classpath.

The body of the test method is written assuming that the application is running and listening on port 8080. It uses Spring's `RestTemplate` to make a request for a non-existent page and asserts that the response from the server is an HTTP 404 (not found). The test will fail if any other response is returned.

4.3.1 *Starting the server on a random port*

As mentioned, the default behavior is to start the server listening on port 8080. That's fine for running a single test at a time on a machine where no other server is already listening on port 8080. But if you're like me, you've probably *always* got something listening on port 8080 on your local machine. In that case, the test would fail because the server wouldn't start due to the port collision. There must be a better way.

Fortunately, it's easy enough to ask Spring Boot to start up the server on a randomly selected port. One way is to set the `server.port` property to 0 to ask Spring Boot to select a random available port. `@WebIntegrationTest` accepts an array of `String` for its `value` attribute. Each entry in the array is expected to be a name/value pair, in the form `name=value`, to set properties for use in the test. To set `server.port` you can use `@WebIntegrationTest` like this:

```
@WebIntegrationTest(value={"server.port=0"})
```

Or, because there's only one property being set, it can take a simpler form:

```
@WebIntegrationTest("server.port=0")
```

Setting properties via the `value` attribute is handy in the general sense, but `@WebIntegrationTest` also offers a `randomPort` attribute for a more expressive way of asking the server to be started on a random port. You can ask for a random port by setting `randomPort` to `true`:

```
@WebIntegrationTest(randomPort=true)
```

Now that we have the server starting on a random port, we need to be sure we use the correct port when making web requests. At the moment, the `getForObject()` method is hard-coded with port 8080 in its URL. If the port is randomly chosen, how can we construct the request to use the right port?

First we'll need to inject the chosen port as an instance variable. To make this convenient, Spring Boot sets a property with the name `local.server.port` to the value of the chosen port. All we need to do is use Spring's `@Value` to inject that property:

```
@Value("${local.server.port}")
private int port;
```

Now that we have the port, we just need to make a slight change to the getForObject() call to use it:

```
rest.getForObject(
    "http://localhost:{port}/bogusPage", String.class, port);
```

Here we've traded the hardcoded 8080 for a {port} placeholder in the URL. By passing the port property as the last parameter in the getForObject() call, we can be assured that the placeholder will be replaced with whatever value was injected into port.

4.3.2   *Testing HTML pages with Selenium*

RestTemplate is fine for simple requests and it's perfect for testing REST endpoints. But even though it can be used to make requests against URLs that return HTML pages, it's not very convenient for asserting the contents of the page or performing operations on the page itself. At best, you'll be able to assert the precise content of the resulting HTML (which will result in fragile tests). But you won't easily be able to assert selected content on the page or perform operations such as clicking links or submitting forms.

A better choice for testing HTML applications is Selenium (www.seleniumhq.org). Selenium does more than just perform requests and fetch the results for you to verify. Selenium actually fires up a web browser and executes your test within the context of the browser. It's as close as you can possibly get to performing the tests manually with your own hands. But unlike manual testing, Selenium tests are automated and repeatable.

To test our reading list application using Selenium, let's write a test that fetches the home page, fills out the form for a new book, posts the form, and then finally asserts that the landing page includes the newly added book.

First we'll need to add Selenium to the build as a test dependency:

```
testCompile("org.seleniumhq.selenium:selenium-java:2.45.0")
```

Now we can write the test class. The following listing shows a basic template for a Selenium test that uses Spring Boot's @WebIntegrationTest.

Listing 4.6   A template for Selenium testing with Spring Boot

```
@RunWith(SpringJUnit4ClassRunner.class)
@SpringApplicationConfiguration(
    classes=ReadingListApplication.class)        Starts on a
@WebIntegrationTest(randomPort=true)      ◁──── random port
public class ServerWebTests {

  private static FirefoxDriver browser;
                                              Injects
  @Value("${local.server.port}")      ◁──── the port
  private int port;
```

```
@BeforeClass
public static void openBrowser() {
  browser = new FirefoxDriver();
  browser.manage().timeouts()
      .implicitlyWait(10, TimeUnit.SECONDS);
}
```
Sets up Firefox driver

```
@AfterClass
public static void closeBrowser() {
  browser.quit();
}
```
Shuts down browser

```
}
```

As with the simpler web test we wrote earlier, this class is annotated with @WebIntegra-tionTest and sets randomPort to true so that the application will be started and run with a server listening on a random port. And, as before, that port is injected into the port property so that we can use it to construct URLs to the running application.

The static openBrowser() method creates a new instance of FirefoxDriver, which will open a Firefox browser (it will need to be installed on the machine running the test). When we write our test method, we'll perform browser operations through the FirefoxDriver instance. The FirefoxDriver is also configured to wait up to 10 seconds when looking for any elements on the page (in case those elements are slow to load).

After the test has completed, we'll need to shut down the Firefox browser. Therefore, closeBrowser() calls quit() on the FirefoxDriver instance to bring it down.

> **PICK YOUR BROWSER** Although we're testing with Firefox, Selenium also provides drivers for several other browsers, including Internet Explorer, Google's Chrome, and Apple's Safari. Not only can you use other browsers, it's probably a good idea to write your tests to use any and all browsers you want to support.

Now we can write our test method. As a reminder, we want to load the home page, fill in and submit the form, and then assert that we land on a page that includes our newly added book in the list. The following listing shows how to do this with Selenium.

Listing 4.7 Testing the reading-list application with Selenium

```
@Test
public void addBookToEmptyList() {
  String baseUrl = "http://localhost:" + port;

  browser.get(baseUrl);
```
Fetches the home page

```
  assertEquals("You have no books in your book list",
           browser.findElementByTagName("div").getText());
```
Asserts an empty book list

```
  browser.findElementByName("title")
```

```
                     .sendKeys("BOOK TITLE");
        browser.findElementByName("author")
                     .sendKeys("BOOK AUTHOR");
        browser.findElementByName("isbn")
                     .sendKeys("1234567890");
        browser.findElementByName("description")
                     .sendKeys("DESCRIPTION");
        browser.findElementByTagName("form")        Fills in and
                     .submit();           ◁──────── submits form

        WebElement dl =
             browser.findElementByCssSelector("dt.bookHeadline");
        assertEquals("BOOK TITLE by BOOK AUTHOR (ISBN: 1234567890)",
                      dl.getText());
        WebElement dt =
             browser.findElementByCssSelector("dd.bookDescription");
        assertEquals("DESCRIPTION", dt.getText());      ◁──────  Asserts new
    }                                                            book in list
```

The very first thing that the test method does is use the `FirefoxDriver` to perform a
GET request for the reading list's home page. It then looks for a `<div>` element on the
page and asserts that its text indicates that no books are in the list.

The next several lines look for the fields in the form and use the driver's `send-Keys()` method to simulate keystroke events on those field elements (essentially filling
in those fields with the given values). Finally, it looks for the `<form>` element and sub-
mits it.

After the form submission is processed, the browser should land on a page with the
new book in the list. So the final few lines look for the `<dt>` and `<dd>` elements in that
list and assert that they contain the data that the test submitted in the form.

When you run this test, you'll see the browser pop up and load the reading-list
application. If you pay close attention, you'll see the form filled out, as if by a ghost.
But it's no spectre using your application—it's the test.

The main thing to notice about this test is that `@WebIntegrationTest` was able to
start up the application and server for us so that Selenium could start poking at it with
a web browser. But what's especially interesting about how this works is that you can use
the test facilities of your IDE to run as many or as few of these tests as you want, without
having to rely on some plugin in your application's build to start a server for you.

If testing with Selenium is something that you think you'll find useful, you should
check out *Selenium WebDriver in Practice* by Yujun Liang and Alex Collins (http://
manning.com/liang/), which goes into far more details about testing with Selenium.

4.4   *Summary*

Testing is an important part of developing quality software. Without a good suite of
tests, you'll never know for sure if your application is doing what it's expected to do.

For unit tests, which focus on a single component or a method of a component,
Spring isn't really necessary. The benefits and techniques promoted by Spring—loose

coupling, dependency injection, and interface-driven design—make writing unit tests easy. But Spring doesn't need to be directly involved in unit tests.

Integration-testing multiple components, however, begs for help from Spring. In fact, if Spring is responsible for wiring those components up at runtime, then Spring should also be responsible for wiring them up in integration tests.

The Spring Framework provides integration-testing support in the form of a JUnit class runner that loads a Spring application context and enables beans from the context to be injected into a test. Spring Boot builds upon Spring integration-testing support with a configuration loader that loads the application context in the same way as Spring Boot itself, including support for externalized properties and Spring Boot logging.

Spring Boot also enables in-container testing of web applications, making it possible to fire up your application to be served by the same container that it will be served by when running in production. This gives your tests the closest thing to a real-world environment for verifying the behavior of the application.

At this point we've built a rather complete (albeit simple) application that leverages Spring Boot starters and auto-configuration to handle the grunt work so that we can focus on writing our application. And we've also seen how to take advantage of Spring Boot's support for testing the application. Coming up in the next couple of chapters, we're going to take a slightly different tangent and explore the ways that Groovy can make developing Spring Boot applications even easier. We'll start in the next chapter by looking at a few features from the Grails framework that have made their way into Spring Boot.

Getting Groovy with the Spring Boot CLI

Some things go really well together. Peanut butter and jelly. Abbott and Costello. Thunder and lightning. Milk and cookies. On their own, these things are great. But when paired up, they're even more awesome.

So far, we've seen a lot of great things that Spring Boot has to offer, including auto-configuration and starter dependencies. When paired up with the elegance of the Groovy language, the result can be greater than the sum of its parts.

In this chapter, we're going to look at the Spring Boot CLI, a command-line tool that brings the power of Spring Boot and Groovy together to form a simple and compelling development tool for creating Spring applications. To demonstrate the power of Spring Boot's CLI, we're going to rewind the reading-list application from chapter 2, rewriting it from scratch in Groovy and taking advantage of the benefits that the CLI has to offer.

5.1   *Developing a Spring Boot CLI application*

Most development projects that target the JVM platform are developed in the Java language and involve a build system such as Maven or Gradle to produce a deployable artifact. In fact, the reading-list application we created in chapter 2 follows this model.

The Java language has seen great improvements in recent versions. Even so, Java has a few strict rules that add noise to the code. Line-ending semicolons, class and method modifiers (such as `public` and `private`), getter and setter methods, and `import` statements serve a purpose in Java, but they distract from the essentials of the code. From a developer's perspective, code noise is friction—friction when writing code and even more friction when trying to read it. If some of this code noise could be eliminated, it'd be easier to develop and read the code.

Likewise, build systems such as Maven and Gradle serve a purpose in a project. But build specifications are also one more thing that must be developed and maintained. If only there were a way to do away with the build, projects would be that much simpler.

When working with the Spring Boot CLI, there is no build specification. The code itself serves as the build specification, providing hints that guide the CLI in resolving dependencies and producing deployment artifacts. Moreover, by teaming up with Groovy, the Spring Boot CLI offers a development model that eliminates almost all code noise, producing a friction-free development experience.

In the very simplest case, writing a CLI-based application could be as easy as writing a single standalone Groovy script like the one we wrote in chapter 1. But when writing a more complete application with the CLI, it makes sense to set up a basic project structure to house the project code. That's where we'll get started with rewriting the reading-list application.

5.1.1   *Setting up the CLI project*

The first thing we'll do is create a directory structure to house the project. Unlike Maven- and Gradle-based projects, Spring Boot CLI projects don't have a strict project structure. In fact, the simplest Spring Boot CLI app could be a single Groovy script living in any directory in the filesystem. For the reading-list project, however, you should create a fresh, clean directory to keep the code separate from anything else you keep on your machine:

```
$ mkdir readinglist
```

Here I've named the directory "readinglist", but feel free to name it however you wish. The name isn't as important as the fact that the project will have a place to live.

We'll need a couple of extra directories to hold the static web content and the Thymeleaf template. Within the readinglist directory, create two new directories named "static" and "templates":

```
$ cd readinglist
$ mkdir static
$ mkdir templates
```

It's no coincidence that these directories are named the same as the directories we created under src/main/resources in the Java-based project. Although Spring Boot doesn't enforce a project structure like Maven and Gradle do, Spring Boot will still auto-configure a Spring `ResourceHttpRequestHandler` that looks for static content in a directory named "static" (among other locations). It will also still configure Thymeleaf to resolve templates from a directory named "templates".

Speaking of static content and Thymeleaf templates, those files will be exactly the same as the ones we created in chapter 2. So that you don't have to worry about remembering them later, go ahead and copy style.css into the static directory and readingList.html into templates.

At this point the reading-list project should be structured like this:

```
.
├──static
│    └── style.css
└──templates
      └── readingList.html
```

Now that the project is set up, we're ready to start writing some Groovy code.

5.1.2   *Eliminating code noise with Groovy*

On its own, Groovy is a very elegant language. Unlike Java, Groovy doesn't require qualifiers such as `public` and `private`. Nor does it demand semicolons at the end of each line. Moreover, thanks to Groovy's simplified property syntax ("GroovyBeans"), the JavaBean standard accessor methods are unnecessary.

Consequently, writing the `Book` domain class in Groovy is extremely easy. Create a new file at the root of the reading-list project named Book.groovy and write the following Groovy class in it.

```groovy
class Book {
    Long id
    String reader
    String isbn
    String title
    String author
    String description
}
```

As you can see, this Groovy class is a mere fraction of the size of its Java counterpart. There are no setter or getter methods, no `public` or `private` modifiers, and no semicolons. The code noise that is so common in Java is squelched, and all that's left is what describes the essence of a book.

JDBC vs. JPA in the Spring Boot CLI

One difference you may have noticed between this Groovy implementation of `Book` and the Java implementation in chapter 2 is that there are no JPA annotations. That's because this time we're going to use Spring's `JdbcTemplate` to access the database instead of Spring Data JPA.

There are a couple of very good reasons why I chose JDBC instead of JPA for this example. First, by mixing things up a little, I can show off a few more auto-configuration tricks that Spring Boot performs when working with Spring's `JdbcTemplate`. But perhaps the most important reason I chose JDBC is that Spring Data JPA requires a .class file when generating on-the-fly implementations of repository interfaces. When you run Groovy scripts via the command line, the CLI compiles the scripts in memory and doesn't produce .class files. Therefore, Spring Data JPA doesn't work well when running scripts through the CLI.

That said, the CLI isn't completely incompatible with Spring Data JPA. If you use the CLI's `jar` command to package your application into a JAR file, the resulting JAR file will contain compiled .class files for all of your Groovy scripts. Building and running a JAR file from the CLI is a handy option when you want to deploy an application developed with the CLI, but it isn't as convenient during development when you want to see the results of your work quickly.

Now that we've defined the `Book` domain class, let's write the repository. First, let's write the `ReadingListRepository` interface (in ReadingListRepository.groovy):

```
interface ReadingListRepository {

    List<Book> findByReader(String reader)

    void save(Book book)

}
```

Aside from a clear lack of semicolons and no `public` modifier on the interface, the Groovy version of `ReadingListRepository` isn't much different from its Java counterpart. The most significant difference is that it doesn't extend `JpaRepository` because we're not working with Spring Data JPA in this chapter. And since we're not using Spring Data JPA, we're going to have to write the implementation of `ReadingListRepository` ourselves. The following listing shows what `JdbcReadingListRepository.groovy` should look like.

Listing 5.1 A Groovy and JDBC implementation of `ReadingListRepository`

```
@Repository
class JdbcReadingListRepository implements ReadingListRepository {

    @Autowired
```

```
JdbcTemplate jdbc                              ◁────┐ Inject
                                                    │ JdbcTemplate
List<Book> findByReader(String reader) {
  jdbc.query(
      "select id, reader, isbn, title, author, description " +
      "from Book where reader=?",
      { rs, row ->
            new Book(id: rs.getLong(1),
                reader: rs.getString(2),
                isbn: rs.getString(3),
                title: rs.getString(4),
                author: rs.getString(5),
                description: rs.getString(6))
      } as RowMapper,                 ◁────┐ RowMapper
      reader)                              │ closure
}

void save(Book book) {
  jdbc.update("insert into Book " +
              "(reader, isbn, title, author, description) " +
              "values (?, ?, ?, ?, ?)",
      book.reader,
      book.isbn,
      book.title,
      book.author,
      book.description)
}

}
```

For the most part, this is a typical `JdbcTemplate`-based repository implementation. It's injected, via autowiring, with a reference to a `JdbcTemplate` object that it uses to query the database for books (in the `findByReader()` method) and to save books to the database (in the `save()` method).

By writing it in Groovy, we're able to apply some Groovy idioms in the implementation. For example, in `findByReader()`, a Groovy closure is given as a parameter in the call to `query()` in place of a `RowMapper` implementation.[1] Also, within the closure, a new `Book` object is created using Groovy's support for setting object properties at construction.

While we're thinking about database persistence, we also need to create a file named schema.sql that will contain the SQL necessary to create the `Book` table that the repository issues queries against:

```
create table Book (
        id identity,
        reader varchar(20) not null,
        isbn varchar(10) not null,
        title varchar(50) not null,
        author varchar(50) not null,
        description varchar(2000) not null
);
```

---

[1] In fairness to Java, we can do something similar in Java 8 using lambdas (and method references).

I'll explain how schema.sql is used later. For now, just know that you need to create it at the root of the classpath (at the root directory of the project) so that there will actually be a Book table to query against.

All of the Groovy pieces are coming together, but there's one more Groovy class we must write to make the Groovy-ified reading-list application complete. We need to write a Groovy implementation of ReadingListController to handle web requests and serve the reading list to the browser. At the root of the project, create a file named ReadingListController.groovy with the following content.

Listing 5.2 ReadingListController handles web requests for displaying and adding

```groovy
@Controller
@RequestMapping("/")
class ReadingListController {

  String reader = "Craig"

  @Autowired
  ReadingListRepository readingListRepository        ⟵⎤ Inject
                                                        ⎦ ReadingListRepository

  @RequestMapping(method=RequestMethod.GET)
  def readersBooks(Model model) {
    List<Book> readingList =
        readingListRepository.findByReader(reader)    ⟵⎤ Fetch
                                                        ⎦ reading list

    if (readingList) {
      model.addAttribute("books", readingList)        ⟵──── Populate model
    }

    "readingList"            ⟵──── Return view name
  }

  @RequestMapping(method=RequestMethod.POST)
  def addToReadingList(Book book) {
    book.setReader(reader)
    readingListRepository.save(book)                 ⟵──── Save book
    "redirect:/"             ⟵⎤
  }                                    ⎦ Redirect after POST

}
```

Comparing this version of ReadingListController with the one from chapter 2, it's easy to see that there's a lot in common. The main difference, once again, is that Groovy's syntax does away with class and method modifiers, semicolons, accessor methods, and other unnecessary code noise.

You'll also notice that both handler methods are declared with def rather than String and both dispense with an explicit return statement. If you prefer explicit typing on the methods and explicit return statements, feel free to include them—Groovy won't mind.

There's one more thing we need to do before we can run the application. Create a new file named Grabs.groovy and put these three lines in it:

```
@Grab("h2")
@Grab("spring-boot-starter-thymeleaf")
class Grabs {}
```

We'll talk more about what this class does later. For now, just know that the `@Grab` annotations on this class tell Groovy to fetch a few dependency libraries on the fly as the application is started.

Believe it or not, we're ready to run the application. We've created a project directory, copied a stylesheet and Thymeleaf template into it, and filled it with Groovy code. All that's left is to run it with the Spring Boot CLI (from within the project directory):

```
$ spring run .
```

After a few seconds, the application should be fully started. Open your web browser and navigate to http://localhost:8080. Assuming everything goes well, you should see the same reading-list application you saw in chapter 2.

Success! In just a few pages of this book, you've written a complete (albeit simple) Spring application!

At this point, however, you might be wondering how it works, considering that...

- *There's no Spring configuration.* How are the beans created and wired together? Where does the `JdbcTemplate` bean come from?
- *There's no build file.* Where do the library dependencies like Spring MVC and Thymeleaf come from?
- *There are no* `import` *statements.* How can Groovy resolve types like `JdbcTemplate` and `RequestMapping` if there are no `import` statements to specify what packages they're in?
- *We never deployed the app.* Where'd the web server come from?

Indeed, the code we've written seems to be missing more than just a few semicolons. How does this code even work?

5.1.3 *What just happened?*

As you've probably surmised, there's more to Spring Boot's CLI than just a convenient means of writing Spring applications with Groovy. The Spring Boot CLI has several tricks in its repertoire, including the following:

- The CLI is able to leverage Spring Boot auto-configuration and starter dependencies.
- The CLI is able to detect when certain types are in use and automatically resolve the appropriate dependency libraries to support those types.
- The CLI knows which packages several commonly used types are in and, if those types are used, adds those packages to Groovy's default packages.

- By applying both automatic dependency resolution and auto-configuration, the CLI can detect that it's running a web application and automatically include an embedded web container (Tomcat by default) to serve the application.

If you think about it, these are the most important features that the CLI offers. The Groovy syntax is just a bonus!

When you run the reading-list application through the Spring Boot CLI, several things happen under the covers to make this magic work. One of the very first things the CLI does is attempt to compile the Groovy code using an embedded Groovy compiler. Without you knowing it, however, the code fails to compile due to several unknown types in the code (such as `JdbcTemplate`, `Controller`, `RequestMapping`, and so on).

But the CLI doesn't give up. The CLI knows that `JdbcTemplate` can be added to the classpath by adding the Spring Boot JDBC starter as a dependency. It also knows that the Spring MVC types can be found by adding the Spring Boot web starter as a dependency. So it grabs those dependencies from the Maven repository (Maven Central, by default).

If the CLI were to try to recompile at this point, it would still fail because of the missing `import` statements. But the CLI also knows the packages of many commonly used types. Taking advantage of the ability to customize the Groovy compiler's default package imports, the CLI adds all of the necessary packages to the Groovy compiler's default imports list.

Now it's time for the CLI to attempt another compile. Assuming there are no other problems outside of the CLI's abilities (such as syntax errors or types that the CLI doesn't know about), the code will compile cleanly and the CLI will run it via an internal bootstrap method similar to the `main()` method we put in Application for the Java-based example.

At this point, Spring Boot auto-configuration kicks in. It sees that Spring MVC is on the classpath (as a result of the CLI resolving the web starter), so it automatically configures the appropriate beans to support Spring MVC, as well as an embedded Tomcat bean to serve the application. It also sees that `JdbcTemplate` is on the classpath, so it automatically creates a `JdbcTemplate` bean, wiring it with a `DataSource` bean that was also automatically created.

Speaking of the `DataSource` bean, it's just one of several other beans that are created via Spring Boot auto-configuration. Spring Boot also automatically configures beans that support Thymeleaf views in Spring MVC. This happens because we used `@Grab` to add H2 and Thymeleaf to the classpath, which triggers auto-configuration for an embedded H2 database and Thymeleaf.

The `@Grab` annotation is an easy way to add dependencies that the CLI isn't able to automatically resolve. In spite of its ease of use, however, there's more to this little annotation than meets the eye. Let's take a closer look at `@Grab` to see what makes it tick, how the Spring Boot CLI makes it even easier by requiring only an artifact name for many commonly used dependencies, and how to configure its dependency-resolution process.

5.2   *Grabbing dependencies*

In the case of Spring MVC and JdbcTemplate, Groovy compilation errors triggered the Spring Boot CLI to go fetch the necessary dependencies and add them to the classpath. But what if a dependency is required but there's no failing code to trigger automatic dependency resolution? Or what if the required dependency isn't among the ones the CLI knows about?

In the reading-list example, we needed Thymeleaf libraries so that we could write our views using Thymeleaf templates. And we needed the H2 database library so that we could have an embedded H2 database. But because none of the Groovy code directly referenced Thymeleaf or H2 classes, there were no compilation failures to trigger them to be resolved automatically. Therefore, we had to help the CLI out a bit by adding the @Grab dependencies in the Grabs class.

> **WHERE SHOULD YOU PLACE @GRAB?**   It's not strictly necessary to put the @Grab annotations in a separate class as we have. They would still do their magic had we put them in ReadingListController or JdbcReadingListRepository. For organization's sake, however, it's useful to create an otherwise empty class definition that has all of the @Grab annotations. This makes it easy to view all of the explicitly declared library dependencies in one place.

The @Grab annotation comes from Groovy's Grape (Groovy Adaptable Packaging Engine or Groovy Advanced Packaging Engine) facility. In a nutshell, Grape enables Groovy scripts to download dependency libraries at runtime without using a build tool like Maven or Gradle. In addition to providing the functionality behind the @Grab annotation, Grape is also used by the Spring Boot CLI to fetch dependencies deduced from the code.

Using @Grab is as simple as expressing the dependency coordinates. For example, suppose you want to add the H2 database to your project. Adding the following @Grab to one of the project's Groovy scripts will do just that:

```
@Grab(group="com.h2database", module="h2", version="1.4.190")
```

Used this way, the group, module, and version attributes explicitly specify the dependency. Alternatively, you can express the same dependency more succinctly using a colon-separated form similar to how dependencies can be expressed in a Gradle build specification:

```
@Grab("com.h2database:h2:1.4.185")
```

These are two textbook examples of using @Grab. But the Spring Boot CLI extends @Grab in a couple of ways to make working with @Grab even easier.

First, for many dependencies it's unnecessary to specify the version. Applying this to the example of the H2 database dependency, it's possible to express the dependency with the following @Grab:

```
@Grab("com.h2database:h2")
```

The specific version of the dependency is determined by the version of the CLI that you're using. In the case of Spring Boot CLI 1.3.0.RELEASE, the H2 dependency resolved will be 1.4.190.

But that's not all. For many commonly used dependencies, it's also possible to leave out the group ID, expressing the dependency by only giving the module ID to @Grab. This is what enabled us to express the following @Grab for H2 in the previous section:

```
@Grab("h2")
```

How can you know which dependencies require a group ID and version and which you can grab using only the module ID? I've included a complete list of all the dependencies the Spring Boot CLI knows about in appendix D. But generally speaking, it's easy enough to try @Grab dependencies with only a module ID first and then only express the group ID and version if the module ID alone doesn't work.

Although it's very convenient to express dependencies giving only their module IDs, what if you disagree with the version chosen by Spring Boot? What if one of Spring Boot's starters transitively pulls in a certain version of a library, but you'd prefer to use a newer version that contains a bug fix?

5.2.1 Overriding default dependency versions

Spring Boot brings a new @GrabMetadata annotation that can be used with @Grab to override the default dependency versions in a properties file.

To use @GrabMetadata, add it to one of the Groovy script files giving it the coordinates for a properties file with the overriding dependency metadata:

```
@GrabMetadata("com.myorg:custom-versions:1.0.0")
```

This will load a properties file named custom-versions.properties from a Maven repository in the com/myorg directory. Each line in the properties file should have a group ID and module ID as the key, and the version as the value. For example, to override the default version for H2 with 1.4.186, you can point @GrabMetadata at a properties file containing the following line:

```
com.h2database:h2=1.4.186
```

Using the Spring IO platform
One way you might want to use @GrabMetadata is to work with dependency versions defined in the Spring IO platform (http://platform.spring.io/platform/). The Spring IO platform offers a curated set of dependencies and versions aimed to give confidence in knowing which versions of Spring and other libraries will work well together. The dependencies and versions specified by the Spring IO platform is a superset of Spring Boot's set of known dependency libraries, and it includes several third-party libraries that are frequently used in Spring applications.

> **(continued)**
> If you'd like to build Spring Boot CLI applications on the Spring IO platform, you'll just need to annotate one of your Groovy scripts with the following `@GrabMetadata`:
>
> ```
> @GrabMetadata('io.spring.platform:platform-versions:1.0.4.RELEASE')
> ```
>
> This overrides the CLI's set of default dependency versions with those defined by the Spring IO platform.

One question you might have is where Grape fetches all of its dependencies from? And is that configurable? Let's see how you can manage the set of repositories that Grape draws dependencies from.

5.2.2 Adding dependency repositories

By default, `@Grab`-declared dependencies are fetched from the Maven Central repository (http://repo1.maven.org/maven2/). In addition, Spring Boot also registers Spring's milestone and snapshot repositories to be able to fetch pre-released dependencies for Spring projects. For many projects, this is perfectly sufficient. But what if your project needs a library that isn't in Central or the Spring repositories? Or what if you're working within a corporate firewall and must use an internal repository?

No problem. The `@GrabResolver` annotation enables you to specify additional repositories from which dependencies can be fetched.

For example, suppose you want to use the latest Hibernate release. Recent Hibernate releases can only be found in the JBoss repository, so you'll need to add that repository via `@GrabResolver`:

```
@GrabResolver(name='jboss', root=
    'https://repository.jboss.org/nexus/content/groups/public-jboss')
```

Here the resolver is named "jboss" with the `name` attribute. The URL to the repository is specified in the `root` attribute.

You've seen how Spring Boot's CLI compiles your code and automatically resolves several known dependency libraries as needed. And with support for `@Grab` to resolve any dependencies that the CLI isn't able to resolve automatically, CLI-based applications have no need for a Maven or Gradle build specification (as is required by traditionally developed Java applications). But resolving dependencies and compiling code aren't the only things that build processes do. Project builds also usually execute automated tests. If there's no build specification, how do the tests run?

5.3 Running tests with the CLI

Tests are an important part of any software project, and they aren't overlooked by the Spring Boot CLI. Because CLI-based applications don't involve a traditional build system, the CLI offers a `test` command for running tests.

Before you can try out the `test` command, you need to write a test. Tests can reside anywhere in the project, but I recommend keeping them separate from the main components of the project by putting them in a subdirectory. You can name the subdirectory anything you want, but I chose to name it "tests":

```
$ mkdir tests
```

Within the tests directory, create a new Groovy script named ReadingListController-Test.groovy and write a test for the `ReadingListController`. To get started, listing 5.3 has a single test method for testing that the controller handles HTTP GET requests properly.

> **Listing 5.3 A Groovy test for `ReadingListController`**

```
import org.springframework.test.web.servlet.MockMvc
import static
    org.springframework.test.web.servlet.setup.MockMvcBuilders.*
import static org.springframework.test.web.servlet.request.
                                    MockMvcRequestBuilders.*
import static org.springframework.test.web.servlet.result.
                                    MockMvcResultMatchers.*
import static org.mockito.Mockito.*

class ReadingListControllerTest {

  @Test
  void shouldReturnReadingListFromRepository() {
    List<Book> expectedList = new ArrayList<Book>()
    expectedList.add(new Book(
        id: 1,
        reader: "Craig",
        isbn: "9781617292545",
        title: "Spring Boot in Action",
        author: "Craig Walls",
        description: "Spring Boot in Action is ..."      Mock
    ))                                          ReadingListRepository

    def mockRepo = mock(ReadingListRepository.class)    <----
    when(mockRepo.findByReader("Craig")).thenReturn(expectedList)

    def controller =
        new ReadingListController(readingListRepository: mockRepo)

    MockMvc mvc = standaloneSetup(controller).build()
    mvc.perform(get("/"))                     <----------   Perform and test
      .andExpect(view().name("readingList"))               GET request
      .andExpect(model().attribute("books", expectedList))
  }

}
```

As you can see, this is a simple JUnit test that uses Spring's support for mock MVC testing to fire a GET request at the controller. It starts by setting up a mock implementation of ReadingListRepository that will return a single-entry list of Book. Then it creates an instance of ReadingListController, injecting the mock repository into the readingListRepository property. Finally, it sets up a MockMvc object, performs a GET request, and asserts expectations with regard to the view name and model contents.

But the specifics of the test aren't as important here as how you run the test. Using the CLI's test command, you can execute the test from the command line like this:

```
$ spring test tests/ReadingListControllerTest.groovy
```

In this case, I'm explicitly selecting ReadingListControllerTest as the test to run. If you have several tests within the tests/ directory and want to run them all, you can give the directory name to the test command:

```
$ spring test tests
```

If you're inclined to write Spock specifications instead of JUnit tests, you may be pleased to know that the CLI's test command can also execute Spock specifications, as demonstrated by ReadingListControllerSpec in the following listing.

Listing 5.4   A Spock specification to test ReadingListController

```
import org.springframework.test.web.servlet.MockMvc
import static
    org.springframework.test.web.servlet.setup.MockMvcBuilders.*
import static org.springframework.test.web.servlet.request.
                                         MockMvcRequestBuilders.*
import static org.springframework.test.web.servlet.result.
                                         MockMvcResultMatchers.*
import static org.mockito.Mockito.*

class ReadingListControllerSpec extends Specification {

  MockMvc mockMvc
  List<Book> expectedList

  def setup() {
    expectedList = new ArrayList<Book>()
    expectedList.add(new Book(
      id: 1,
      reader: "Craig",
      isbn: "9781617292545",
      title: "Spring Boot in Action",
      author: "Craig Walls",
      description: "Spring Boot in Action is ..."              Mock
    ))                                           ReadingListRepository
                                                         ◁───────┐
    def mockRepo = mock(ReadingListRepository.class)
    when(mockRepo.findByReader("Craig")).thenReturn(expectedList)
```

```
    def controller =
        new ReadingListController(readingListRepository: mockRepo)
    mockMvc = standaloneSetup(controller).build()
}

def "Should put list returned from repository into model"() {
    when:
        def response = mockMvc.perform(get("/"))        ◁──────  Perform GET
                                                                  request
    then:
        response.andExpect(view().name("readingList"))
                .andExpect(model().attribute("books", expectedList))    ◁──  Test
}                                                                            results

}
```

`ReadingListControllerSpec` is a simple translation of `ReadingListControllerTest` from a JUnit test into a Spock specification. As you can see, its one test very plainly states that when a `GET` request is performed against "/", then the response should have a view named `readingList` and the expected list of books should be in the model at the key `books`.

Even though it's a Spock specification, `ReadingListControllerSpec` can be run with `spring test` tests the same way as a JUnit-based test.

Once the code is written and the tests are all passing, you might want to deploy your project. Let's see how the Spring Boot CLI can help produce a deployable artifact.

5.4   *Creating a deployable artifact*

In conventional Java projects based on Maven or Gradle, the build system is responsible for producing a deployment unit; typically a JAR file or a WAR file. With Spring Boot CLI, however, we've simply been running our application from the command line with the `spring` command.

Does that mean that if you want to deploy a Spring Boot CLI application you must install the CLI on your server and fire up the application manually from the command line? That seems awfully inconvenient (not to mention risky) when deploying to production environments.

We'll talk more about options for deploying Spring Boot applications in chapter 8. For now, though, let me show you one more trick that the CLI has up its sleeve. From within the CLI-based reading-list application, issue the following at the command line:

```
$ spring jar ReadingList.jar .
```

This will package up the entire project, including all dependencies, Groovy, and an embedded Tomcat, into a single executable JAR file. Once complete, you'll be able to run the app at the command line (without the CLI) like this:

```
$ java -jar ReadingList.jar
```

In addition to being run at the command line, the executable JAR can be deployed to several Platform-as-a-Service (PaaS) cloud platforms including Pivotal Cloud Foundry and Heroku. You'll see how in chapter 8.

5.5   Summary

The Spring Boot CLI takes the simplicity offered by Spring Boot auto-configuration and starter dependencies and turns it up a notch. Using the elegance of the Groovy language, the CLI makes it possible to develop Spring applications with minimal code noise.

In this chapter we completely rewrote the reading-list application from chapter 2. But this time we developed it in Groovy as a Spring Boot CLI application. You saw how the CLI makes Groovy even more elegant by automatically adding `import` statements for many commonly used packages and types. And the CLI is also able to automatically resolve several dependency libraries.

For libraries that the CLI is unable to automatically resolve, CLI-based applications can take advantage of the Grape `@Grab` annotation to explicitly declare dependencies without a build specification. Spring Boot's CLI extends `@Grab` so that, for many commonly needed library dependencies, you only need to declare the module ID.

Finally, you also saw how to execute tests and build deployable artifacts, tasks commonly handled by build systems, with the Spring Boot CLI.

Spring Boot and Groovy go well together, each boosting the other's simplicity. We're going to take another look at how Spring Boot and Groovy play well together in the next chapter as we explore how Spring Boot is at the core of the latest version of Grails.

6

Applying Grails in Spring Boot

This chapter covers

- Persisting data with GORM
- Defining GSP views
- An introduction to Grails 3 and Spring Boot

When I was growing up, there was a series of television advertisements involving two people, one enjoying a chocolate bar and another eating peanut butter out of a jar. By way of some sort of comedic mishap, the two would collide, resulting in the peanut butter and chocolate getting mixed.

One would proclaim, "You got your chocolate in my peanut butter!" The other would respond, "You got peanut butter on my chocolate!"

After initially being angry with their circumstances, the two would conclude that the combination of peanut butter and chocolate is a good thing. Then a voice-over would suggest that the viewer should eat a Reese's Peanut Butter Cup.

From the moment that Spring Boot was announced, I've been frequently asked how to choose between Spring Boot and Grails. Both are built upon the Spring Framework and both help ease application development. Indeed, they're very much like peanut butter and chocolate. Both are great, but the choice is largely a personal one.

As it turns out, there's no reason to choose one or the other. Just like the chocolate vs. peanut butter debate, Spring Boot and Grails are two great choices that work great together.

In this chapter, we're going to look at the connection between Grails and Spring Boot. We'll start by looking at a few Grails features like GORM and Groovy Server Pages (GSP) that are available in Spring Boot. Then we'll flip it around and see how Grails 3 has been reinvented by being built upon Spring Boot.

6.1 *Using GORM for data persistence*

Probably one of the most intriguing pieces of Grails is GORM (Grails object-relational mapping). GORM makes database work as simple as declaring the entities that will be persisted. For example, listing 6.1 shows how the `Book` entity from the reading-list example could be written in Groovy as a GORM entity.

Listing 6.1   A GORM Book entity

```
package readinglist

import grails.persistence.*                    This is a GORM
                                                entity
@Entity
class Book {

    Reader reader
    String isbn
    String title
    String author
    String description

}
```

Just like its Java equivalent, this `Book` class has a handful of properties that describe a book. Unlike the Java version, however, it's not littered with semicolons, `public` or `private` modifiers, setter and getter methods, or any of the other noise that's common in Java. But what makes it a GORM entity is that it's annotated with the `@Entity` annotation from Grails. This simple entity does a lot, including mapping the object to the database and enabling `Book` with persistence methods through which it can be saved and retrieved.

To use GORM with a Spring Boot project, all you must do is add the GORM dependency to your build. In Maven, the `<dependency>` looks like this:

```
<dependency>
  <groupId>org.grails</groupId>
  <artifactId>gorm-hibernate4-spring-boot</artifactId>
  <version>1.1.0.RELEASE</version>
</dependency>
```

The same dependency can be expressed in a Gradle build like this:

```
compile("org.grails:gorm-hibernate4-spring-boot:1.1.0.RELEASE")
```

This library carries some Spring Boot auto-configuration with it that will automatically configure all of the necessary beans to support working with GORM. All you need to do is start writing the code.

Another GORM option for Spring Boot

As its name suggests, the `gorm-hibernate4-spring-boot` dependency enables GORM for data persistence via Hibernate. For many projects, this will be fine. If, however, you're interested in working with the MongoDB document database, you'll be pleased to know that GORM for MongoDB is also available for Spring Boot.

The Maven dependency looks like this:

```
<dependency>
  <groupId>org.grails</groupId>
  <artifactId>gorm-mongodb-spring-boot</artifactId>
  <version>1.1.0.RELEASE</version>
</dependency>
```

Likewise, the Gradle dependency is as follows:

```
compile("org.grails:gorm-mongodb-spring-boot:1.1.0.RELEASE")
```

Due to the nature of how GORM works, it requires that at least the entity class be written in Groovy. We've already written the `Book` entity in listing 6.1. As for the `Reader` entity, it's shown in the following listing.

Listing 6.2 A GORM Reader entity

```
package readinglist

import grails.persistence.*

import org.springframework.security.core.GrantedAuthority
import
    org.springframework.security.core.authority.SimpleGrantedAuthority
import org.springframework.security.core.userdetails.UserDetails

@Entity                                          ⟵  This is
class Reader implements UserDetails {               an entity

  String username
  String fullname
  String password

  Collection<? extends GrantedAuthority> getAuthorities() {
```

```
    Arrays.asList(new SimpleGrantedAuthority("READER"))
  }

  boolean isAccountNonExpired() {        ◄─┐   Implement
    true                                     │   UserDetails
  }

  boolean isAccountNonLocked() {
    true
  }

  boolean isCredentialsNonExpired() {
    true
  }

  boolean isEnabled() {
    true
  }

}
```

Now that we've written the two GORM entities for the reading-list application, we'll need to rewrite the rest of the app to use them. Because working with Groovy is such a pleasant experience (and very Grails-like), we'll continue writing the other classes in Groovy as well.

First up is `ReadingListController`, as shown next.

Listing 6.3   A Groovy reading-list controller

```
package readinglist

import org.springframework.beans.factory.annotation.Autowired
import
    org.springframework.boot.context.properties.ConfigurationProperties
import org.springframework.http.HttpStatus
import org.springframework.stereotype.Controller
import org.springframework.ui.Model
import org.springframework.web.bind.annotation.ExceptionHandler
import org.springframework.web.bind.annotation.RequestMapping
import org.springframework.web.bind.annotation.RequestMethod
import org.springframework.web.bind.annotation.ResponseStatus

@Controller
@RequestMapping("/")
@ConfigurationProperties("amazon")
class ReadingListController {

  @Autowired
  AmazonProperties amazonProperties

  @ExceptionHandler(value=RuntimeException.class)
  @ResponseStatus(value=HttpStatus.BANDWIDTH_LIMIT_EXCEEDED)
  def error() {
```

```
      "error"
}

@RequestMapping(method=RequestMethod.GET)
def readersBooks(Reader reader, Model model) {
  List<Book> readingList = Book.findAllByReader(reader)        ◁─── Find all
  model.addAttribute("reader", reader)                             reader books
  if (readingList) {
    model.addAttribute("books", readingList)
    model.addAttribute("amazonID", amazonProperties.getAssociateId())
  }
  "readingList"
}

@RequestMapping(method=RequestMethod.POST)
def addToReadingList(Reader reader, Book book) {
  Book.withTransaction {
    book.setReader(reader)
    book.save()        ◁───┐  Save a
  }                        │  book
  "redirect:/"
}

}
```

The most obvious difference between this version of `ReadingListController` and the one from chapter 3 is that it's written in Groovy and lacks much of the code noise from Java. But the most significant difference is that it doesn't work with an injected `ReadingListRepository` anymore. Instead, it works directly with the `Book` type for persistence.

In the `readersBooks()` method, it calls the static `findAllByReader()` method on `Book` to fetch all books for the given reader. Although we didn't write a `findAllBy-Reader()` method in listing 6.1, this will work because GORM will implement it for us.

Likewise, the `addToReadingList()` method uses the static `withTransaction()` and the instance `save()` methods, both provided by GORM, to save a `Book` to the database.

And all we had to do was declare a few properties and annotate `Book` with `@Entity`. A pretty good payoff, if you ask me.

A similar change must be made to `SecurityConfig` to fetch a `Reader` via GORM rather than using `ReadingListRepository`. The following listing shows the new Groovy `SecurityConfig`.

Listing 6.4 `SecurityConfig` in Groovy

```
package readinglist

import org.springframework.context.annotation.Configuration
import org.springframework.security.config.annotation.authentication.
                          builders.AuthenticationManagerBuilder
import org.springframework.security.config.annotation.web.
                          builders.HttpSecurity
```

```
import org.springframework.security.config.annotation.web.
                          configuration.WebSecurityConfigurerAdapter
import org.springframework.security.core.userdetails.UserDetailsService

@Configuration
class SecurityConfig extends WebSecurityConfigurerAdapter {

  void configure(HttpSecurity http) throws Exception {
    http
      .authorizeRequests()
        .antMatchers("/").access("hasRole('READER')")
        .antMatchers("/**").permitAll()
      .and()
      .formLogin()
        .loginPage("/login")
        .failureUrl("/login?error=true")
  }

  void configure(AuthenticationManagerBuilder auth) throws Exception {
    auth
      .userDetailsService(
        { username -> Reader.findByUsername(username) }      ◁———┐ Find a reader
        as UserDetailsService)                                    │ by username
  }

}
```

Aside from being rewritten in Groovy, the most significant change in `SecurityConfig` is the second `configure()` method. As you can see, it uses a closure (as the implementation of `UserDetailsService`) that looks up a `Reader` by calling the static `findByUsername()` method, which is provided by GORM.

You may be wondering what becomes of `ReadingListRepository` in this GORM-enabled application. With GORM handling all of the persistence for us, `ReadingListRepository` is no longer needed. Neither are any of its implementations. I think you'll agree that less code is a good thing.

As for the remaining code in the application, it should also be rewritten in Groovy to match the classes we've changed thus far. But none of it deals with GORM and is therefore out of scope for this chapter. The complete Groovy application is available in the example code download.

At this point, you can fire up the reading-list application using any of the ways we've already discussed for running Spring Boot applications. Once it starts, the application should work as it always has. Only you and I know that the persistence mechanism has been changed.

In addition to GORM, Grails apps usually use Groovy Server Pages to render model data as HTML served to the browser. The Grails-ification of our application continues in the next section, where we'll replace the Thymeleaf templates with equivalent GSP.

6.2   *Defining views with Groovy Server Pages*

Up until now, we've been using Thymeleaf templates to define the view for the reading-list application. In addition to Thymeleaf, Spring Boot also offers Freemarker, Velocity, and Groovy-based templates. For any of those choices, all you must do is add the appropriate starter to your build and start writing templates in the templates/ directory at the root of the classpath. Auto-configuration takes care of the rest.

The Grails project also offers auto-configuration for Groovy Server Pages (GSP). If you want to use GSP in your Spring Boot application, all you must do is add the GSP for Spring Boot library to your build:

```
compile("org.grails:grails-gsp-spring-boot:1.0.0")
```

Just like the other view template options offered by Spring Boot, simply having this library in your classpath triggers auto-configuration that sets up the view resolvers necessary for GSP to work as the view layer of Spring MVC.

All that's left is to write the GSP templates for your application. For the reading-list application, we'll need to rewrite the Thymeleaf readingList.html file in GSP form as readingList.gsp (in src/main/resources/templates). The following listing shows the new GSP-enabled reading-list template.

Listing 6.5   The reading-list app's main view written in GSP

```html
<!DOCTYPE html>
<html>
  <head>
    <title>Reading List</title>
    <link rel="stylesheet" href="/style.css"></link>
  </head>

  <body>
    <h2>Your Reading List</h2>

    <g:if test="${books}">                          ◁────┐ List the
    <g:each in="${books}" var="book">                     │ books
      <dl>
        <dt class="bookHeadline">
          ${book.title} by ${book.author}
          (ISBN: ${book.isbn}")
        </dt>
        <dd class="bookDescription">
          <g:if test="book.description">
            ${book.description}
          </g:if>
          <g:else>
            No description available
          </g:else>
        </dd>
      </dl>
    </g:each>
```

```
</g:if>
<g:else>
  <p>You have no books in your book list</p>
</g:else>

<hr/>

<h3>Add a book</h3>

<form method="POST">                                    The book
  <label for="title">Title:</label>                     form
  <input type="text" name="title"
                     value="${book?.title}"/><br/>
  <label for="author">Author:</label>
  <input type="text" name="author"
                     value="${book?.author}"/><br/>
  <label for="isbn">ISBN:</label>
  <input type="text" name="isbn"
                     value="${book?.isbn}"/><br/>
  <label for="description">Description:</label><br/>
  <textarea name="description" rows="5" cols="80">
    ${book?.description}
  </textarea>                                            The CSRF
  <input type="hidden" name="${_csrf.parameterName}"    token
      value="${_csrf.token}" />
  <input type="submit" value="Add Book" />
</form>

  </body>
</html>
```

As you can see, the GSP template is sprinkled with expression language references (the parts wrapped in ${}) and tags from the GSP tag library such as <g:if> and <g:each>. It's not quite pure HTML as is the case with Thymeleaf, but it's a familiar and comfortable option if you're used to working with JSP.

For the most part, it's rather straightforward to map the elements on this GSP template with the corresponding Thymeleaf templates from chapters 2 and 3. One thing to note, however, is that you have to put in a hidden field to carry the CSRF (Cross-Site Request Forgery) token. Spring Security requires this token on POST requests, and Thymeleaf is able to automatically include it in the rendered HTML. With GSP, however, you must explicitly include the CSRF token in a hidden field.

Figure 6.1 shows the results of the GSP rendered as HTML in the browser after a few books have been entered.

Although Grails features like GORM and GSP are appealing and go a long way toward making a Spring Boot application even simpler, it's not quite the complete Grails experience. We've seen how to put a little Grails chocolate in the Spring Boot peanut butter. Now we'll turn it around and see how Grails 3 gives you the best of both worlds: a development experience that's both fully Spring Boot and fully Grails.

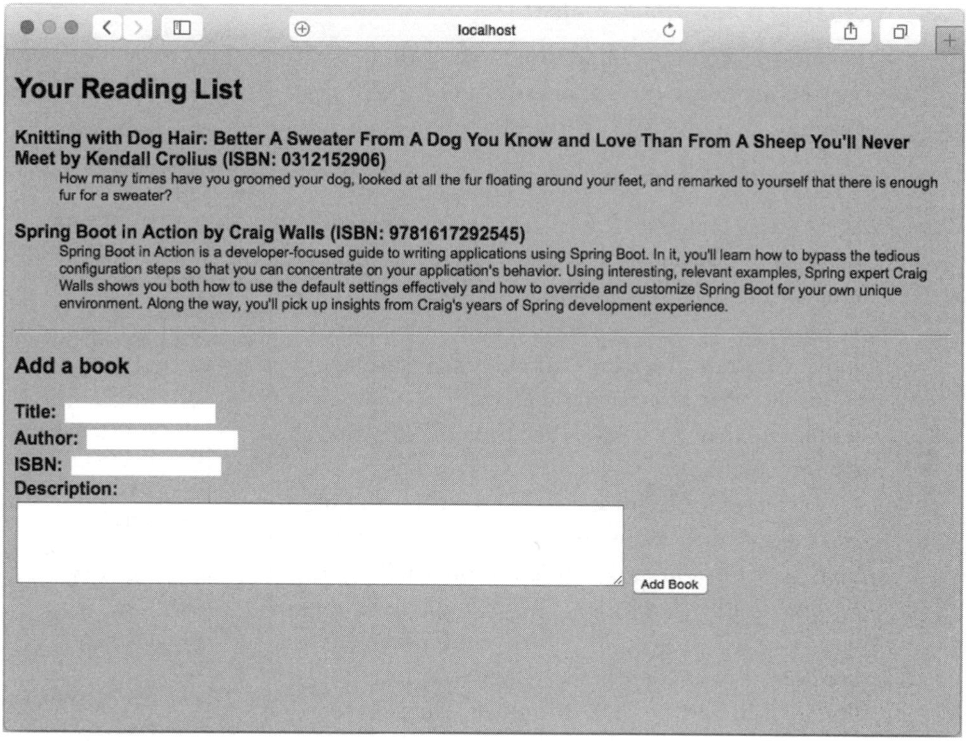

Figure 6.1 The reading list rendered from a GSP template

6.3 *Mixing Spring Boot with Grails 3*

Grails has always been a higher-level framework built upon the giants of Spring, Groovy, Hibernate, and others. With Grails 3, Grails is now built upon Spring Boot, enabling a very compelling developer experience that makes both Grails developers and Spring Boot developers feel at home.

The first step toward working with Grails 3 is to install it. On Mac OS X and most Unix systems, the easiest way to install Grails is to use SDKMAN at the command line:

```
$ sdk install grails
```

If you're using Windows or otherwise can't use SDKMAN, you'll need to download the binary distribution, unzip it, and add the bin directory to your system path.

Whichever installation choice you use, you can verify the installation by checking the Grails version at the command line:

```
$ grails -version
```

Assuming the installation went well, you're now ready to start creating a Grails project.

6.3.1   *Creating a new Grails project*

The `grails` command-line tool is what you'll use to perform many tasks with a Grails project, including the initial creation of the project. To kick off the reading-list application project, use `grails` like this:

```
$ grails create-app readinglist
```

As its name suggests, the `create-app` command creates a new application project. In this case, the name of the project is "readinglist".

Once the `grails` tool has created the application, `cd` into the `readinglist` directory and take a look at what was created. Figure 6.2 shows a high-level view of what the project structure should look like.

You should recognize a few familiar entries in the project's directory structure. There's a Gradle build specification and configuration (build.gradle and gradle.properties). There's also a standard Gradle project structure under the src directory. But grails-app is the most interesting directory in the project. If you've ever worked with any previous version of Grails, you'll know what this directory is for. It's where you'll write the controllers, domain types, and other code that makes up the Grails project.

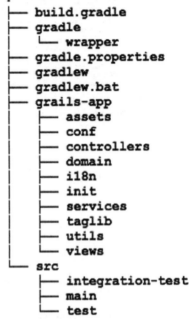

Figure 6.2   The directory structure of a Grails 3 project

If you dig a little deeper and open up the build.gradle file, you'll find a few more familiar items. To start with, the build specification uses the Spring Boot plugin for Gradle:

```
apply plugin: "spring-boot"
```

This means that you'll be able to build and run the Grails application just as you would any other Spring Boot application.

You'll also notice that there are a handful of Spring Boot libraries among the other dependencies:

```
dependencies {
  compile 'org.springframework.boot:spring-boot-starter-logging'
  compile("org.springframework.boot:spring-boot-starter-actuator")
  compile "org.springframework.boot:spring-boot-autoconfigure"
  compile "org.springframework.boot:spring-boot-starter-tomcat"

  ...
}
```

This provides your Grails application with Spring Boot auto-configuration and logging, as well as the Actuator and an embedded Tomcat to serve the application when run as an executable JAR.

Indeed, this is a Spring Boot project. It's also a Grails project. As of Grails 3, Grails is built upon a foundation of Spring Boot.

RUNNING THE APPLICATION

The most straightforward way to run a Grails application is with the `run-app` command of the `grails` tool at the command line:

```
$ grails run-app
```

Even though we've not written a single line of code, we're already able to run the application and view it in the browser. Once the application starts up, you can navigate to http://localhost:8080 in your web browser. You should see something similar to what's shown in figure 6.3.

Figure 6.3   Running a freshly created Grails application

The `run-app` command is the Grails way of running the application and has been the way to run Grails applications for years, even in previous versions of Grails. But because this Grails 3 project's Gradle specification uses the Spring Boot plugin for Gradle, you can also run the application using any of the means available to a Spring Boot project. This includes the `bootRun` task via Gradle:

```
$ gradle bootRun
```

You can also build the project and run the resulting executable JAR file:

```
$ gradle build
...
$ java -jar build/lib/readingList-0.1.jar
```

Of course, the WAR file produced by the build can also be deployed to a servlet 3.0 container of your choice.

It's very convenient to be able to run the application this early in the development process. It helps you know that the project has been properly initialized. But the application doesn't do much interesting yet. It's up to us to build upon the initial project. We'll start by defining the domain.

6.3.2   *Defining the domain*

The central domain type in the reading-list application is the `Book` class. Although we could manually create a Book.groovy file, it's usually better to use the `grails` tool to create domain types. That's because it knows where the source files go and it's also able to generate any related artifacts for us at the same time.

To create the `Book` class, we'll use the `create-domain-class` command of the `grails` tool:

```
$ grails create-domain-class Book
```

This will generate two source files: a Book.groovy file and a BookSpec.groovy file. The latter is a Spock specification for testing the `Book` class. It's initially empty, but you can fill it with any tests you need to verify the functionality of a `Book`.

The Book.groovy file defines the `Book` class itself. You'll find it in grails-app/domain/readingList. Initially, it's rather empty and looks like this:

```
package readinglist
class Book {

  static constraints = {
  }
}
```

We'll need to add the fields that define a book, such as the title, author, and ISBN. After adding the fields, Book.groovy looks like this:

```
package readinglist
class Book {

  static constraints = {
  }

  String reader
  String isbn
  String title
  String author
  String description

}
```

The static `constraints` variable is where you can define any validation constraints to be enforced on instances of `Book`. In this chapter, we're primarily interested in building out the reading-list application to see how it's built upon Spring Boot and not so much on validation. Therefore, we'll leave the `constraints` empty. Feel free to add constraints if you wish, though. Have a look at *Grails in Action, Second Edition,* by Glen Smith and Peter Ledbrook (Manning, 2014) for more information.[1]

For the purpose of working with Grails, we're going to keep the reading-list application simple and in line with what we wrote in chapter 2. Therefore, we'll forego creating a `Reader` domain and go ahead and create the controller.

6.3.3 *Writing a Grails controller*

As with domain types, it's easy to create controllers using the `grails` tool. In the case of controllers, you have a few choices of commands, however:

- `create-controller`—Creates an empty controller, leaving it to the developer to write the controller's functionality
- `generate-controller`—Generates a controller with scaffolded CRUD operations for a given domain type
- `generate-all`—Generates a scaffolded CRUD controller and associated views for a given domain type

Although scaffolded controllers are very handy and are certainly one of the most well-known features of Grails, we're going to keep it simple and write a controller that has just enough functionality to mimic the behavior of the application we created in chapter 2. Therefore, we'll use the `create-controller` command to create a bare-bones controller and then fill it in with the methods we need:

```
$ grails create-controller ReadingList
```

This command creates a controller named `ReadingListController` in grails-app/controllers/readingList that looks like this:

---

[1] Although *Grails in Action, Second Edition,* covers Grails 2, much of what you learn about Grails 2 applies to Grails 3.

```
package readinglist
class ReadingListController {

  def index() { }
}
```

Without making any changes, this controller is ready to run, although it won't do much. At this point, it will handle requests whose path is /readingList and forward the request to the view defined at grails-app/views/readingList/index.gsp (which doesn't yet exist, but we'll create soon).

But what we need our controller to do is display a list of books and a form to add a new book. We also need it to handle the form submission and save a book to the database. The following listing shows the `ReadingListController` that we need.

> **Listing 6.6   Fleshing out the ReadingListController**

```
package readinglist

import static org.springframework.http.HttpStatus.*
import grails.transaction.Transactional

class ReadingListController {

  def index() {
    respond Book.list(params), model:[book: new Book()]    ◁──┐ Fetch books
  }                                                            │ into model

  @Transactional
  def save(Book book) {
    book.reader = 'Craig'                                       Save the
    book.save flush:true    ◁──┐                                book
    redirect(action: "index")  │
  }

}
```

Although it's much shorter than the equivalent Java controller, this version of `Reading-ListController` is almost completely functionally equivalent. It handles GET requests for /readingList and fetches a list of books to be displayed. And when the form is submitted, it handles the POST request, saves the book, then redirects to the index action (which is handled by the `index()` method).

Incredibly, we're almost finished with the Grails version of the reading-list application. The only thing left is to create the view that displays the list of books and the form.

6.3.4   Creating the view

Grails applications typically use GSP templates for their views. You've already seen how to use GSP in a Spring Boot application, so the template we need won't be much different from the one in section 6.2.

What we might want to do, however, is take advantage of the layout facilities offered in Grails to apply a common design to all of the pages in the application. As you can see in listing 6.7, it's a rather straightforward and simple change.

Listing 6.7 A Grails-ready GSP template, including layout

```
<!DOCTYPE html>
<html>
  <head>
    <meta name="layout" content="main"/>                          Use the main
    <title>Reading List</title>                                   layout
    <link rel="stylesheet"
        href="/assets/main.css?compile=false"  />
    <link rel="stylesheet"
        href="/assets/mobile.css?compile=false"  />
    <link rel="stylesheet"
        href="/assets/application.css?compile=false"  />
  </head>

  <body>
    <h2>Your Reading List</h2>
                                                                  List the
    <g:if test="${bookList && !bookList.isEmpty()}">              books
      <g:each in="${bookList}" var="book">
      <dl>
        <dt class="bookHeadline">
          ${book.title}</span> by ${book.author}
          (ISBN: ${book.isbn}")
        </dt>
        <dd class="bookDescription">
          <g:if test="${book.description}">
          ${book.description}
          </g:if>
          <g:else>
          No description available
          </g:else>
        </dd>
      </dl>
      </g:each>
    </g:if>
    <g:else>
      <p>You have no books in your book list</p>
    </g:else>

    <hr/>

    <h3>Add a book</h3>
                                                                  The book
    <g:form action="save">                                        form
    <fieldset class="form">
      <label for="title">Title:</label>
      <g:field type="text" name="title" value="${book?.title}"/><br/>
      <label for="author">Author:</label>
      <g:field type="text" name="author"
```

```
                        value="${book?.author}"/><br/>
    <label for="isbn">ISBN:</label>
    <g:field type="text" name="isbn" value="${book?.isbn}"/><br/>
    <label for="description">Description:</label><br/>
    <g:textArea name="description" value="${book?.description}"
                              rows="5" cols="80"/>
  </fieldset>
  <fieldset class="buttons">
    <g:submitButton name="create" class="save"
      value="${message(code: 'default.button.create.label',
                              default: 'Create')}" />
  </fieldset>
  </g:form>

  </body>
</html>
```

Within the `<head>` element we've removed the `<link>` tag that references our stylesheet. In its place, we've put in a `<meta>` tag that references the "main" layout of the Grails application. As a consequence, the application will take on the Grails look and feel, as shown in figure 6.4, when you run it.

Although the Grails style is more eye-catching than the simple stylesheet we've been using, there is obviously still a little work to do to make the reading-list application look

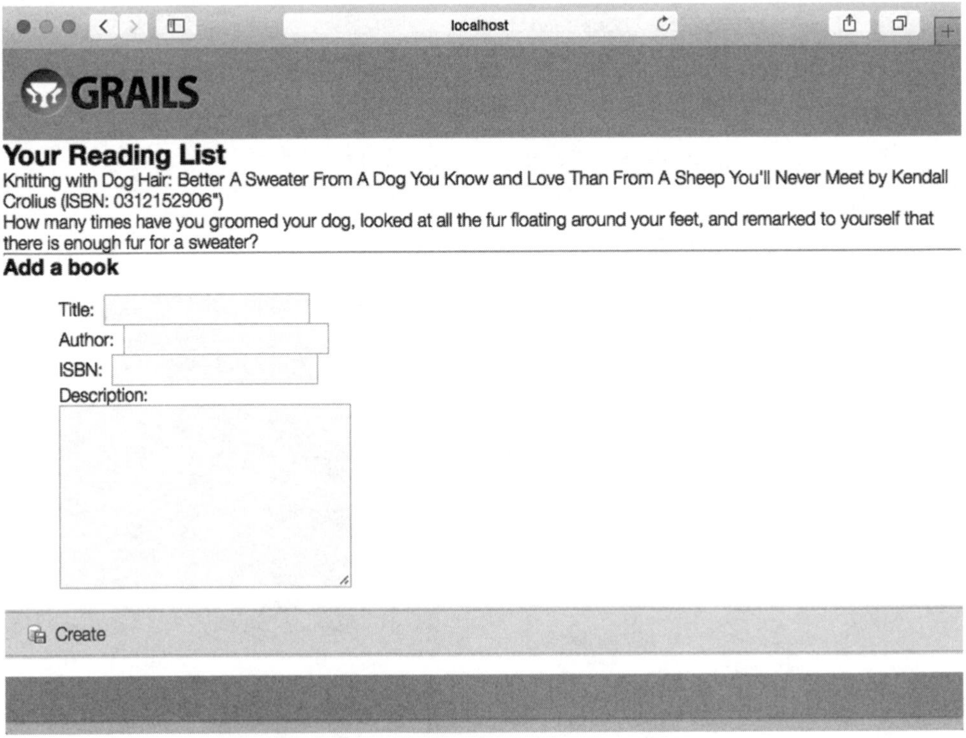

Figure 6.4   The reading-list application with the common Grails styling

good. And we'll probably want to start making the application look a little less like Grails and more like what we want our application to look like. Manipulating the application's stylesheets is well outside of the scope of this book, but if you're interested in tweaking the look and feel, you'll find the stylesheets in the grails-app/assets/stylesheets directory.

6.4 *Summary*

Both Grails and Spring Boot aim to make developers' lives easy, providing a greatly simplified development model on top of Spring, so it may appear that these are competing frameworks. But in this chapter, we've seen how to get the best of both worlds by bringing Spring Boot and Grails together.

We looked at how to add GORM and GSP views, two well-known Grails features, to an otherwise typical Spring Boot application. GORM is an especially welcome feature in Spring Boot, enabling you to perform persistence directly with the domain and eliminating the need for a repository.

Then we looked at Grails 3, the latest incarnation of Grails, built upon Spring Boot. When developing a Grails 3 application, you're also working with Spring Boot and are afforded all of the features of Spring Boot, including auto-configuration.

In all cases, both in this and the previous chapter, you've seen how mixing Groovy and Spring Boot helps squelch the code noise that's required in the Java language.

Coming up in the next chapter, we're going to shift our attention away from coding Spring Boot applications and look at the Spring Boot Actuator to see how it gives us insights into the inner workings of our running applications.

7
Taking a peek inside with the Actuator

This chapter covers

- Actuator web endpoints
- Adjusting the Actuator
- Shelling into a running application
- Securing the Actuator

Have you ever tried to guess what's inside a wrapped gift? You shake it, weigh it, and measure it. And you might even have a solid idea as to what's inside. But until you open it up, there's no way of knowing for sure.

A running application is kind of like a wrapped gift. You can poke at it and make reasonable guesses as to what's going on under the covers. But how can you know for sure? If only there were some way that you could peek inside a running application, see how it's behaving, check on its health, and maybe even trigger operations that influence how it runs?

In this chapter, we're going to explore Spring Boot's Actuator. The Actuator offers production-ready features such as monitoring and metrics to Spring Boot applications. The Actuator's features are provided by way of several REST endpoints, a remote shell, and Java Management Extensions (JMX). We'll start by looking at the Actuator's REST endpoints, which offer the most complete and well-known way of working with the Actuator.

7.1 Exploring the Actuator's endpoints

The key feature of Spring Boot's Actuator is that it provides several web endpoints in your application through which you can view the internals of your running application. Through the Actuator, you can find out how beans are wired together in the Spring application context, determine what environment properties are available to your application, get a snapshot of runtime metrics, and more.

The Actuator offers a baker's dozen of endpoints, as described in table 7.1.

Table 7.1 Actuator endpoints

HTTP method	Path	Description
GET	/autoconfig	Provides an auto-configuration report describing what auto-configuration conditions passed and failed.
GET	/configprops	Describes how beans have been injected with configuration properties (including default values).
GET	/beans	Describes all beans in the application context and their relationship to each other.
GET	/dump	Retrieves a snapshot dump of thread activity.
GET	/env	Retrieves all environment properties.
GET	/env/{name}	Retrieves a specific environment value by name.
GET	/health	Reports health metrics for the application, as provided by HealthIndicator implementations.
GET	/info	Retrieves custom information about the application, as provided by any properties prefixed with info.
GET	/mappings	Describes all URI paths and how they're mapped to controllers (including Actuator endpoints).
GET	/metrics	Reports various application metrics such as memory usage and HTTP request counters.
GET	/metrics/{name}	Reports an individual application metric by name.
POST	/shutdown	Shuts down the application; requires that endpoints.shutdown.enabled be set to true.
GET	/trace	Provides basic trace information (timestamp, headers, and so on) for HTTP requests.

To enable the Actuator endpoints, all you must do is add the Actuator starter to your build. In a Gradle build specification, that dependency looks like this:

```
compile 'org.springframework.boot:spring-boot-starter-actuator'
```

For a Maven build, the required dependency is as follows:

```
<dependency>
  <groupId>org.springframework.boot</groupId>
  <artifactId>spring-boot-starter-actuator</artifactId>
</dependency>
```

Or, if you're using the Spring Boot CLI, the following @Grab should do the trick:

```
@Grab('spring-boot-starter-actuator')
```

No matter which technique you use to add the Actuator to your build, auto-configuration will kick in when the application is running and you enable the Actuator.

The endpoints in table 7.1 can be organized into three distinct categories: configuration endpoints, metrics endpoints, and miscellaneous endpoints. Let's take a look at each of these endpoints, starting with the endpoints that provide insight into the configuration of your application.

7.1.1 Viewing configuration details

One of the most common complaints lodged against Spring component-scanning and autowiring is that it's hard to see how all of the components in an application are wired together. Spring Boot auto-configuration makes this problem even worse, as there's even less Spring configuration. At least with explicit configuration, you could look at the XML file or the configuration class and get an idea of the relationships between the beans in the Spring application context.

Personally, I've never had this concern. Maybe it's because I realize that before Spring came along there wasn't any map of the components in my applications.

Nevertheless, if it concerns you that auto-configuration hides how beans are wired up in the Spring application context, then I have some good news! The Actuator has endpoints that give you that missing application component map as well as some insight into the decisions that auto-configuration made when populating the Spring application context.

GETTING A BEAN WIRING REPORT

The most essential endpoint for exploring an application's Spring context is the /beans endpoint. This endpoint returns a JSON document describing every single bean in the application context, its Java type, and any of the other beans it's injected with. By performing a GET request to /beans (http://localhost:8080/beans when running locally), you'll be given information similar to what's shown in the following listing.

> **Listing 7.1   The /beans endpoint exposes the beans in the Spring application context**

```
[
  {
    "beans": [
      {
```

```
      "bean": "application",          ⟵——— Bean ID
      "dependencies": [],
      "resource": "null",
      "scope": "singleton",                       ⟵——| Resource file
      "type": "readinglist.Application$$EnhancerBySpringCGLIB$$f363c202"
    },
    {
      "bean": "amazonProperties",
      "dependencies": [],
      "resource": "URL [jar:file:/../readinglist-0.0.1-SNAPSHOT.jar!
                             /readinglist/AmazonProperties.class]", ⟵—┐
      "scope": "singleton",
      "type": "readinglist.AmazonProperties"                 Dependencies │
    },
    {
      "bean": "readingListController",
      "dependencies": [              ⟵——— Bean scope
        "readingListRepository",
        "amazonProperties"
      ],
      "resource": "URL [jar:file:/../readinglist-0.0.1-SNAPSHOT.jar!
                          /readinglist/ReadingListController.class]",
      "scope": "singleton",
      "type": "readinglist.ReadingListController"
    },
    {
      "bean": "readerRepository",
      "dependencies": [
        "(inner bean)#219df4f5",
        "(inner bean)#2c0e7419",
        "(inner bean)#7d86037b",
        "jpaMappingContext"
      ],
      "resource": "null",
      "scope": "singleton",
      "type": "readinglist.ReaderRepository"          ⟵——— Java type
    },
    {
      "bean": "readingListRepository",
      "dependencies": [
        "(inner bean)#98ce66",
        "(inner bean)#1fd7add0",
        "(inner bean)#59faabb2",
        "jpaMappingContext"
      ],
      "resource": "null",
      "scope": "singleton",
      "type": "readinglist.ReadingListRepository"
    },
    ...
  ],
  "context": "application",
  "parent": null
}
]
```

Listing 7.1 is an abridged listing of the beans from the reading-list application. As you can see, all of the bean entries carry five pieces of information about the bean:

- `bean`—The name or ID of the bean in the Spring application context
- `resource`—The location of the physical .class file (often a URL into the built JAR file, but this might vary depending on how the application is built and run)
- `dependencies`—A list of bean IDs that this bean is injected with
- `scope`—The bean's scope (usually singleton, as that is the default scope)
- `type`—The bean's Java type

Although the beans report doesn't draw a specific picture of how the beans are wired together (for example, via properties or constructor arguments), it does help you visualize the relationships of the beans in the application context. Indeed, it would be reasonably easy to write a utility that processes the beans report and produces a graphical representation of the bean relationships. Be aware, however, that the full bean report includes many beans, including many auto-configured beans, so such a graphic could be quite busy.

EXPLAINING AUTO-CONFIGURATION

Whereas the `/beans` endpoint produces a report telling you what beans are in the Spring application context, the `/autoconfig` endpoint might help you figure out why they're there—or not there.

As mentioned in chapter 2, Spring Boot auto-configuration is built upon Spring conditional configuration. It provides several configuration classes with `@Conditional` annotations referencing conditions that decide whether or not beans should be automatically configured. The `/autoconfig` endpoint provides a report of all the conditions that are evaluated, grouping them by which conditions passed and which failed.

Listing 7.2 shows an excerpt from the auto-configuration report produced for the reading-list application with one passing and one failing condition.

Listing 7.2 An auto-configuration report for the reading-list app

```
{
  "positiveMatches": {          ◁──── Successful conditions
  ...
  "DataSourceAutoConfiguration.JdbcTemplateConfiguration
                                       #jdbcTemplate": [
    {
      "condition": "OnBeanCondition",
      "message": "@ConditionalOnMissingBean (types:
          org.springframework.jdbc.core.JdbcOperations;
          SearchStrategy: all) found no beans"
    }
  ],
  ...
  },
  "negativeMatches": {          ◁──── Failed conditions
  "ActiveMQAutoConfiguration": [
```

```
    {
      "condition": "OnClassCondition",
      "message": "required @ConditionalOnClass classes not found:
          javax.jms.ConnectionFactory,org.apache.activemq
          .ActiveMQConnectionFactory"
    }
  ],
  ...
  }
}
```

In the `positiveMatches` section, you'll find a condition used to decide whether or not Spring Boot should auto-configure a `JdbcTemplate` bean. The match is named `Data-SourceAutoConfiguration.JdbcTemplateConfiguration#jdbcTemplate`, which indicates the specific configuration class where this condition is applied. The type of condition is an `OnBeanCondition`, which means that the condition's outcome is determined by the presence or absence of a bean. In this case, the `message` property makes it clear that the condition checks for the absence of a bean of type `JdbcOperations` (the interface that `JbdcTemplate` implements). If no such bean has already been configured, then this condition passes and a `JdbcTemplate` bean will be created.

Similarly, under `negativeMatches`, there's a condition that decides whether or not to configure an ActiveMQ. This decision is an `OnClassCondition`, and it hinges on the presence of `ActiveMQConnectionFactory` in the classpath. Because `ActiveMQConnectionFactory` isn't in the classpath, the condition fails and ActiveMQ will not be auto-configured.

INSPECTING CONFIGURATION PROPERTIES

In addition to knowing how your application beans are wired together, you might also be interested in learning what environment properties are available and what configuration properties were injected on the beans.

The `/env` endpoint produces a list of all of the environment properties available to the application, whether they're being used or not. This includes environment variables, JVM properties, command-line parameters, and any properties provided in an application.properties or application.yml file.

The following listing shows an abridged example of what you might get from the `/env` endpoint.

Listing 7.3 The `/env` endpoint reports all properties available

```
{
  "applicationConfig: [classpath:/application.yml]": {        ◁─── Application
    "amazon.associate_id": "habuma-20",                            properties
    "error.whitelabel.enabled": false,
    "logging.level.root": "INFO"
  },
  "profiles": [],
  "servletContextInitParams": {},           Environment
  "systemEnvironment": {              ◁──┘   variables
```

```
    "BOOK_HOME": "/Users/habuma/Projects/BookProjects/walls6",
    "GRADLE_HOME": "/Users/habuma/.sdkman/gradle/current",
    "GRAILS_HOME": "/Users/habuma/.sdkman/grails/current",
    "GROOVY_HOME": "/Users/habuma/.sdkman/groovy/current",
    ...
  },
  "systemProperties": {                    ⟵──────────┐  JVM system
    "PID": "682",                                      │  properties
    "file.encoding": "UTF-8",
    "file.encoding.pkg": "sun.io",
    "file.separator": "/",
    ...
  }
}
```

Essentially, any property source that can provide properties to a Spring Boot application will be listed in the results of the /env endpoint along with the properties provided by that endpoint.

In listing 7.3, properties come from application configuration (application.yml), Spring profiles, servlet context initialization parameters, the system environment, and JVM system properties. (In this case, there are no profiles or servlet context initialization parameters.)

It's common to use properties to carry sensitive information such as database or API passwords. To keep that kind of information from being exposed by the /env endpoint, any property named (or whose last segment is) "password", "secret", or "key" will be rendered as "" in the response from /env. For example, if there's a property named "database.password", it will be rendered in the /env response like this:

```
"database.password":"******"
```

The /env endpoint can also be used to request the value of a single property. Just append the property name to /env when making the request. For example, requesting /env/amazon.associate_id will yield a response of "habuma-20" (in plain text) when requested against the reading-list application.

As you'll recall from chapter 3, these environment properties come in handy when using the @ConfigurationProperties annotation. Beans annotated with @ConfigurationProperties can have their instance properties injected with values from the environment. The /configprops endpoint produces a report of how those properties are set, whether from injection or otherwise. Listing 7.4 shows an excerpt from the configuration properties report for the reading-list application.

Listing 7.4   A configuration properties report

```
{
  "amazonProperties": {                    ⟵──────────┐  Amazon
    "prefix": "amazon",                                │  configuration
    "properties": {
      "associateId": "habuma-20"
```

```
    }
  },
  ...
  "serverProperties": {                    ◁──────────┐  Server
    "prefix": "server",                                │  configuration
    "properties": {
      "address": null,
      "contextPath": null,
      "port": null,
      "servletPath": "/",
      "sessionTimeout": null,
      "ssl": null,
      "tomcat": {
        "accessLogEnabled": false,
        "accessLogPattern": null,
        "backgroundProcessorDelay": 30,
        "basedir": null,
        "compressableMimeTypes": "text/html,text/xml,text/plain",
        "compression": "off",
        "maxHttpHeaderSize": 0,
        "maxThreads": 0,
        "portHeader": null,
        "protocolHeader": null,
        "remoteIpHeader": null,
        "uriEncoding": null
      },
      ...
    }
  },
  ...
}
```

The first item in this excerpt is the amazonProperties bean we created in chapter 3. This report tells us that it's annotated with @ConfigurationProperties to have a prefix of "amazon". And it shows that the associateId property is set to "habuma-20". This is because in application.yml, we set the amazon.associateId property to "habuma-20".

You can also see an entry for serverProperties—it has a prefix of "server" and several properties that we can work with. Here they all have default values, but you can change any of them by setting a property prefixed with "server". For example, you could change the port that the server listens on by setting the server.port property.

Aside from giving insight into how configuration properties are set in the running application, this report is also useful as a quick reference showing all of the properties that you *could* set. For example, if you weren't sure how to set the maximum number of threads in the embedded Tomcat server, a quick look at the configuration properties report would give you a clue that server.tomcat.maxThreads is the property you're looking to set.

PRODUCING ENDPOINT-TO-CONTROLLER MAP

When an application is relatively small, it's usually easy to know how all of its controllers are mapped to endpoints. But once the web interface exceeds more than a handful of controllers and request-handling methods, it might be helpful to have a list of all of the endpoints exposed by the application.

The /mappings endpoint provides such a list. Listing 7.5 shows an excerpt of the mappings report from the reading-list application.

Listing 7.5 The controller/endpoint mappings for the reading-list app

```
{
    ...                                                    ReadingListController
                                                                      mappings
    "{[/],methods=[GET],params=[],headers=[],consumes=[],produces=[],  ◄──┐
                                                custom=[]}": {
        "bean": "requestMappingHandlerMapping",
        "method": "public java.lang.String readinglist.ReadingListController.
                   readersBooks(readinglist.Reader,org.springframework.ui.Model)"
    },
    "{[/],methods=[POST],params=[],headers=[],consumes=[],produces=[],
                                                custom=[]}": {
        "bean": "requestMappingHandlerMapping",
        "method": "public java.lang.String readinglist.ReadingListController
                        .addToReadingList(readinglist.Reader,readinglist.
        Book)"
    },
    "{[/autoconfig],methods=[GET],params=[],headers=[],consumes=[]   ◄─────┐
                                ,produces=[],custom=[]}": {
        "bean": "endpointHandlerMapping",
        "method": "public java.lang.Object org.springframework.boot
                    .actuate.endpoint.mvc.EndpointMvcAdapter.invoke()"
    },
    ...                                                    Auto-configuration
}                                                          report mapping
```

Here we see a handful of endpoint mappings. The key for each mapping is a string containing what appears to be the attributes of Spring MVC's @RequestMapping annotation. Indeed, this string gives you a good idea of how the controller is mapped, even if you haven't seen the source code. The value of each mapping has two properties: bean and method. The bean property identifies the name of the Spring bean that the mapping comes from. The method property gives the fully qualified method signature of the method for which the mapping is being reported.

The first two mappings are for the request-handing methods in our application's ReadingListController. The first shows that an HTTP GET request for the root path ("/") will be handled by the readersBooks() method. The second shows that a POST request is mapped to the addToReadingList() method.

The next mapping is for an Actuator-provided endpoint. An HTTP GET request for the /autoconfig endpoint will be handled by the invoke() method of Spring Boot's EndpointMvcAdapter class. There are, of course, many other Actuator endpoints that aren't shown in listing 7.5, but those were omitted from the listing for brevity's sake.

The Actuator's configuration endpoints are great for seeing how your application is configured. But it's also interesting and useful to see what's actually happening within your application while it's running. The metrics endpoints help give a snapshot into an application's runtime internals.

7.1.2 *Tapping runtime metrics*

When you go to the doctor for a physical exam, the doctor performs a battery of tests to see how your body is performing. Some of them, such as determining your blood type, are important but will not change over time. These kinds of tests give the doctor insight into how your body is configured. Other tests give the doctor a snapshot into how your body is performing during the visit. Your heart rate, blood pressure, and cholesterol level are useful in helping the doctor evaluate your health. These metrics are temporal and likely to change over time, but they're still helpful runtime metrics.

Similarly, taking a snapshot of the runtime metrics is helpful in evaluating the health of an application. The Actuator offers a handful of endpoints that enable you to perform a quick checkup on your application while it's running. Let's take a look at them, starting with the /metrics endpoint.

VIEWING APPLICATION METRICS

There are a lot of interesting and useful bits of information about any running application. Knowing the application's memory circumstances (available vs. free), for instance, might help you decide if you need to give the JVM more or less memory to work with. For a web application, it can be helpful knowing at a glance, without scouring web server log files, if there are any requests that are failing or taking too long to serve.

The /metrics endpoint provides a snapshot of various counters and gauges in a running application. The following listing shows a sample of what the /metrics endpoint might give you.

Listing 7.6 The metrics endpoint provides several useful pieces of runtime data

```
{
  mem: 198144,
  mem.free: 144029,
  processors: 8,
  uptime: 1887794,
  instance.uptime: 1871237,
  systemload.average: 1.33251953125,
  heap.committed: 198144,
  heap.init: 131072,
  heap.used: 54114,
  heap: 1864192,
  threads.peak: 21,
  threads.daemon: 19,
  threads: 21,
  classes: 9749,
  classes.loaded: 9749,
  classes.unloaded: 0,
```

```
  gc.ps_scavenge.count: 22,
  gc.ps_scavenge.time: 122,
  gc.ps_marksweep.count: 2,
  gc.ps_marksweep.time: 156,
  httpsessions.max: -1,
  httpsessions.active: 1,
  datasource.primary.active: 0,
  datasource.primary.usage: 0,
  counter.status.200.beans: 1,
  counter.status.200.env: 1,
  counter.status.200.login: 3,
  counter.status.200.metrics: 2,
  counter.status.200.root: 6,
  counter.status.200.star-star: 9,
  counter.status.302.login: 3,
  counter.status.302.logout: 1,
  counter.status.302.root: 5,
  gauge.response.beans: 169,
  gauge.response.env: 165,
  gauge.response.login: 3,
  gauge.response.logout: 0,
  gauge.response.metrics: 2,
  gauge.response.root: 11,
  gauge.response.star-star: 2
}
```

As you can see, a lot of information is provided by the /metrics endpoint. Rather than examine these metrics line by line, which would be tedious, table 7.2 groups them into categories by the type of information they offer.

Table 7.2 Gauges and counters reported by the /metrics endpoint

Category	Prefix	What it reports
Garbage collector	gc.*	The count of garbage collections that have occurred and the elapsed garbage collection time for both the mark-sweep and scavenge garbage collectors (from java.lang.management.GarbageCollectorMXBean)
Memory	mem.*	The amount of memory allotted to the application and the amount of memory that is free (from java.lang.Runtime)
Heap	heap.*	The current memory usage (from java.lang.management.MemoryUsage)
Class loader	classes.*	The number of classes that have been loaded and unloaded by the JVM class loader (from java.lang.management.ClassLoadingMXBean)
System	processors uptime instance.uptime systemload.average	System information such as the number of processors (from java.lang.Runtime), uptime (from java.lang.management.RuntimeMXBean), and average system load (from java.lang.management.OperatingSystemMXBean)

Table 7.2   Gauges and counters reported by the `/metrics` endpoint *(continued)*

Category	Prefix	What it reports
Thread pool	`threads.*`	The number of threads, daemon threads, and the peak count of threads since the JVM started (from `java.lang.management.ThreadMXBean`)
Data source	`datasource.*`	The number of data source connections (from the data source's metadata and only available if there are one or more `DataSource` beans in the Spring application context)
Tomcat sessions	`httpsessions.*`	The active and maximum number of sessions in Tomcat (from the embedded Tomcat bean and only available if the application is served via an embedded Tomcat server)
HTTP	`counter.status.*` `gauge.response.*`	Various gauges and counters for HTTP requests that the application has served

Notice that some of these metrics, such as the data source and Tomcat session metrics, are only available if the necessary components are in play in the running application. You can also register your own custom application metrics, as you'll see in section 7.4.3.

The HTTP counters and gauges demand a bit more explanation. The number following the `counter.status` prefix is the HTTP status code. What follows that is the path requested. For instance, the metric named `counter.status.200.metrics` indicates the number of times that the `/metrics` endpoint was served with an HTTP status of 200 (OK).

The HTTP gauges are similarly structured but report a different kind of metrics. They're all prefixed with `gauge.response`, indicating that they are gauges for HTTP responses. Following that prefix is the path that the gauge refers to. The value of the metric indicates the time in milliseconds that it took to serve that path the most recent time it was served. For instance, the `gauge.response.beans` metric in table 7.6 indicates that it took 169 milliseconds to serve that request the last time it was served.

You'll notice that there are a few special cases for the counter and gauge paths. The `root` path refers to the root path or `/`. And `star-star` is a catchall that refers to any path that Spring determines is a static resource, including images, JavaScript, and stylesheets. It also includes any resource that can't be found, which is why you'll often see a `counter.status.404.star-star` metric indicating the count of requests that were met with HTTP 404 (NOT FOUND) status.

Whereas the `/metrics` endpoint fetches a full set of all available metrics, you may only be interested in a single metric. To fetch only one metric value, append the metric's key to the URL path when making the request. For example, to fetch only the amount of free memory, perform a GET request for `/metrics/mem.free`:

```
$ curl localhost:8080/metrics/mem.free
144029
```

It may be useful to know that even though the result from /metrics/{name} appears to be plain text, the Content-Type header in the response is set to "application/json;charset=UTF-8". Therefore, it can be processed as JSON if you need to do so.

TRACING WEB REQUESTS

Although the /metrics endpoint gives you some basic counters and timers for web requests, those metrics lack any details. Sometimes it can be helpful, especially when debugging, to know more about the requests that were handled. That's where the /trace endpoint can be handy.

The /trace endpoint reports details of all web requests, including details such as the request method, path, timestamp, and request and response headers. Listing 7.7 shows an excerpt of the /trace endpoint's output containing a single request trace entry.

Listing 7.7   The /trace endpoint records web request details

```
[
  ...
  {
    "timestamp": 1426378239775,
    "info": {
      "method": "GET",
      "path": "/metrics",
      "headers": {
        "request": {
          "accept": "*/*",
          "host": "localhost:8080",
          "user-agent": "curl/7.37.1"
        },
        "response": {
          "X-Content-Type-Options": "nosniff",
          "X-XSS-Protection": "1; mode=block",
          "Cache-Control":
                    "no-cache, no-store, max-age=0, must-revalidate",
          "Pragma": "no-cache",
          "Expires": "0",
          "X-Frame-Options": "DENY",
          "X-Application-Context": "application",
          "Content-Type": "application/json;charset=UTF-8",
          "Transfer-Encoding": "chunked",
          "Date": "Sun, 15 Mar 2015 00:10:39 GMT",
          "status": "200"
        }
      }
    }
  }
]
```

As indicated by the method and path properties, you can see that this trace entry is for a /metrics request. The timestamp property (as well as the Date header in the response) tells you when the request was handled. The `headers` property carries header details for both the request and the response.

Although listing 7.7 only shows a single trace entry, the `/trace` endpoint will report trace details for the 100 most recent requests, including requests for the `/trace` endpoint itself. It maintains the trace data in an in-memory trace repository. Later, in section 7.4.4, you'll see how to create a custom trace repository implementation for a more permanent tracing of requests.

DUMPING THREAD ACTIVITY

In addition to request tracing, thread activity can also be useful in determining what's going on in a running application. The `/dump` endpoint produces a snapshot of current thread activity.

Listing 7.8 The `/dump` endpoint provides a snapshot of an application's threads

```
[
  {
    "threadName": "container-0",
    "threadId": 19,
    "blockedTime": -1,
    "blockedCount": 0,
    "waitedTime": -1,
    "waitedCount": 64,
    "lockName": null,
    "lockOwnerId": -1,
    "lockOwnerName": null,
    "inNative": false,
    "suspended": false,
    "threadState": "TIMED_WAITING",
    "stackTrace": [
      {
        "className": "java.lang.Thread",
        "fileName": "Thread.java",
        "lineNumber": -2,
        "methodName": "sleep",
        "nativeMethod": true
      },
      {
        "className": "org.apache.catalina.core.StandardServer",
        "fileName": "StandardServer.java",
        "lineNumber": 407,
        "methodName": "await",
        "nativeMethod": false
      },
      {
        "className": "org.springframework.boot.context.embedded.
                      tomcat.TomcatEmbeddedServletContainer$1",
        "fileName": "TomcatEmbeddedServletContainer.java",
        "lineNumber": 139,
        "methodName": "run",
        "nativeMethod": false
      }
  }
```

```
      ],
      "lockedMonitors": [],
      "lockedSynchronizers": [],
      "lockInfo": null
    },
    ...
]
```

The complete thread dump report includes every thread in the running application. To save space, listing 7.8 shows an abridged entry for a single thread. As you can see, it includes details regarding the blocking and locking status of the thread, among other thread specifics. There's also a stack trace that, in this case, indicates the thread is a Tomcat container thread.

MONITORING APPLICATION HEALTH

If you're ever wondering if your application is up and running or not, you can easily find out by requesting the /health endpoint. In the simplest case, the /health endpoint reports a simple JSON structure like this:

```
{"status":"UP"}
```

The status property reports that the application is up. Of course it is. It doesn't really matter what the response is; any response at all is an indication that the application is running. But the /health endpoint has more information than a simple "UP" status.

Some of the information offered by the /health endpoint can be sensitive, so unauthenticated requests are only given the simple health status response. If the request is authenticated (for example, if you're logged in), more health information is exposed. Here's some sample health information reported for the reading-list application:

```
{
  "status":"UP",
  "diskSpace": {
    "status":"UP",
    "free":377423302656,
    "threshold":10485760
  },
  "db":{
    "status":"UP",
    "database":"H2",
    "hello":1
  }
}
```

Along with the basic health status, you're also given information regarding the amount of available disk space and the status of the database that the application is using.

All of the information reported by the /health endpoints is provided by one or more health indicators, including those listed in table 7.3, that come with Spring Boot.

Table 7.3 Spring Boot's out-of-the-box health indicators

Health indicator	Key	Reports
ApplicationHealthIndicator	none	Always "UP"
DataSourceHealthIndicator	db	"UP" and database type if the database can be contacted; "DOWN" status otherwise
DiskSpaceHealthIndicator	diskSpace	"UP" and available disk space, and "UP" if available space is above a threshold; "DOWN" if there isn't enough disk space
JmsHealthIndicator	jms	"UP" and JMS provider name if the message broker can be contacted; "DOWN" otherwise
MailHealthIndicator	mail	"UP" and the mail server host and port if the mail server can be contacted; "DOWN" otherwise
MongoHealthIndicator	mongo	"UP" and the MongoDB server version; "DOWN" otherwise
RabbitHealthIndicator	rabbit	"UP" and the RabbitMQ broker version; "DOWN" otherwise
RedisHealthIndicator	redis	"UP" and the Redis server version; "DOWN" otherwise
SolrHealthIndicator	solr	"UP" if the Solr server can be contacted; "DOWN" otherwise

These health indicators will be automatically configured as needed. For example, `Data-SourceHealthIndicator` will be automatically configured if `javax.sql.DataSource` is available in the classpath. `ApplicationHealthIndicator` and `DiskSpaceHealth-Indicator` will always be configured.

In addition to these out-of-the-box health indicators, you'll see how to create custom health indicators in section 7.4.5.

7.1.3 *Shutting down the application*

Suppose you need to kill your running application. In a microservice architecture, for instance, you might have multiple instances of a microservice application running in the cloud. If one of those instances starts misbehaving, you might decide to shut it down and let the cloud provider restart the failed application for you. In that scenario, the Actuator's `/shutdown` endpoint will prove useful.

In order to shut down your application, you can send a POST request to `/shutdown`. For example, you can shut down your application using the `curl` command-line tool like this:

```
$ curl -X POST http://localhost:8080/shutdown
```

Obviously, the ability to shut down a running application is a dangerous thing, so it's disabled by default. Unless you've explicitly enabled it, you'll get the following response from the POST request:

```
{"message":"This endpoint is disabled"}
```

To enable the /shutdown endpoint, configure the endpoints.shutdown.enabled property to true. For example, add the following lines to application.yml to enable the /shutdown endpoint:

```
endpoints:
  shutdown:
    enabled: true
```

Once the /shutdown endpoint is enabled, you want to make sure that not just anybody can kill your application. You should secure the /shutdown endpoint, requiring that only authorized users are allowed to bring the application down. You'll see how to secure Actuator endpoints in section 7.5.

7.1.4 *Fetching application information*

Spring Boot's Actuator has one more endpoint you might find useful. The /info endpoint reports any information about your application that you might want to expose to callers. The default response to a GET request to /info looks like this:

```
{}
```

Obviously, an empty JSON object isn't very useful. But you can add any information to the /info endpoint's response by simply configuring properties prefixed with info. For example, suppose you want to provide a contact email in the /info endpoint response. You could set a property named info.contactEmail like this in application.yml:

```
info:
  contactEmail: support@myreadinglist.com
```

Now if you request the /info endpoint, you'll get the following response:

```
{
  "contactEmail":"support@myreadinglist.com"
}
```

Properties in the /info response can also be nested. For example, suppose that you want to provide both a support email and a support phone number. In application.yml, you might configure the following properties:

```
info:
  contact:
    email: support@myreadinglist.com
    phone: 1-888-555-1971
```

The JSON returned from the /info endpoint will include a contact property that itself has email and phone properties:

```
{
  "contact":{
    "email":"support@myreadinglist.com",
    "phone":"1-888-555-1971"
  }
}
```

Adding properties to the /info endpoint is just one of many ways you can customize Actuator behavior. Later in section 7.4, we'll look at other ways that you can configure and extend the Actuator. But first, let's see how to secure the Actuator's endpoints.

7.2 *Connecting to the Actuator remote shell*

You've seen how the Actuator provides some very useful information over REST endpoints. An optional way to dig into the internals of a running application is by way of a remote shell. Spring Boot integrates with CRaSH, a shell that can be embedded into any Java application. Spring Boot also extends CRaSH with a handful of Spring Boot-specific commands that offer much of the same functionality as the Actuator's endpoints.

In order to use the remote shell, you'll need to add the remote shell starter as a dependency. The Gradle dependency you'll need looks like this:

```
compile("org.springframework.boot:spring-boot-starter-remote-shell")
```

If you're building your project with Maven, you'll need the following dependency in your pom.xml file:

```
<dependency>
  <groupId>org.springframework.boot</groupId>
  <artifactId>spring-boot-starter-remote-shell</artifactId>
</dependency>
```

And if you're developing an application to run with the Spring Boot CLI, the following @Grab is what you'll need:

```
@Grab("spring-boot-starter-remote-shell")
```

With the remote shell added as a dependency, you can now build and run the application. As it's starting up, watch for the password to be written to the log in a line that looks something like this:

```
Using default security password: efe30c70-5bf0-43b1-9d50-c7a02dda7d79
```

The username that goes with that password is "user". The password itself is randomly generated and will be different each time you run the application.

Now you can use an SSH utility to connect to the shell, which is listening for con-nections on port 2000. If you use the UNIX ssh command to connect to the shell, it might look something like this:

```
~% ssh user@localhost -p 2000
Password authentication
Password:
    .    ____
   /\\ / ___'_ _ _ _(_)_ __ __ _ \ \ \ \
  ( ( )\___ | '_ | '_| | '_ \/ _` | \ \ \ \
   \\/  ___)| |_)| | | | | | || (_| |  ) ) ) )
    '  |____| .__|_| |_|_| |_\__, | / / / /
   =========|_|==============|___/=/_/_/_/
   :: Spring Boot ::   (v1.3.0.RELEASE) on habuma.local
>
```

Great! You're connected to the shell. Now what?

The remote shell offers almost two dozen commands that you can execute within the context of the running application. Most of those commands come out of the box with CRaSH, but Spring Boot adds a handful of commands. These Spring Boot-specific commands are listed in table 7.4.

Table 7.4 CRaSH shell commands provided by Spring Boot

Command	Description
autoconfig	Produces an auto-configuration explanation report. Similar to the /autoconfig end-point, except that the results are plain text instead of JSON.
beans	Displays the beans in the Spring application context. Similar to the /beans endpoint.
endpoint	Invokes an Actuator endpoint.
metrics	Displays Spring Boot metrics. Similar to the /metrics endpoint, except presented as a live list of metrics that's updated as the values change.

Let's take a look at how to use each of the shell commands added by Spring Boot.

7.2.1 *Viewing the autoconfig report*

The autoconfig command produces a report that's very similar to the report pro-duced by the Actuator's /autoconfig endpoint. Figure 7.1 shows an abridged screen-shot of the output produced by the autoconfig command.

As you can see, the results are split into two groups—positive matches and negative matches—just like the results from the /autoconfig endpoint. In fact, the only signif-icant difference is that the autoconfig command produces a textual report whereas the /autoconfig endpoint produces JSON output. Otherwise, they are the same.

Figure 7.1 Output of `autoconfig` command

We're not going to dwell on any of the shell commands provided natively by CRaSH, but you might want to consider piping the results of the `autoconfig` command to CRaSH's `less` command:

```
> autoconfig | less
```

The `less` command is much like the same-named command in Unix shells; it enables you to page back and forth through a file. The `autoconfig` output is lengthy, but piping it to `less` will make it easier to read and navigate.

7.2.2 Listing application beans

The output from the `autoconfig` shell command and the `/autoconfig` endpoint were similar but different. In contrast, you'll find that the results from the `beans` command are exactly the same as those from the `/beans` endpoint, as the screenshot in figure 7.2 shows.

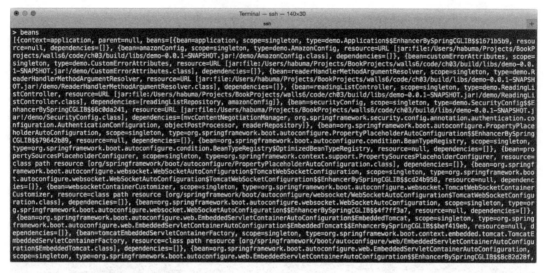

Figure 7.2   Output of `beans` command

Just like the `/beans` endpoint, the `beans` command produces a list of all beans in the
Spring application context, along with any dependency beans, in JSON format.

7.2.3   *Watching application metrics*

The `metrics` shell command produces the same information as the Actuator
`/metrics` endpoint. But unlike the `/metrics` endpoint, which produces a snapshot of
the current metrics in JSON format, the `metrics` command takes over the shell and
displays its results in a live dashboard. Figure 7.3 shows what the `metrics` dashboard
looks like.

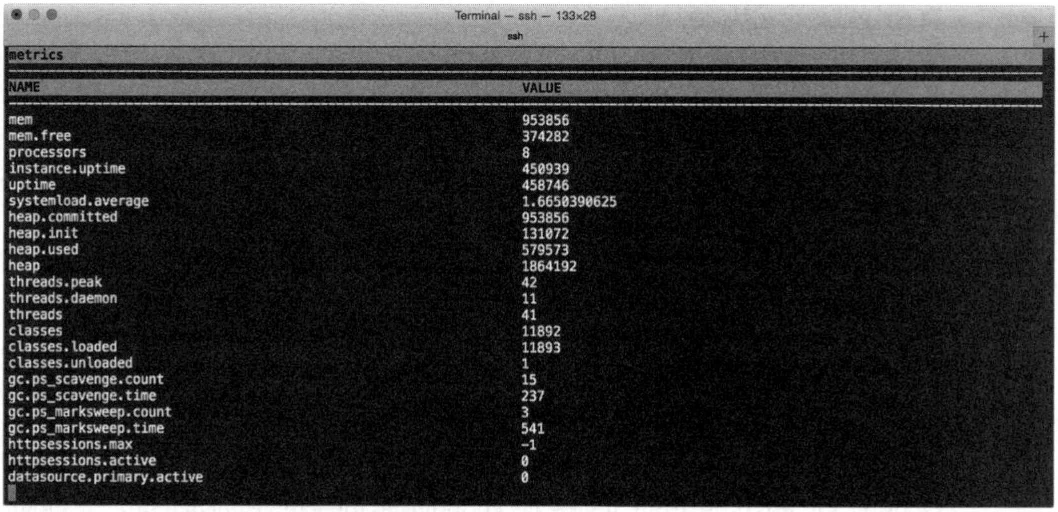

Figure 7.3   The `metrics` dashboard

It's difficult to demonstrate the live dashboard behavior of the `metrics` command with a static figure in a book. But try to imagine that as memory, heap, and threads are consumed and released and as classes are loaded, the numbers shown in the dashboard will change to reflect the current values.

Once you're finished looking at the metrics offered by the `metrics` command, press Ctrl-C to return to the shell.

7.2.4 Invoking Actuator endpoints

You've probably realized by now that not all of the Actuator's endpoints have corresponding commands in the shell. Does that mean that the shell can't be a full replacement for the Actuator endpoints? Will you still have to query the endpoints directly for some of the internals offered by the Actuator? Although the shell doesn't pair a command up with each of the endpoints, the `endpoint` command enables you to invoke Actuator endpoints from within the shell.

First, you need to know which endpoint you want to invoke. You can get a list of endpoints by issuing `endpoint list` at the shell prompt, as shown in figure 7.4. Notice that the endpoints listed are referred to by their bean names, not by their URL paths.

When you want to call one of the endpoints from the shell, you'll use the `endpoint invoke` command, giving it the endpoint's bean name without the "Endpoint" suffix. For example, to invoke the health endpoint, you'd issue `endpoint invoke health` at the shell prompt, as shown in figure 7.5.

Notice that the results coming back from the endpoint are in the form of a raw, unformatted JSON document. Although it may be nice to be able to invoke the Actuator's endpoints from within the shell, the results can be a bit difficult to read. Out of the box, there's not much that can be done about that. But if you're feeling adventurous, you can create a custom CRaSH shell command that accepts the unformatted JSON via

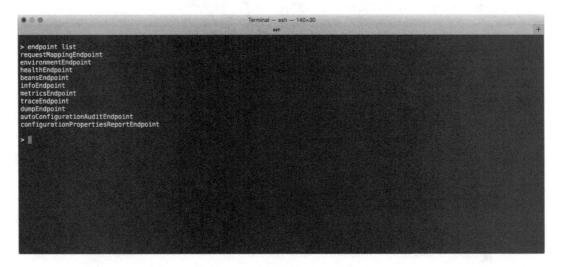

Figure 7.4 Getting a list of endpoints

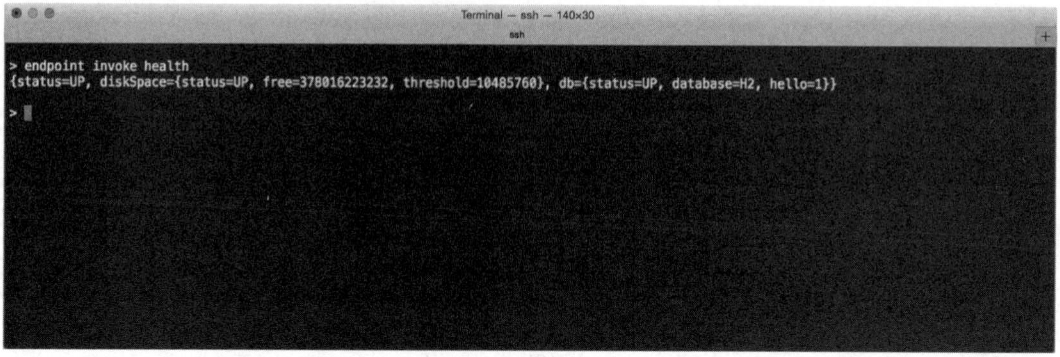

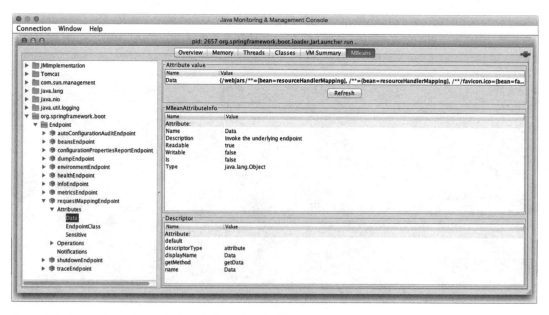

Figure 7.5 Invoking the health endpoint

a pipe and pretty-prints it. And you can always cut and paste it into a tool of your choosing for further review or formatting.

7.3 *Monitoring your application with JMX*

In addition to the endpoints and the remote shell, the Actuator also exposes its endpoints as MBeans to be viewed and managed through JMX (Java Management Extensions). JMX is an attractive option for managing your Spring Boot application, especially if you're already using JMX to manage other MBeans in your applications.

All of the Actuator's endpoints are exposed under the org.springframework.boot domain. For example, suppose you want to view the request mappings for your application. Figure 7.6 shows the request mapping endpoint as viewed in JConsole.

Figure 7.6 Request mapping endpoint as viewed in JConsole

As you can see, the request mapping endpoint is found under `requestMappingEnd-point`, which is under `Endpoint` in the org.springframework.boot domain. The `Data` attribute contains the JSON reported by the endpoint.

As with any MBean, the endpoint MBeans have operations that you can invoke. Most of the endpoint MBeans only have accessor operations that return the value of one of their attributes. But the shutdown endpoint offers a slightly more interesting (and destructive!) operation, as shown in figure 7.7

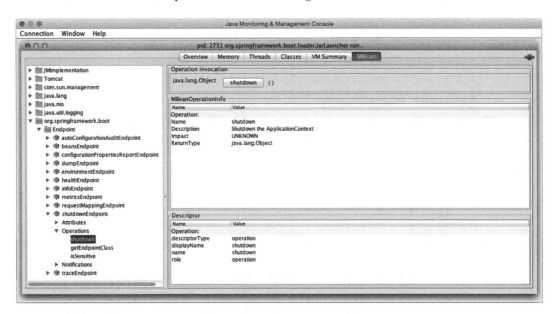

Figure 7.7   Shutdown button invokes the endpoint.

If you ever need to shut down your application (or just like living dangerously), the shutdown endpoint is there for you. As shown in figure 7.7, it's waiting for you to click the "shutdown" button to invoke the endpoint. Be careful, though—there's no turning back or "Are you sure?" prompt. The very next thing you'll see is shown in figure 7.8.

After that, your application will have been shut down. And because it's dead, there's no way it could possibly expose another MBean operation for restarting it. You'll have to restart it yourself, the same way you started it in the first place.

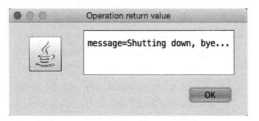

Figure 7.8   Application immediately shuts down.

7.4   *Customizing the Actuator*

Although the Actuator offers a great deal of insight into the inner workings of a running Spring Boot application, it may not be a perfect fit for your needs. Maybe you don't need everything it offers and want to disable some of it. Or maybe you need to extend it with metrics custom-suited to your application.

As it turns out, the Actuator can be customized in several ways, including the following:

- Renaming endpoints
- Enabling and disabling endpoints
- Defining custom metrics and gauges
- Creating a custom repository for storing trace data
- Plugging in custom health indicators

We're going to see how to customize the Actuator, bending it to meet our needs. We'll start with one of the simplest customizations: renaming the Actuator's endpoints.

7.4.1   *Changing endpoint IDs*

Each of the Actuator endpoints has an ID that's used to determine that endpoint's path. For example, the /beans endpoint has beans as its default ID.

If an endpoint's path is determined by its ID, then it stands to reason that you can change an endpoint's path by changing its ID. All you need to do is set a property whose name is endpoints.*endpoint-id*.id.

To demonstrate how this works, consider the /shutdown endpoint. It responds to POST requests sent to /shutdown. Suppose, however, that you'd rather have it handle POST requests sent to /kill. The following YAML shows how you might assign a new ID, and therefore a new path, to the /shutdown endpoint:

```
endpoints:
  shutdown:
    id: kill
```

There are a couple of reasons you might want to rename an endpoint and change its path. The most obvious is that you might simply want to name the endpoints to match the terminology used by your team. But you might also think that renaming an endpoint will hide it from anyone who might be familiar with the default names, thus creating a sense of security by obscurity.

Unfortunately, renaming an endpoint doesn't really secure it. At best, it will only slow down a hacker looking to gain access to an endpoint. We'll look at how you can secure Actuator endpoints in section 7.5. For now, let's see how to completely disable any (or all) endpoints that you don't want anyone to have access to.

7.4.2 *Enabling and disabling endpoints*

Although all of the Actuator endpoints are useful, you may not want or need all of them. By default, all of the endpoints (except for /shutdown) are enabled. We've already seen how to enable the /shutdown endpoint by setting endpoints.shutdown .enabled to true (in section 7.1.1). In the same way, you can disable any of the other endpoints by setting endpoints._endpoint-id.enabled to false.

For example, suppose you want to disable the /metrics endpoint. All you need to do is set the endpoints.metrics.enabled property to false. In application.yml, that would look like this:

```
endpoints:
  metrics:
    enabled: false
```

If you find that you only want to leave one or two of the endpoints enabled, it might be easier to disable them all and then opt in to the ones you want to enable. For example, consider the following snippet from application.yml:

```
endpoints:
  enabled: false
  metrics:
    enabled: true
```

As shown here, all of the Actuator's endpoints are disabled by setting endpoints.enabled to false. Then the /metrics endpoint is re-enabled by setting endpoints.metrics .enabled to true.

7.4.3 *Adding custom metrics and gauges*

In section 7.1.2, you saw how to use the /metrics endpoint to fetch information about the internal metrics of a running application, including memory, garbage collection, and thread metrics. Although these are certainly useful and informative metrics, you may want to define custom metrics to capture information specific to your application.

Suppose, for instance, that we want a metric that reports how many times a user has saved a book to their reading list. The easiest way to capture this number is to increment a counter every time the addToReadingList() method is called on ReadingListController. A counter is simple enough to implement, but how would you expose the running total along with the other metrics exposed by the /metrics endpoint?

Let's also suppose that we want to capture a timestamp for the last time a book was saved. We could easily capture that by calling System.currentTimeMillis(), but how could we report that time in the /metrics endpoint?

As it turns out, the auto-configuration that enables the Actuator also creates an instance of `CounterService` and registers it as a bean in the Spring application context. `CounterService` is an interface that defines three methods for incrementing, decrementing, or resetting a named metric, as shown here:

```
package org.springframework.boot.actuate.metrics;

public interface CounterService {
  void increment(String metricName);
  void decrement(String metricName);
  void reset(String metricName);
}
```

Actuator auto-configuration will also configure a bean of type `GaugeService`, an interface similar to `CounterService` that lets you record a single value to a named gauge metric. `GaugeService` looks like this:

```
package org.springframework.boot.actuate.metrics;

public interface GaugeService {
  void submit(String metricName, double value);
}
```

We don't need to implement either of these interfaces; Spring Boot already provides implementations for them both. All we must do is inject the `CounterService` and `GaugeService` instances into any other bean where they're needed, and call the methods to update whichever metrics we want.

For the metrics we want, we'll need to inject the `CounterService` and `GaugeService` beans into `ReadingListController` and call their methods from the `addToReading-List()` method. Listing 7.9 shows the necessary changes to `ReadingListController`.

Listing 7.9 Using injected gauge and counter services

```
@Controller
@RequestMapping("/")
@ConfigurationProperties("amazon")
public class ReadingListController {

  ...

  private CounterService counterService;

  @Autowired
  public ReadingListController(
      ReadingListRepository readingListRepository,
      AmazonProperties amazonProperties,
      CounterService counterService,                    ◁─────┐  Inject the
      GaugeService gaugeService) {                             │  counter and
    this.readingListRepository = readingListRepository;       │  gauge services
    this.amazonProperties = amazonProperties;
    this.counterService = counterService;
    this.gaugeService = gaugeService;
```

```
    }

    ...

    @RequestMapping(method=RequestMethod.POST)
    public String addToReadingList(Reader reader, Book book) {
      book.setReader(reader);
      readingListRepository.save(book);

      counterService.increment("books.saved");

      gaugeService.submit(
              "books.last.saved", System.currentTimeMillis());
      return "redirect:/";
    }

  }
```

Increment
"books.saved"

Record
"books.last.saved"

This change to ReadingListController uses autowiring to inject the CounterService and GaugeService beans via the controller's constructor, which then stores them in instance variables. Then, each time that the addToReadingList() method handles a request, it will call counterService.increment("books.saved") and gaugeService .submit("books.last.saved") to adjust our custom metrics.

Although CounterService and GaugeService are simple to use, there are some metrics that are hard to capture by incrementing a counter or recording a gauge value. For those cases, we can implement the PublicMetrics interface and provide as many custom metrics as we want. The PublicMetrics interface defines a single metrics() method that returns a collection of Metric objects:

```
package org.springframework.boot.actuate.endpoint;

public interface PublicMetrics {
  Collection<Metric<?>> metrics();
}
```

To put PublicMetrics to work, suppose that we want to be able to report some metrics from the Spring application context. The time when the application context was started and the number of beans and bean definitions might be interesting metrics to include. And, just for grins, let's also report the number of beans that are annotated as @Controller. Listing 7.10 shows the implementation of PublicMetrics that will do the job.

Listing 7.10 Publishing custom metrics

```
package readinglist;
import java.util.ArrayList;
import java.util.Collection;
import java.util.List;
import org.springframework.beans.factory.annotation.Autowired;
import org.springframework.boot.actuate.endpoint.PublicMetrics;
import org.springframework.boot.actuate.metrics.Metric;
```

```
import org.springframework.context.ApplicationContext;
import org.springframework.stereotype.Component;
import org.springframework.stereotype.Controller;

@Component
public class ApplicationContextMetrics implements PublicMetrics {

  private ApplicationContext context;

  @Autowired
  public ApplicationContextMetrics(ApplicationContext context) {
    this.context = context;
  }

  @Override
  public Collection<Metric<?>> metrics() {
    List<Metric<?>> metrics = new ArrayList<Metric<?>>();
    metrics.add(new Metric<Long>("spring.context.startup-date",      ⟵──┐   Record
        context.getStartupDate()));                                       startup
                                                                          date

    metrics.add(new Metric<Integer>("spring.beans.definitions",      ⟵──   Record bean
        context.getBeanDefinitionCount()));                                definition
                                                                           count

    metrics.add(new Metric<Integer>("spring.beans",
        context.getBeanNamesForType(Object.class).length));         ⟵──┐  Record bean
                                                                         count
    metrics.add(new Metric<Integer>("spring.controllers",
        context.getBeanNamesForAnnotation(Controller.class).length)); ⟵─┐

    return metrics;                                                       Record controller
  }                                                                       bean count

}
```

The metrics() method will be called by the Actuator to get any custom metrics that ApplicationContextMetrics provides. It makes a handful of calls to methods on the injected ApplicationContext to fetch the numbers we want to report as metrics. For each one, it creates an instance of Metric, specifying the metric's name and the value, and adds the Metric to the list to be returned.

As a consequence of creating ApplicationContextMetrics as well as using CounterService and GaugeService in ReadingListController, we get the following entries in the response from the /metrics endpoint:

```
{
  ...
  spring.context.startup-date: 1429398980443,
  spring.beans.definitions: 261,
  spring.beans: 272,
  spring.controllers: 2,
  books.count: 1,
  gauge.books.save.time: 1429399793260,
  ...
}
```

Of course, the actual values for these metrics will vary, depending on how many books you've added and the times when you started the application and last saved a book. In case you're wondering, `spring.controllers` is 2 because it's counting `ReadingList-Controller` as well as the Spring Boot–provided `BasicErrorController`.

7.4.4 *Creating a custom trace repository*

By default, the traces reported by the `/trace` endpoint are stored in an in-memory repository that's capped at 100 entries. Once it's full, it starts rolling off older trace entries to make room for new ones. This is fine for development purposes, but in a production application the higher traffic may result in traces being discarded before you ever get a chance to see them.

One way to remedy that problem is to declare your own `InMemoryTraceRepository` bean and set its capacity to some value higher than 100. The following configuration class should increase the capacity to 1000 entries:

```
package readinglist;
import org.springframework.boot.actuate.trace.InMemoryTraceRepository;
import org.springframework.context.annotation.Bean;
import org.springframework.context.annotation.Configuration;

@Configuration
public class ActuatorConfig {

  @Bean
  public InMemoryTraceRepository traceRepository() {
    InMemoryTraceRepository traceRepo = new InMemoryTraceRepository();
    traceRepo.setCapacity(1000);
    return traceRepo;
  }

}
```

Although a tenfold increase in the repository's capacity should keep a few of those trace entries around a bit longer, a sufficiently busy application might still discard traces before you get a chance to review them. And because this is an in-memory trace repository, we should be careful about increasing the capacity too much, as it will have an impact on our application's memory footprint.

Alternatively, we could store those trace entries elsewhere—somewhere that's not consuming memory and that will be more permanent. All we need to do is implement Spring Boot's `TraceRepository` interface:

```
package org.springframework.boot.actuate.trace;
import java.util.List;
import java.util.Map;

public interface TraceRepository {
  List<Trace> findAll();
  void add(Map<String, Object> traceInfo);
}
```

As you can see, `TraceRepository` only requires that we implement two methods: one that finds all stored `Trace` objects and another that saves a `Trace` given a `Map` containing trace information.

For demonstration purposes, perhaps we could create an instance of `TraceRepository` that stores trace entries in a MongoDB database. Listing 7.11 shows such an implementation of `TraceRepository`.

Listing 7.11   Saving trace data to Mongo

```
package readinglist;
import java.util.Date;
import java.util.List;
import java.util.Map;
import org.springframework.beans.factory.annotation.Autowired;
import org.springframework.boot.actuate.trace.Trace;
import org.springframework.boot.actuate.trace.TraceRepository;
import org.springframework.data.mongodb.core.MongoOperations;
import org.springframework.stereotype.Service;

@Service
public class MongoTraceRepository implements TraceRepository {

  private MongoOperations mongoOps;

  @Autowired
  public MongoTraceRepository(MongoOperations mongoOps) {     ◁─── Inject MongoOperations
    this.mongoOps = mongoOps;
  }

  @Override
  public List<Trace> findAll() {                              ◁─── Fetch all trace entries
    return mongoOps.findAll(Trace.class);
  }

  @Override
  public void add(Map<String, Object> traceInfo) {           ◁─── Save a trace entry
    mongoOps.save(new Trace(new Date(), traceInfo));
  }

}
```

The `findAll()` method is straightforward enough, asking the injected `MongoOperations` to find all `Trace` objects. The `add()` method is only slightly more interesting, instantiating a `Trace` object given the current date/time and the `Map` of trace info before saving it via `MongoOperations.save()`. The only question you might have is where `MongoOperations` comes from.

In order for `MongoTraceRepository` to work, we're going to need to make sure that we have a `MongoOperations` bean in the Spring application context. Thanks to Spring Boot starters and auto-configuration, that's simply a matter of adding the MongoDB starter as a dependency. The Gradle dependency you need is as follows:

```
compile("org.springframework.boot:spring-boot-starter-data-mongodb")
```

If your project is built with Maven, this is the dependency you'll need:

```
<dependency>
  <groupId>org.springframework.boot</groupId>
  <artifactId>spring-boot-starter-data-mongodb</artifactId>
</dependency>
```

By adding this starter, Spring Data MongoDB and supporting libraries will be added to the application's classpath. And because those are in the classpath, Spring Boot will auto-configure the beans necessary to support working with a MongoDB database, including a `MongoOperations` bean. The only other thing you'll need to do is be sure that there's a MongoDB server running for `MongoOperations` to talk to.

7.4.5   *Plugging in custom health indicators*

As we've seen, the Actuator comes with a nice set of out-of-the-box health indicators for common needs such as reporting the health of a database or message broker that the application is using. But what if your application interacts with some system for which there's no health indicator?

Because our application includes links to Amazon for books in the reading list, it might be interesting to report whether or not Amazon is reachable. Sure, it's not likely that Amazon will go down, but stranger things have happened. So let's create a health indicator that reports whether Amazon is available. Listing 7.12 shows a `HealthIndicator` implementation that should do the job.

Listing 7.12   Defining a custom Amazon health indicator

```
package readinglist;
import org.springframework.boot.actuate.health.Health;
import org.springframework.boot.actuate.health.HealthIndicator;
import org.springframework.stereotype.Component;
import org.springframework.web.client.RestTemplate;

@Component
public class AmazonHealth implements HealthIndicator {

  @Override
  public Health health() {

    try {
      RestTemplate rest = new RestTemplate();
      rest.getForObject("http://www.amazon.com", String.class);    ⟵─── Send request to Amazon
      return Health.up().build();
    } catch (Exception e) {
      return Health.down().build();    ⟵─── Report "down" health
    }
  }

}
```

The `AmazonHealth` class isn't terribly fancy. The `health()` method simply uses Spring's `RestTemplate` to perform a `GET` request to Amazon's home page. If it works, it returns a `Health` object indicating that Amazon is "UP". On the other hand, if an exception is thrown while requesting Amazon's home page, then `health()` returns a `Health` object indicating that Amazon is "DOWN".

The following excerpt from the `/health` endpoint's response shows what you might see if Amazon is unreachable:

```
{
    "amazonHealth": {
        "status": "DOWN"
    },
    ...
}
```

You wouldn't believe how long I had to wait for Amazon to crash so that I could get that result![1]

If you'd like to add additional information to the health record beyond a simple status, you can do so by calling `withDetail()` on the `Health` builder. For example, to add the exception's message as a `reason` field in the health record, the `catch` block could be changed to return a `Health` object created like this:

```
return Health.down().withDetail("reason", e.getMessage()).build();
```

As a result of this change, the health record might look like this when the request to Amazon fails:

```
"amazonHealth": {
    "reason": "I/O error on GET request for
            \"http://www.amazon.com\":www.amazon.com;
            nested exception is java.net.UnknownHostException:
            www.amazon.com",
    "status": "DOWN"
},
```

You can add as many additional details as you want by calling `withDetail()` for each additional field you want included in the health record.

7.5   *Securing Actuator endpoints*

We've seen that many of the Actuator endpoints expose information that may be considered sensitive. And some, such as the `/shutdown` endpoint, are dangerous and can be used to bring your application down. Therefore, it's very important to be able to secure these endpoints so that they're only available to authorized clients.

As it turns out, the Actuator endpoints can be secured the same way as any other URL path: with Spring Security. In a Spring Boot application, this means adding the

---

[1]   Not really. I just disconnected my computer from the network. No network, no Amazon.

Security starter as a build dependency and letting security auto-configuration take care of locking down the application, including the Actuator endpoints.

In chapter 3, we saw how the default security auto-configuration results in all URL paths being secured, requiring HTTP Basic authentication where the username is "user" and the password is randomly generated at startup and written to the log file. This was not how we wanted to secure the application, and it's likely not how you want to secure the Actuator either.

We've already added some custom security configuration to restrict the root URL path (/) to only authenticated users with READER access. To lock down Actuator endpoints, we'll need to make a few changes to the `configure()` method in `Security-Config.java`.

Suppose, for instance, that we want to lock down the `/shutdown` endpoint, requiring that the user have ADMIN access. Listing 7.13 shows the changes required in the `configure()` method.

Listing 7.13 Securing the `/shutdown` endpoint

```
@Override
protected void configure(HttpSecurity http) throws Exception {
  http
    .authorizeRequests()
      .antMatchers("/").access("hasRole('READER')")
      .antMatchers("/shutdown").access("hasRole('ADMIN')")    ◁——  Require ADMIN
      .antMatchers("/**").permitAll()                                 access
    .and()
    .formLogin()
      .loginPage("/login")
      .failureUrl("/login?error=true");
}
```

Now the only way to access the `/shutdown` endpoint is to authenticate as a user with ADMIN access.

The custom `UserDetailsService` we created in chapter 3, however, is coded to only apply READER access to users it looks up via the `ReaderRepository`. Therefore, you may want to create a smarter `UserDetailsService` implementation that is able to apply ADMIN access to some users. Optionally, you can configure an additional authentication implementation, such as the in-memory authentication shown in listing 7.14.

Listing 7.14 Adding an in-memory admin authentication user

```
@Override
protected void configure(
          AuthenticationManagerBuilder auth) throws Exception {
  auth
    .userDetailsService(new UserDetailsService() {         ◁——  Reader
      @Override                                                   authentication
      public UserDetails loadUserByUsername(String username)
```

```
        throws UsernameNotFoundException {
        UserDetails user = readerRepository.findOne(username);
        if (user != null) {
          return user;
        }
        throw new UsernameNotFoundException(
                    "User '" + username + "' not found.");
      }
    })
    .and()
    .inMemoryAuthentication()
      .withUser("admin").password("s3cr3t")
                  .roles("ADMIN", "READER");            Admin
                                                        authentication
}
```

With the in-memory authentication added, you can authenticate with "admin" as the username and "s3cr3t" as the password and be granted both ADMIN and READER access.

Now the /shutdown endpoint is locked down for everyone except users with ADMIN access. But what about the Actuator's other endpoints? Assuming you want to lock them down with ADMIN access as for /shutdown, you can list each of them in the call to antMatchers(). For example, to lock down /metrics and /configprops as well as /shutdown, call antMatchers() like this:

```
.antMatchers("/shutdown", "/metrics", "/configprops")
                  .access("hasRole('ADMIN')")
```

Although this approach will work, it's only suitable if you want to secure a small subset of the Actuator endpoints. It becomes unwieldy if you use it to lock down all of the Actuator's endpoints.

Rather than explicitly list all of the Actuator endpoints when calling antMatchers(), it's much easier to use wildcards to match them all with a simple Ant-style expression. This is challenging, however, because there's not a lot in common between the endpoint paths. And we can't apply ADMIN access to "/**" because then everything except for the root path (/) would require ADMIN access.

Instead, consider setting the endpoint's context path by setting the management.context-path property. By default, this property is empty, which is why all of the Actuator's endpoint paths are relative to the root path. But the following entry in application.yaml will prefix them all with /mgmt.

```
management:
  context-path: /mgmt
```

Optionally, you can set it in application.properties like this:

```
management.context-path=/mgmt
```

With `management.context-path` set to /mgmt, all Actuator endpoints will be relative to the /mgmt path. For example, the `/metrics` endpoint will be at /mgmt/metrics.

With this new path, we now have a common prefix to work with when assigning ADMIN access restriction to the Actuator endpoints:

```
.antMatchers("/mgmt/**").access("hasRole('ADMIN')")
```

Now all requests beginning with /mgmt, which includes all Actuator endpoints, will require an authenticated user who has been granted ADMIN access.

7.6 *Summary*

It can be difficult to know for sure what's going on inside a running application. Spring Boot's Actuator opens a portal into the inner workings of a Spring Boot application, exposing components, metrics, and gauges to help understand what makes the application tick.

In this chapter, we started by looking at the Actuator's web endpoints—REST endpoints that expose runtime details over HTTP. These include endpoints for viewing all of the beans in the Spring application context, auto-configuration decisions, Spring MVC mappings, thread activity, application health, and various metrics, gauges, and counters.

In addition to web endpoints, the Actuator also offers two alternative ways to dig into the information it provides. The remote shell offers a way to securely shell into the application itself and issue commands that expose much of the same data as the Actuator's endpoints. Meanwhile, all of the Actuator's endpoints are exposed as MBeans that can be monitored and managed by a JMX client.

Next, we took a look at how to customize the Actuator. We saw how to change Actuator endpoint paths by changing the endpoint IDs as well as how to enable and disable endpoints. We also plugged in a few custom metrics and created a custom trace repository to replace the default in-memory trace repository.

Finally, we looked at how to secure the Actuator's endpoints, restricting access to authorized users.

Coming up in the next chapter, we'll see how to take an application from the coding phase to production, looking at how Spring Boot helps when deploying an application to a variety of platforms, including traditional application servers and the cloud.

Deploying Spring Boot applications

This chapter covers

- Deploying WAR files
- Database migration
- Deploying to the cloud

Think of your favorite action movie. Now imagine going to see that movie in the theater and being taken on a thrilling audio-visual ride with high-speed chases, explosions, and battles, only to have it come to a sudden end just before the good guys take down the bad guys. Instead of seeing the movie's conflict resolved, the theater lights come on and everyone is ushered out the door.

Although the lead-up was exciting, it's the climax of the movie that's important. Without it, it's action for action's sake.

Now imagine developing applications and putting a lot of effort and creativity into solving the business problem, but then never deploying the application for others to use and enjoy. Sure, most applications we write don't involve car chases or explosions (at least I hope not), but there's a certain rush we get along the way. Of course, not every line of code we write is destined for production, but it'd be a big let-down if none of it ever was deployed.

Up to this point we've been focused on using features of Spring Boot that help us develop an application. There have been some exciting steps along the way. But it's all for nothing if we don't cross the finish line and deploy the application.

In this chapter we're going to step beyond developing applications with Spring Boot and look at how to deploy those applications. Although this may seem obvious for anyone who has ever deployed a Java-based application, there are some unique features of Spring Boot and related Spring projects we can draw on that make deploying Spring Boot applications unique.

In fact, unlike most Java web applications, which are typically deployed to an application server as WAR files, Spring Boot offers several deployment options. Before we look at how to deploy a Spring Boot application, let's consider all of the options and choose a few that suit our needs best.

8.1 *Weighing deployment options*

There are several ways to build and run Spring Boot applications. You've already seen a few of them:

- Running the application in the IDE (either Spring ToolSuite or IntelliJ IDEA)
- Running from the command line using the Maven `spring-boot:run` goal or Gradle `bootRun` task
- Using Maven or Gradle to produce an executable JAR file that can be run at the command line
- Using the Spring Boot CLI to run Groovy scripts at the command line
- Using the Spring Boot CLI to produce an executable JAR file that can be run at the command line

Any of these choices is suitable for running the application while you're still developing it. But what about when you're ready to deploy the application into a production or other non-development environment?

Although none of the choices listed seems fitting for deploying an application beyond development, the truth is that all but one of them is a valid choice. Running an application within the IDE is certainly ill-suited for a production deployment. Executable JAR files and the Spring Boot CLI, however, are still on the table and are great choices when deploying to a cloud environment.

That said, you're probably wondering how to deploy a Spring Boot application to a more traditional application server environment such as Tomcat, WebSphere, or WebLogic. In those cases, executable JAR files and Groovy source code won't work. For application server deployment, you'll need your application wrapped up in a WAR file.

As it turns out, Spring Boot applications can be packaged for deployment in several ways, as described in table 8.1.

Table 8.1 Spring Boot deployment choices

Deployment artifact	Produced by	Target environment
Raw Groovy source	Written by hand	Cloud Foundry and container deployment, such as with Docker
Executable JAR	Maven, Gradle, or Spring Boot CLI	Cloud environments, including Cloud Foundry and Heroku, as well as container deployment, such as with Docker
WAR	Maven or Gradle	Java application servers or cloud environments such as Cloud Foundry

As you can see in table 8.1, your target environment will need to be a factor in your choice. If you're deploying to a Tomcat server running in your own data center, then the choice of a WAR file has been made for you. On the other hand, if you'll be deploying to Cloud Foundry, you're welcome to choose any of the deployment options shown.

In this chapter, we're going to focus our attention on the following options:

- Deploying a WAR file to a Java application server
- Deploying an executable JAR file to Cloud Foundry
- Deploying an executable JAR file to Heroku (where the build is performed by Heroku)

As we explore these scenarios, we're also going to have to deal with the fact that we've been using an embedded H2 database as we've developed the application, and we'll look at ways to replace it with a production-ready database.

To get started, let's take a look at how we can build our reading-list application into a WAR file that can be deployed to a Java application server such as Tomcat, WebSphere, or WebLogic.

8.2   *Deploying to an application server*

Thus far, every time we've run the reading-list application, the web application has been served from a Tomcat server embedded in the application. Compared to a conventional Java web application, the tables were turned. The application has not been deployed in Tomcat; rather, Tomcat has been deployed in the application.

Thanks in large part to Spring Boot auto-configuration, we've not been required to create a web.xml file or servlet initializer class to declare Spring's `DispatcherServlet` for Spring MVC. But if we're going to deploy the application to a Java application server, we're going to need to build a WAR file. And so that the application server will know how to run the application, we'll also need to include a servlet initializer in that WAR file.

8.2.1   *Building a WAR file*

As it turns out, building a WAR file isn't that difficult. If you're using Gradle to build the application, you simply must apply the "war" plugin:

```
apply plugin: 'war'
```

Then, replace the existing `jar` configuration with the following `war` configuration in build.gradle:

```
war {
    baseName = 'readinglist'
    version = '0.0.1-SNAPSHOT'
}
```

The only difference between this `war` configuration and the previous `jar` configuration is the change of the letter *j* to *w*.

If you're using Maven to build the project, then it's even easier to get a WAR file. All you need to do is change the `<packaging>` element's value from `jar` to `war`.

```
<packaging>war</packaging>
```

Those are the only changes required to produce a WAR file. But that WAR file will be useless unless it includes a web.xml file or a servlet initializer to enable Spring MVC's `DispatcherServlet`.

Spring Boot can help here. It provides `SpringBootServletInitializer`, a special Spring Boot-aware implementation of Spring's `WebApplicationInitializer`. Aside from configuring Spring's `DispatcherServlet`, `SpringBootServletInitializer` also looks for any beans in the Spring application context that are of type `Filter`, `Servlet`, or `ServletContextInitializer` and binds them to the servlet container.

To use `SpringBootServletInitializer`, simply create a subclass and override the `configure()` method to specify the Spring configuration class. Listing 8.1 shows `ReadingListServletInitializer`, a subclass of `SpringBootServletInitializer` that we'll use for the reading-list application.

Listing 8.1 Extending `SpringBootServletInitializer` for the reading-list application

```
package readinglist;
import org.springframework.boot.builder.SpringApplicationBuilder;
import org.springframework.boot.context.web.SpringBootServletInitializer;

public class ReadingListServletInitializer
        extends SpringBootServletInitializer {

  @Override
  protected SpringApplicationBuilder configure(
                                SpringApplicationBuilder builder) {
    return builder.sources(Application.class);    ◁─────┐  Specify Spring
  }                                                      │  configuration
}
```

As you can see, the `configure()` method is given a `SpringApplicationBuilder` as a parameter and returns it as a result. In between, it calls the `sources()` method to register any Spring configuration classes. In this case, it only registers the `Application` class, which, as you'll recall, served dual purpose as both a bootstrap class (with a `main()` method) and a Spring configuration class.

Even though the reading-list application has other Spring configuration classes, it's not necessary to register them all with the `sources()` method. The `Application` class is annotated with `@SpringBootApplication`, which implicitly enables component-scanning. Component-scanning will discover and pull in any other configuration classes that it finds.

Now we're ready to build the application. If you're using Gradle to build the project, simply invoke the `build` task:

```
$ gradle build
```

Assuming no problems, the build will produce a file named readinglist-0.0.1-SNAP-SHOT.war in build/libs.

For a Maven-based build, use the `package` goal:

```
$ mvn package
```

After a successful Maven build, the WAR file will be found in the "target" directory.

All that's left is to deploy the application. The deployment procedure varies across application servers, so consult the documentation for your application server's specific deployment procedure.

For Tomcat, you can deploy an application by copying the WAR file into Tomcat's webapps directory. If Tomcat is running (or once it starts up if it isn't currently running), it will detect the presence of the WAR file, expand it, and install it.

Assuming that you didn't rename the WAR file before deploying it, the servlet context path will be the same as the base name of the WAR file, or /readinglist-0.0.1-SNAPSHOT in the case of the reading-list application. Point your browser at http://*server*._port_/readinglist-0.0.1-SNAPSHOT to kick the tires on the app.

One other thing worth noting: even though we're building a WAR file, it may still be possible to run it without deploying to an application server. Assuming you don't remove the `main()` method from `Application`, the WAR file produced by the build can also be run as if it were an executable JAR file:

```
$ java -jar readinglist-0.0.1-SNAPSHOT.war
```

In effect, you get two deployment options out of a single deployment artifact!

At this point, the application should be up and running in Tomcat. But it's still using the embedded H2 database. An embedded database was handy while developing the application, but it's not a great choice in production. Let's see how to wire in a different data source when deploying to production.

8.2.2 *Creating a production profile*

Thanks to auto-configuration, we have a `DataSource` bean that references an embedded H2 database. More specifically, the `DataSource` bean is a data source pool, typically `org.apache.tomcat.jdbc.pool.DataSource`. Therefore, it may seem obvious that in order to use some database other than the embedded H2 database, we simply need to declare our own `DataSource` bean, overriding the auto-configured `DataSource`, to reference a production database of our choosing.

For example, suppose that we wanted to work with a PostgreSQL database running on `localhost` with the name "readingList". The following `@Bean` method would declare our `DataSource` bean:

```
@Bean
@Profile("production")
public DataSource dataSource() {
  DataSource ds = new DataSource();
  ds.setDriverClassName("org.postgresql.Driver");
  ds.setUrl("jdbc:postgresql://localhost:5432/readinglist");
  ds.setUsername("habuma");
  ds.setPassword("password");
  return ds;
}
```

Here the `DataSource` type is Tomcat's `org.apache.tomcat.jdbc.pool.DataSource`, not to be confused with `javax.sql.DataSource`, which it ultimately implements. The details required to connect to the database (including the JDBC driver class name, the database URL, and the database credentials) are given to the `DataSource` instance. With this bean declared, the default auto-configured `DataSource` bean will be passed over.

The key thing to notice about this `@Bean` method is that it is also annotated with `@Profile` to specify that it should only be created if the "production" profile is active. Because of this, we can still use the embedded H2 database while developing the application, but use the PostgreSQL database in production by activating the profile.

Although that should do the trick, there's a better way to configure the database details without explicitly declaring our own `DataSource` bean. Rather than replace the auto-configured `DataSource` bean, we can configure it via properties in application.yml or application.properties. Table 8.2 lists all of the properties that are useful for configuring the `DataSource` bean.

Table 8.2 `DataSource` **configuration properties**

Property (prefixed with `spring.datasource.`)	Description
`name`	The name of the data source
`initialize`	Whether or not to populate using data.sql (default: `true`)
`schema`	The name of a schema (DDL) script resource
`data`	The name of a data (DML) script resource
`sql-script-encoding`	The character set for reading SQL scripts

Table 8.2 `DataSource` **configuration properties** *(continued)*

Property (prefixed with `spring.datasource.`)	Description
`platform`	The platform to use when reading the schema resource (for example, "schema-{platform}.sql")
`continue-on-error`	Whether or not to continue if initialization fails (default: `false`)
`separator`	The separator in the SQL scripts (default: ;)
`driver-class-name`	The fully qualified class name of the JDBC driver (can often be automatically inferred from the URL)
`url`	The database URL
`username`	The database username
`password`	The database password
`jndi-name`	A JNDI name for looking up a datasource via JNDI
`max-active`	Maximum active connections (default: 100)
`max-idle`	Maximum idle connections (default: 8)
`min-idle`	Minimum idle connections (default: 8)
`initial-size`	The initial size of the connection pool (default: 10)
`validation-query`	A query to execute to verify the connection
`test-on-borrow`	Whether or not to test a connection as it's borrowed from the pool (default: `false`)
`test-on-return`	Whether or not to test a connection as it's returned to the pool (default: `false`)
`test-while-idle`	Whether or not to test a connection while it is idle (default: `false`)
`time-between-eviction-runs-millis`	How often (in milliseconds) to evict connections (default: `5000`)
`min-evictable-idle-time-millis`	The minimum time (in milliseconds) that a connection can be idle before being tested for eviction (default: `60000`)
`max-wait`	The maximum time (in milliseconds) that the pool will wait when no connections are available before failing (default: `30000`)
`jmx-enabled`	Whether or not the data source is managed by JMX (default: `false`)

Most of the properties in table 8.2 are for fine-tuning the connection pool. I'll leave it to you to tinker with those settings as you see fit. What we're interested in now, however, is setting a few properties that will point the `DataSource` bean at PostgreSQL instead of the embedded H2 database. Specifically, the `spring.datasource.url`, `spring.datasource.username`, and `spring.datasource.password` properties are what we need.

As I'm writing this, I have a PostgreSQL database running locally, listening on port 5432, with a username and password of "habuma" and "password". Therefore, the following "production" profile in application.yml is what I used:

```
---
spring:
  profiles: production
  datasource:
    url: jdbc:postgresql://localhost:5432/readinglist
    username: habuma
    password: password
  jpa:
    database-platform: org.hibernate.dialect.PostgreSQLDialect
```

Notice that this excerpt starts with `---` and the first property set is `spring.profiles`. This indicates that the properties that follow will only be applied if the "production" profile is active.

Next, the `spring.datasource.url`, `spring.datasource.username`, and `spring.datasource.password` properties are set. Note that it's usually unnecessary to set the `spring.datasource.driver-class-name` property, as Spring Boot can infer it from the value of the `spring.datasource.url` property. I also had to set some JPA properties. The `spring.jpa.database-platform` property sets the underlying JPA engine to use Hibernate's PostgreSQL dialect.

To enable this profile, we'll need to set the `spring.profiles.active` property to "production". There are several ways to set this property, but the most convenient way is by setting a system environment variable on the machine running the application server. To enable the "production" profile before starting Tomcat, I exported the `SPRING_PROFILES_ACTIVE` environment variable like this:

```
$ export SPRING_PROFILES_ACTIVE=production
```

You probably noticed that `SPRING_PROFILES_ACTIVE` is different from `spring.profiles.active`. It's not possible to export an environment variable with periods in the name, so it was necessary to alter the name slightly. From Spring's point of view, the two names are equivalent.

We're almost ready to deploy the application to an application server and see it run. In fact, if you are feeling adventurous, go ahead and try it. You'll run into a small problem, however.

By default, Spring Boot configures Hibernate to create the schema automatically when using the embedded H2 database. More specifically, it sets Hibernate's `hibernate.hbm2ddl.auto` to `create-drop`, indicating that the schema should be created when Hibernate's `SessionFactory` is created and dropped when it is closed.

But it's set to do nothing if you're not using an embedded H2 database. This means that our application's tables won't exist and you'll see errors as it tries to query those nonexistent tables.

8.2.3 *Enabling database migration*

One option is to set the `hibernate.hbm2ddl.auto` property to `create`, `create-drop`, or `update` via Spring Boot's `spring.jpa.hibernate.ddl-auto` property. For instance, to set `hibernate.hbm2ddl.auto` to `create-drop` we could add the following lines to application.yml:

```
spring:
  jpa:
    hibernate:
      ddl-auto: create-drop
```

This, however, is not ideal for production, as the database schema would be wiped clean and rebuilt from scratch any time the application was restarted. It may be tempting to set it to `update`, but even that isn't recommended in production.

Alternatively, we could define the schema in schema.sql. This would work fine the first time, but every time we started the application thereafter, the initialization scripts would fail because the tables in question would already exist. This would force us to take special care in writing our initialization scripts to not attempt to repeat any work that has already been done.

A better choice is to use a database migration library. Database migration libraries work from a set of database scripts and keep careful track of the ones that have already been applied so that they won't be applied more than once. By including the scripts within each deployment of the application, the database is able to evolve in concert with the application.

Spring Boot includes auto-configuration support for two popular database migration libraries:

- Flyway (http://flywaydb.org)
- Liquibase (www.liquibase.org)

All you need to do to use either of these database migration libraries with Spring Boot is to include them as dependencies in the build and write the scripts. Let's see how they work, starting with Flyway.

DEFINING DATABASE MIGRATION WITH FLYWAY

Flyway is a very simple, open source database migration library that uses SQL for defining the migration scripts. The idea is that each script is given a version number, and Flyway will execute each of them in order to arrive at the desired state of the database. It also records the status of scripts it has executed so that it won't run them again.

For the reading-list application, we're starting with an empty database with no tables or data. Therefore, the script we'll need to get started will need to create the Reader and Book tables, including any foreign-key constraints and initial data. Listing 8.2 shows the Flyway script we'll need to go from an empty database to one that our application can use.

Listing 8.2   A database initialization script for Flyway

```
create table Reader (
  id serial primary key,                              Create Reader
  username varchar(25) unique not null,               table
  password varchar(25) not null,
  fullname varchar(50) not null
);

create table Book (          Create Book table
  id serial primary key,
  author varchar(50) not null,
  description varchar(1000) not null,
  isbn varchar(10) not null,
  title varchar(250) not null,
  reader_username varchar(25) not null,
  foreign key (reader_username) references Reader(username)
);

create sequence hibernate_sequence;      Define a sequence

insert into Reader (username, password, fullname)
            values ('craig', 'password', 'Craig Walls');
                                                         An initial
                                                         Reader
```

As you can see, the Flyway script is just SQL. What makes it work with Flyway is where it's placed in the classpath and how it's named. Flyway scripts follow a naming convention that includes the version number, as illustrated in figure 8.1.

All Flyway scripts have names that start with a capital V which precedes the script's version number. That's followed by two underscores and a description of the script. Because this is the first script in the

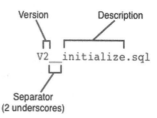

Figure 8.1   Flyway scripts are named with their version number.

migration, it will be version 1. The description given can be flexible and is primarily to provide some understanding of the script's purpose. Later, should we need to add a new table to the database or a new column to an existing table, we can create another script named with 2 in the version place.

Flyway scripts need to be placed in the path /db/migration relative to the application's classpath root. Therefore, this script needs to be placed in src/main/resources/db/migration within the project.

You'll also need to tell Hibernate to not attempt to create the tables by setting `spring.jpa.hibernate.ddl-auto` to none. The following lines in application.yml take care of that:

```
spring:
  jpa:
    hibernate:
      ddl-auto: none
```

All that's left is to add Flyway as a dependency in the project build. Here's the dependency that's required for Gradle:

```
compile("org.flywaydb:flyway-core")
```

In a Maven build, the <dependency> is as follows:

```
<dependency>
  <groupId>org.flywayfb</groupId>
  <artifactId>flyway-core</artifactId>
</dependency>
```

When the application is deployed and running, Spring Boot will detect Flyway in the classpath and auto-configure the beans necessary to enable it. Flyway will step through any scripts in /db/migration and apply them if they haven't already been applied. As each script is executed, an entry will be written to a table named schema_version. The next time the application starts, Flyway will see that those scripts have been recorded in schema_version and skip over them.

DEFINING DATABASE MIGRATION WITH LIQUIBASE

Flyway is simple to use, especially with help from Spring Boot auto-configuration. But defining migration scripts with SQL is a two-edged sword. Although it's easy and natural to work with SQL, you run the risk of defining a migration script that works with one database platform but not another.

Rather than be limited to platform-specific SQL, Liquibase supports several formats for writing migration scripts that are agnostic to the underlying platform. These include XML, YAML, and JSON. And, if you really want it, Liquibase also supports SQL scripts.

The first step to using Liquibase with Spring Boot is to add it as a dependency in your build. The Gradle dependency is as follows:

```
compile("org.liquibase:liquibase-core")
```

For Maven, here's the <dependency> you'll need:

```
<dependency>
  <groupId>org.liquibase</groupId>
  <artifactId>liquibase-core</artifactId>
</dependency>
```

Spring Boot auto-configuration takes it from there, wiring up the beans that support Liquibase. By default, those beans are wired to look for all of the migration scripts in a single file named db.changelog-master.yaml in /db/changelog (relative to the classpath

root). The migration script in listing 8.3 includes instructions to initialize the database
for the reading-list application.

Listing 8.3 A Liquibase script for initializing the reading-list database

```
databaseChangeLog:
  - changeSet:
      id: 1                           ◁——— Changeset ID
      author: habuma
      changes:
        - createTable:
            tableName: reader          ◁———┐ Create reader
            columns:                        │ table
              - column:
                  name: username
                  type: varchar(25)
                  constraints:
                    unique: true
                    nullable: false
              - column:
                  name: password
                  type: varchar(25)
                  constraints:
                    nullable: false
              - column:
                  name: fullname
                  type: varchar(50)
                  constraints:
                    nullable: false
        - createTable:
            tableName: book            ◁———┐ Create book
            columns:                        │ table
              - column:
                  name: id
                  type: bigserial
                  autoIncrement: true
                  constraints:
                    primaryKey: true
                    nullable: false
              - column:
                  name: author
                  type: varchar(50)
                  constraints:
                    nullable: false
              - column:
                  name: description
                  type: varchar(1000)
                  constraints:
                    nullable: false
              - column:
                  name: isbn
                  type: varchar(10)
                  constraints:
                    nullable: false
```

```
        - column:
            name: title
            type: varchar(250)
            constraints:
              nullable: false
        - column:
            name: reader_username
            type: varchar(25)
            constraints:
              nullable: false
              references: reader(username)
              foreignKeyName: fk_reader_username
    - createSequence:                                    ◁────────┐ Define a
        sequenceName: hibernate_sequence                          │ sequence
    - insert:
        tableName: reader                ◁────────┐ Insert an initial
        columns:                                  │ reader
          - column:
              name: username
              value: craig
          - column:
              name: password
              value: password
          - column:
              name: fullname
              value: Craig Walls
```

As you can see, the YAML format is a bit more verbose than the equivalent Flyway SQL script. But it's still fairly clear as to its purpose and it isn't coupled to any specific database platform.

Unlike Flyway, which has multiple scripts, one for each change set, Liquibase changesets are all collected in the same file. Note the id property on the line following the changeset command. Future changes to the database can be included by adding a new changeset with a different id. Also note that the id property isn't necessarily numeric and may contain any text you'd like.

When the application starts up, Liquibase will read the changeset instructions in db.changelog-master.yaml, compare them with what it may have previously written to the databaseChangeLog table, and apply any changesets that have not yet been applied.

Although the example given here is expressed in YAML format, you're welcome to choose one of Liquibase's other supported formats, such as XML or JSON. Simply set the liquibase.change-log property (in application.properties or application.yml) to reflect the file you want Liquibase to load. For example, to use an XML changeset file, set liquibase.change-log like this:

```
liquibase:
  change-log: classpath:/db/changelog/db.changelog-master.xml
```

Spring Boot auto-configuration makes both Liquibase and Flyway a piece of cake to work with. But there's a lot more to what each of these database migration libraries can do beyond what we've seen here. I encourage you to refer to each project's documentation for more details.

We've seen how building Spring Boot applications for deployment into a conventional Java application server is largely a matter of creating a subclass of `Spring-BootServletInitializer` and adjusting the build specification to produce a WAR file instead of a JAR file. But as we'll see next, Spring Boot applications are even easier to build for the cloud.

8.3 *Pushing to the cloud*

Server hardware can be expensive to purchase and maintain. Properly scaling servers to handle heavy loads can be tricky and even prohibitive for some organizations. These days, deploying applications to the cloud is a compelling and cost-effective alternative to running your own data center.

There are several cloud choices available, but those that offer a platform as a service (PaaS) are among the most compelling. PaaS offers a ready-made application deployment platform with several add-on services (such as databases and message brokers) to bind to your applications. In addition, as your application requires additional horsepower, cloud platforms make it easy to scale up (or down) your application on the fly by adding and removing instances.

Now that we've deployed the reading-list application to a traditional application server, we're going to try deploying it to the cloud. Specifically, we're going to deploy our application to two of the most popular PaaS platforms available: Cloud Foundry and Heroku.

8.3.1 *Deploying to Cloud Foundry*

Cloud Foundry is a PaaS platform from Pivotal, the same company that sponsors the Spring Framework and the other libraries in the Spring platform. One of the most compelling things about Cloud Foundry is that it is both open source and has several commercial distributions, giving you the choice of how and where you use Cloud Foundry. It can even be run inside the firewall in a corporate datacenter, offering a private cloud.

For the reading-list application, we're going to deploy to Pivotal Web Services (PWS), a public Cloud Foundry hosted by Pivotal at http://run.pivotal.io. If you want to work with PWS, you'll need to sign up for an account. PWS offers a 60-day free trial and doesn't even require you to give any credit card information during the trial.

Once you've signed up for PWS, you'll need to download and install the `cf` command-line tool from https://console.run.pivotal.io/tools. You'll use the `cf` tool to push applications to Cloud Foundry. But the first thing you'll use it for is to log into your PWS account:

```
$ cf login -a https://api.run.pivotal.io
API endpoint: https://api.run.pivotal.io

Email> {your email}

Password> {your password}
Authenticating...
OK
```

Now we're ready to take the reading-list application to the cloud. As it turns out, our reading-list project is already ready to be deployed to Cloud Foundry. All we need to do is use the cf push command:

```
$ cf push sbia-readinglist -p build/libs/readinglist.war
```

The first argument to cf push is the name given to the application in Cloud Foundry. Among other things, this name will be used as the subdomain that the application will be hosted at. In this case, the full URL for the application will be http://sbia-readinglist .cfapps.io. Therefore, it's important that the name you give the application be unique so that it doesn't collide with any other application deployed in Cloud Foundry (including those deployed by other Cloud Foundry users).

Because dreaming up a unique name may be tricky, the cf push command offers a --random-route option that will randomly produce a subdomain for you. Here's how to push the reading-list application so that a random route is generated:

```
$ cf push sbia-readinglist -p build/libs/readinglist.war --random-route
```

When using --random-route, the application name is still required, but two randomly chosen words will be appended to it to produce the subdomain. (When I tried it, the resulting subdomain was sbia-readinglist-gastroenterological-stethoscope.)

> **NOT JUST WAR FILES** Although we're going to deploy the reading-list application as a WAR file, Cloud Foundry will be happy to deploy Spring Boot applications in any form they come in, including executable JAR files and even uncompiled Groovy scripts run via the Spring Boot CLI.

Assuming everything goes well, the application should be deployed and ready to handle requests. Supposing that the subdomain is sbia-readinglist, you can point your browser at http://sbia-readinglist.cfapps.io to see it in action. You should be prompted with the login page. As you'll recall, the database migration script inserted a user named "craig" with a password of "password". Use those to log into the application.

Go ahead and play around with the application and add a few books to the reading list. Everything should work. But something still isn't quite right. If you were to restart the application (using the cf restart command) and then log back into the application, you'd see that your reading list is empty. Any book you've added before restarting the application will be gone.

The reason the data doesn't survive an application restart is because we're still using the embedded H2 database. You can verify this by requesting the Actuator's /health endpoint, which will reply with something like this:

```
{
  "status": "UP",
  "diskSpace": {
    "status": "UP",
    "free": 834236510208,
    "threshold": 10485760
  },
  "db": {
    "status": "UP",
    "database": "H2",
    "hello": 1
  }
}
```

Notice the value of the db.database property. It confirms any suspicion we might have had that the database is an embedded H2 database. We need to fix that.

As it turns out, Cloud Foundry offers a few database options to choose from in the form of marketplace services, including MySQL and PostgreSQL. Because we already have the PostgreSQL JDBC driver in our project, we'll use the PostgreSQL service from the marketplace, which is named "elephantsql".

The elephantsql service comes with a handful of different plans to choose from, ranging from small development-sized databases to large industrial-strength production databases. You can get a list of all of the elephantsql plans with the cf market-place command like this:

```
$ cf marketplace -s elephantsql
Getting service plan information for service elephantsql as craig@habuma.com...
OK

service plan    description           free or paid
turtle          Tiny Turtle           free
panda           Pretty Panda          paid
hippo           Happy Hippo           paid
elephant        Enormous Elephant     paid
```

As you can see, the more serious production-sized database plans require payment. You're welcome to choose one of those plans if you want, but for now I'll assume that you're choosing the free "turtle" plan.

To create an instance of the database service, you can use the cf create-service command, specifying the service name, the plan name, and an instance name:

```
$ cf create-service elephantsql turtle readinglistdb
Creating service readinglistdb in org habuma /
    space development as craig@habuma.com...
OK
```

Once the service has been created, we'll need to bind it to our application with the
`cf bind-service` command:

```
$ cf bind-service sbia-readinglist readinglistdb
```

Binding a service to an application merely provides the application with details on
how to connect to the service within an environment variable named VCAP_SERVICES.
It doesn't change the application to actually use that service.

We *could* rewrite the reading-list application to read VCAP_SERVICES and use the
information it provides to access the database service, but that's completely unnecessary. Instead, all we need to do is restage the application with the `cf restage` command:

```
$ cf restage sbia-readinglist
```

The `cf restage` command forces Cloud Foundry to redeploy the application and
reevaluate the VCAP_SERVICES value. As it does, it will see that our application declares
a DataSource bean in the Spring application context and replaces it with a DataSource
that references the bound database service. As a consequence, our application will now
be using the PostgreSQL service known as elephantsql rather than the embedded
H2 database.

Go ahead and try it out now. Log into the application, add a few books to the reading list, and then restart the application. Your books should still be in your reading list
after the restart. That's because they were persisted to the bound database service
rather than to an embedded H2 database. Once again, the Actuator's /health endpoint will back up that claim:

```
{
  "status": "UP",
  "diskSpace": {
    "status": "UP",
    "free": 834331525120,
    "threshold": 10485760
  },
  "db": {
    "status": "UP",
    "database": "PostgreSQL",
    "hello": 1
  }
}
```

Cloud Foundry is a great PaaS for Spring Boot application deployment. Its associa-
tion with the Spring projects affords some synergy between the two. But it's
not the only PaaS where Spring Boot applications can be deployed. Let's see what
needs to be done to deploy the reading-list application to Heroku, another popular
PaaS platform.

8.3.2   *Deploying to Heroku*

Heroku takes a unique approach to application deployment. Rather than deploy a completely built deployment artifact, Heroku arranges a Git repository for your application and builds and deploys the application for you every time you push it to the repository.

If you've not already done so, you'll want to initialize the project directory as a Git repository:

```
$ git init
```

This will enable the Heroku command-line tool to add the remote Heroku Git repository to the project automatically.

Now it's time to set up the application in Heroku using the Heroku command-line tool's apps:create command:

```
$ heroku apps:create sbia-readinglist
```

Here I've asked Heroku to name the application "sbia-readinglist". This name will be used as the name of the Git repository as well as the subdomain of the application at herokuapps.com. You'll want to be sure to pick a unique name, as there can't be more than one application with the same name. Alternatively, you can leave off the name and Heroku will generate a unique name for you (such as "fierce-river-8120" or "serene-anchorage-6223").

The apps:create command creates a remote Git repository at https://git.heroku .com/sbia-readinglist.git and adds a remote reference to the repository named "heroku" in the local project's Git configuration. That will enable us to push our project into Heroku using the git command.

The project has been set up in Heroku, but we're not quite ready to push it yet. Heroku asks that you provide a file named Procfile that tells Heroku how to run the application after it has been built. For our reading-list application, we need to tell Heroku to run the WAR file produced by the build as an executable JAR file using the java command.[1] Assuming that the application will be built with Gradle, the following one-line Procfile is what we'll need:

```
web: java -Dserver.port=$PORT -jar build/libs/readinglist.war
```

On the other hand, if you're using Maven to build the project, then the path to the JAR file will be slightly different. Instead of referencing the executable WAR file in build/libs, Heroku will need to find it in the target directory, as shown in the following Procfile:

```
web: java -Dserver.port=$PORT -jar target/readinglist.war
```

---

[1]   The project we're working with actually produces an executable WAR file, but as far as Heroku knows, it's no different than an executable JAR file.

In either case, you'll also need to set the `server.port` property as shown so that the embedded Tomcat server starts up on the port that Heroku assigns to the application (provided by the `$PORT` variable).

We're almost ready to push the application to Heroku, but there's a small change required in the Gradle build specification. When Heroku tries to build our application, it will do so by executing a task named `stage`. Therefore, we'll need to add a `stage` task to `build.gradle`:

```
task stage(dependsOn: ['build']) {
}
```

As you can see, this `stage` task doesn't do much. But it does depend on the `build` task. Therefore, the `build` task will be triggered when Heroku tries to build the application with the `stage` task, and the resulting JAR will be ready to run in the build/libs directory.

You may also need to inform Heroku of the Java version we're building the application with so that it runs the application with the appropriate version of Java. The easiest way to do that is to create a file named system.properties at the root of the project that sets a `java.runtime.version` property:

```
java.runtime.version=1.7
```

Now we're ready to push the project into Heroku. As I said before, this is just a matter of pushing the code into the remote Git repository that Heroku set up for us:

```
$ git commit -am "Initial commit"
$ git push heroku master
```

After the code is pushed into Heroku, Heroku will build it using either Maven or Gradle (depending on which kind of build file it finds) and then run it using the instructions in `Procfile`. Once it's ready, you should be able to try it out by pointing your browser at http://{app name}.herokuapp.com, where "{app name}" is the name given to the application when you used `apps:create`. For example, I named the application "sbia-readinglist" when I deployed it, so the application's URL is http://sbia-readinglist.herokuapps.com.

Feel free to poke about in the application as much as you'd like. But then go take a look at the /`health` endpoint. The `db.database` property should tell you that the application is using the embedded H2 database. We should change that to use a PostgreSQL service instead.

We can create and bind to a PostgreSQL service using the Heroku command-line tool's `addons:add` command like this:

```
$ heroku addons:add heroku-postgresql:hobby-dev
```

Here we're asking for the addon service named `heroku-postgresql`, which is the PostgreSQL service offered by Heroku. We're also asking for the `hobby-dev` plan for that service, which is the free plan.

Now the PostgreSQL service is created and bound to our application, and Heroku will automatically restart the application to ensure that binding. But even so, if we were to go look at the /health endpoint, we'd see that the application is still using the embedded H2 database. That's because the auto-configuration for H2 is still in play, and there's nothing to tell Spring Boot to use PostgreSQL instead.

One option is to set the spring.datasource.* properties like we did when deploying to an application server. The information we'd need can be found on the database service's dashboard, which can be opened with the addons:open command:

```
$ heroku addons:open waking-carefully-3728
```

In this case, the name of the database instance is "waking-carefully-3728". This command will open a dashboard page in your web browser that includes all of the necessary connection information, including the hostname, database name, and credentials—everything we'd need to set the spring.datasource.* properties.

But there's an easier way. Rather than look up that information for ourselves and set those properties, why can't Spring look them up for us? In fact, that's what the Spring Cloud Connectors project does. It works with both Cloud Foundry and Heroku to look up any services bound to an application and automatically configure the application to use those services.

We just need to add Spring Cloud Connectors as a dependency in the build. For a Gradle build, add the following to build.gradle:

```
compile(
        "org.springframework.boot:spring-boot-starter-cloud-connectors")
```

If you're using Maven, the following <dependency> will add Spring Cloud Connectors to the build:

```
<dependency>
  <groupId>org.springframework.boot</groupId>
  <artifactId>spring-boot-starter-cloud-connectors</artifactId>
</dependency>
```

Spring Cloud Connectors will only work if the "cloud" profile is active. To activate the "cloud" profile in Heroku, use the config:set command:

```
$ heroku config:set SPRING_PROFILES_ACTIVE="cloud"
```

Now that the Spring Cloud Connectors dependency is in the build and the "cloud" profile is active, we're ready to push the application again:

```
$ git commit -am "Add cloud connector"
$ git push heroku master
```

After the application starts up, sign in to the application and view the /health endpoint. It should indicate that the application is connected to a PostgreSQL database:

```
"db": {
  "status": "UP",
  "database": "PostgreSQL",
  "hello": 1
}
```

Now our application is deployed in the cloud, ready to take requests from the world!

8.4   Summary

There are several options for deploying Spring Boot applications, including traditional application servers and PaaS options in the cloud. In this chapter, we looked at a few of those options, deploying the reading-list application as a WAR file to Tomcat and in the cloud to both Cloud Foundry and Heroku.

Spring Boot applications are often given a build specification that produces an executable JAR file. But we've seen how to tweak the build and write a `Spring-BootServletInitializer` implementation to produce a WAR file suitable for deployment to an application server.

We then took a first step toward deploying our application to Cloud Foundry. Cloud Foundry is flexible enough to accept Spring Boot applications in any form, including executable JAR files, traditional WAR files, or even raw Spring Boot CLI Groovy scripts. We also saw how Cloud Foundry is able to automatically swap out our embedded data source bean with one that references a database service bound to the application.

Finally we saw how although Heroku doesn't offer automatic swapping of data source beans like Cloud Foundry, by adding the Spring Cloud Connectors library to our deployment we can achieve the same effect, enabling a bound database service instead of an embedded database.

Along the way, we also looked at how to enable database migration tools such as Flyway and Liquibase in Spring Boot. We used database migration to initialize our database on the first deployment and now are ready to evolve our database as needed on future deployments.

appendix A
Spring Boot Developer Tools

Spring Boot 1.3 introduced a new set of developer tools that make it even easier to work with Spring Boot at development time. Among its many capabilities are

- *Automatic restart*—Restarts a running application when files are changed in the classpath
- *LiveReload support*—Changes to resources trigger a browser refresh automatically
- *Remote development*—Supports automatic restart and LiveReload when deployed remotely
- *Development property defaults*—Provides sensible development defaults for some configuration properties

Spring Boot's developer tools come in the form of a library that can be added to a project as a dependency. If you're using Gradle to build your project, the development tools can be added with the following line in your build.gradle file:

```
compile "org.springframework.boot:spring-boot-devtools"
```

Or it can be added as a <dependency> in a Maven POM:

```
<dependency>
  <groupId>org.springframework.boot</groupId>
  <artifactId>spring-boot-devtools</artifactId>
</dependency>
```

The developer tools will be disabled when your application is running from a fully packaged JAR or WAR file, so it's unnecessary to remove this dependency before building a production deployment.

Automatic restart

With the developer tools active, any changes to files on the classpath will trigger an application restart. To make the restart as fast as possible, classes that won't change (such as those in third-party JAR files) will be loaded into a base classloader, whereas application code that is being worked on will be loaded into a separate restart classloader. When changes are detected, only the restart classloader is restarted.

There are some classpath resources that don't require an application restart when they change. View templates, such as Thymeleaf templates, can be edited on the fly without restarting the application. Static resources in /static or /public likewise don't require an application restart, so Spring Boot developer tools exclude the following paths from restart consideration: /META-INF/resources, /resources, /static, /public, /templates.

The default set of restart path exclusions can be overridden by setting the `spring.devtools.restart.exclude` property. For example, to only exclude /static and /templates, set `spring.devtools.restart.exclude` like this:

```
spring:
  devtools:
    restart:
      exclude: /static/**,/templates/**
```

On the other hand, if you'd rather disable automatic restart completely, you can set `spring.devtools.restart.enabled` to `false`:

```
spring:
  devtools:
    restart:
      enabled: false
```

Another option is to set a trigger file that must be changed in order for the restart to take place. For example, suppose you don't want a restart to happen unless a change is made to a file named .trigger. All you must do is set the `spring.devtools.restart.trigger-file` property like this:

```
spring:
  devtools:
    restart:
      trigger-file: .trigger
```

A trigger file is useful if your IDE continuously compiles changed files. Without a trigger file, every change would trigger a restart. With a trigger file, you can be sure that a restart doesn't happen unless you want it to (by making a change to the trigger file).

LiveReload

One of the most common rituals of web application development involves the following steps:

1 Make a change to rendered content (such as images, stylesheets, templates).
2 Click Refresh in the browser to see the results of the change.
3 Repeat starting at step 1.

Although it's not an arduous process, it would be nice if you could see the results of a change immediately, without clicking Refresh.

Spring Boot's developer tools integrate with LiveReload (http://livereload.com) to eliminate the Refresh step. When the developer tools are active, Spring Boot will start an embedded LiveReload server that can trigger a browser refresh whenever a resource is changed. All you need to do is install the LiveReload plugin into your web browser.

If you'd like to disable the embedded LiveReload server, you can do so by setting `spring.devtools.livereload.enabled` to `false`:

```
spring:
  devtools:
    livereload:
      enabled: false
```

Remote development

The automatic restart and LiveReload features of the developer tools are also optionally available when running the applications remotely (such as when deployed on a server or in a cloud environment). In addition, Spring Boot's developer tools enable remote debugging of Spring Boot applications.

In a typical deployment, you won't want the remote development feature enabled, as it will hinder performance. But in special cases, such as when developing an application that's deployed in a non-production environment set aside for development purposes, these tools can come in handy. This is especially useful if your application uses a cloud service that isn't available in your local development environment.

You must opt in to remote development by setting a remote secret:

```
spring:
  devtools:
    remote:
      secret: myappsecret
```

By setting this property, a server component is enabled in the running application to support remote development. This server will listen for requests asking it to accept incoming changes and will either restart the application or trigger a browser refresh.

In order to put this remote server to use, you'll need to run the remote development tools client locally. The remote client comes in the form of a class whose fully qualified name is `org.springframework.boot.devtools.RemoteSpringApplication`. It's designed to run in your IDE with an argument telling it where your remote application is deployed.

For example, suppose you're running the reading-list application remotely, deployed on Cloud Foundry at https://readinglist.cfapps.io. If you're using Eclipse or Spring ToolSuite, you can start the remote client with the following steps:

1 Select the Run > Run Configurations menu item.
2 Create a new Java Application launch configuration.
3 Select the Reading List project in the Project field (either by typing the project name or clicking the Browse button and finding it). See figure A.1.
4 Enter `org.springframework.boot.devtools.RemoteSpringApplication` into the Main Class field. See figure A.1.
5 On the Arguments tab, enter `https://readinglist.cfapps.io` into the Program Arguments field. See figure A.2.

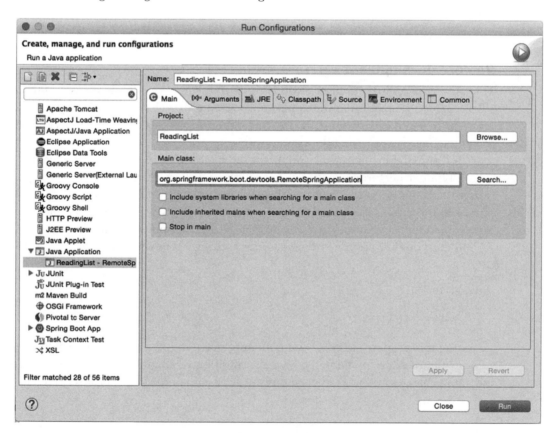

Figure A.1 `RemoteSpringApplication` **is the remote developer tools client.**

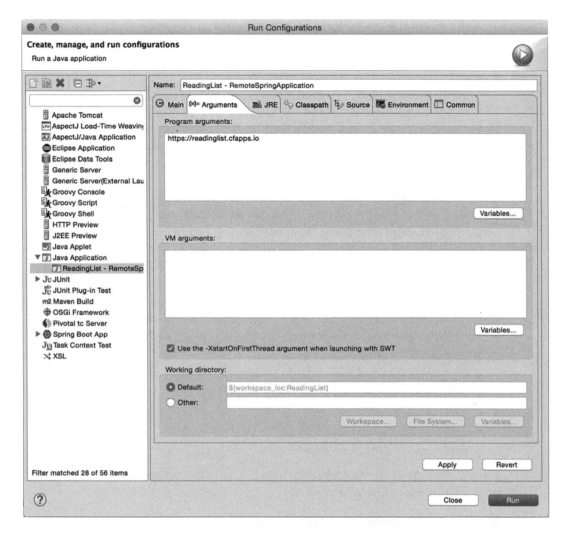

Figure A.2 `RemoteSpringApplication` **takes the remote app's URL as an argument.**

Once the client has started, you can start making changes to the application in your IDE. As changes are detected, they'll be pushed to the remote server and applied. If changes are made to a rendered web resource (such as a stylesheet or JavaScript), they'll also trigger a browser refresh using LiveReload.

The remote client will also enable tunneling of remote debug traffic over HTTP so that you can debug a remotely deployed application in your IDE. All you must do is ensure that the remote application has remote debugging enabled. This can usually be done by configuring `JAVA_OPTS`.

For example, if your application is deployed to Cloud Foundry, you can set JAVA_OPTS in your application's manifest.yml file like this:

```
---
  env:
    JAVA_OPTS: "-Xdebug -Xrunjdwp:server=y,transport=dt_socket,suspend=n"
```

Once the remote application is started and a connection is established with the local debug server, you should be able to set breakpoints and step through the code of the remote application much as if it were local (albeit a bit slower due to network latency).

Development property defaults

There are some configuration properties that are usually set at development time, but never in a production setting. View template caching, for instance, is best disabled during development so that you can see the results of any changes you make immediately. But in production, view template caching should be left enabled for better performance.

By default, Spring Boot will enable caching for any of the supported view template options (Thymeleaf, Freemarker, Velocity, Mustache, and Groovy templates). But if Spring Boot's developer tools are in play, that caching will be disabled.

Essentially what this means is that when the developer tools are active, the following properties are set to `false`:

- spring.thymeleaf.cache
- spring.freemarker.cache
- spring.velocity.cache
- spring.mustache.cache
- spring.groovy.template.cache

This saves you from having to disable them (likely in a development-profiled configuration) for development time.

Globally configuring developer tools

As you work with the developer tools, you'll probably find that you regularly use the same settings across multiple projects. For instance, if you use a restart trigger file, you're likely to name the trigger file consistently across projects. Rather than repeat developer tool configuration in each project, it may be more convenient to configure the developer tools globally.

To do this, create a file named .spring-boot-devtools.properties in your home directory. (Note that the name starts with a period.) In that file, set whatever developer tool properties you want to have applied across all of your projects.

For example, suppose that you want to set a trigger file named .trigger and disable LiveReload across all of your Spring Boot projects. To do that, you can create a .spring-boot-devtools.properties file with the following lines:

```
spring.devtools.restart.trigger-file=.trigger
spring.devtools.livereload.enabled=false
```

Then, should you want to override any of these properties, you can do so on a project-by-project basis by setting them in each project's application.properties or application.yml file.

appendix B
Spring Boot starters

Spring Boot starter dependencies greatly simplify the dependencies section of your project's build specification by aggregating commonly used dependencies under more coarse-grained dependencies. Your build will transitively resolve the dependencies that are declared in the starter dependency.

Not only do starter dependencies keep the dependencies section of the build smaller, they are typically organized by the type of functionality they bring to an application. For example, rather than specify specific libraries required for validation (such as Hibernate Validator and Tomcat's embedded expression language), you can simply add the `spring-boot-starter-validation` starter as a dependency.

Table B.1 lists all of Spring Boot's starter dependencies along with the dependencies that they transitively declare.

Table B.1 Spring Boot starters

Starter *(Group ID: org.springframework.boot)*	Transitively depends on
spring-boot-starter	▪ org.springframework.boot:spring-boot ▪ org.springframework.boot:spring-boot-autoconfigure ▪ org.springframework.boot:spring-boot-starter-logging ▪ org.springframework:spring-core *(excludes commons-logging:commons-logging)* ▪ org.yaml:snakeyaml
spring-boot-starter-actuator	▪ org.springframework.boot:spring-boot-starter ▪ org.springframework.boot:spring-boot-actuator
spring-boot-starter-amqp	▪ org.springframework.boot:spring-boot-starter ▪ org.springframework:spring-messaging ▪ org.springframework.amqp:spring-rabbit

Table B.1 Spring Boot starters *(continued)*

Starter *(Group ID: org.springframework.boot)*	Transitively depends on
spring-boot-starter-aop	▪ org.springframework.boot:spring-boot-starter ▪ org.springframework:spring-aop ▪ org.aspectj:aspectjrt ▪ org.aspectj:aspectjweaver
spring-boot-starter-artemis	▪ org.springframework.boot:spring-boot-starter ▪ org.springframework:spring-jms ▪ org.apache.activemq:artemis-jms-client
spring-boot-starter-batch	▪ org.springframework.boot:spring-boot-starter ▪ org.hsqldb:hsqldb ▪ org.springframework:spring-jdbc ▪ org.springframework.batch:spring-batch-core
spring-boot-starter-cache	▪ org.springframework.boot:spring-boot-starter ▪ org.springframework:spring-context ▪ org.springframework:spring-context-support
spring-boot-starter-cloud-connectors	▪ org.springframework.boot:spring-boot-starter ▪ org.springframework.cloud:spring-cloud-spring-service-connector ▪ org.springframework.cloud:spring-cloud-cloudfoundry-connector ▪ org.springframework.cloud:spring-cloud-heroku-connector ▪ org.springframework.cloud:spring-cloud-localconfig-connector
spring-boot-starter-data-elasticsearch	▪ org.springframework.boot:spring-boot-starter ▪ org.springframework.data:spring-data-elasticsearch
spring-boot-starter-data-gemfire	▪ org.springframework.boot:spring-boot-starter ▪ com.gemstone.gemfire:gemfire *(excludes commons-logging:commons-logging)* ▪ org.springframework.data:spring-data-gemfire
spring-boot-starter-data-jpa	▪ org.springframework.boot:spring-boot-starter ▪ org.springframework.boot:spring-boot-starter-aop ▪ org.springframework.boot:spring-boot-starter-jdbc ▪ org.hibernate:hibernate-entitymanager *(excludes org.jboss.spec.javax.transaction:jboss-transaction-api_1.2_spec)* ▪ javax.transaction:javax.transaction-api ▪ org.springframework.data:spring-data-jpa ▪ org.springframework:spring-aspects
spring-boot-starter-data-mongodb	▪ org.springframework.boot:spring-boot-starter ▪ org.mongodb:mongo-java-driver ▪ org.springframework.data:spring-data-mongodb

Table B.1   Spring Boot starters *(continued)*

Starter *(Group ID: org.springframework.boot)*	Transitively depends on
spring-boot-starter-data-rest	▪ org.springframework.boot:spring-boot-starter ▪ org.springframework.boot:spring-boot-starter-web ▪ com.fasterxml.jackson.core:jackson-annotations ▪ com.fasterxml.jackson.core:jackson-databind ▪ org.springframework.data:spring-data-rest-webmvc
spring-boot-starter-data-solr	▪ org.springframework.boot:spring-boot-starter ▪ org.apache.solr:solr-solrj *(excludes log4j:log4j)* ▪ org.springframework.data:spring-data-solr ▪ org.apache.httpcomponents:httpmime
spring-boot-starter-freemarker	▪ org.springframework.boot:spring-boot-starter ▪ org.springframework.boot:spring-boot-starter-web ▪ org.freemarker:freemarker ▪ org.springframework:spring-context-support
spring-boot-starter-groovy-templates	▪ org.springframework.boot:spring-boot-starter ▪ org.springframework.boot:spring-boot-starter-web ▪ org.codehaus.groovy:groovy-templates
spring-boot-starter-hateoas	▪ org.springframework.boot:spring-boot-starter-web ▪ org.springframework.hateoas:spring-hateoas ▪ org.springframework.plugin:spring-plugin-core
spring-boot-starter-hornetq	▪ org.springframework.boot:spring-boot-starter ▪ org.springframework:spring-jms ▪ org.hornetq:hornetq-jms-client
spring-boot-starter-integration	▪ org.springframework.boot:spring-boot-starter ▪ org.springframework.boot:spring-boot-starter-aop ▪ org.springframework.integration:spring-integration-core ▪ org.springframework.integration:spring-integration-file ▪ org.springframework.integration:spring-integration-http ▪ org.springframework.integration:spring-integration-ip ▪ org.springframework.integration:spring-integration-stream
spring-boot-starter-jdbc	▪ org.springframework.boot:spring-boot-starter ▪ org.apache.tomcat:tomcat-jdbc ▪ org.springframework:spring-jdbc

Table B.1   Spring Boot starters *(continued)*

Starter *(Group ID: org.springframework.boot)*	Transitively depends on
spring-boot-starter-jersey	<ul><li>org.springframework.boot:spring-boot-starter</li><li>org.springframework.boot:spring-boot-starter-tomcat</li><li>org.springframework.boot:spring-boot-starter-validation</li><li>com.fasterxml.jackson.core:jackson-databind</li><li>org.springframework:spring-web</li><li>org.glassfish.jersey.core:jersey-server</li><li>org.glassfish.jersey.containers:jersey-container-servlet-core</li><li>org.glassfish.jersey.containers:jersey-container-servlet</li><li>org.glassfish.jersey.ext:jersey-bean-validation *(excludes javax.el:javax.el-api, org.glassfish.web:javax.el)*</li><li>org.glassfish.jersey.ext:jersey-spring3</li><li>org.glassfish.jersey.media:jersey-media-json-jackson</li></ul>
spring-boot-starter-jetty	<ul><li>org.eclipse.jetty:jetty-servlets</li><li>org.eclipse.jetty:jetty-webapp</li><li>org.eclipse.jetty.websocket:websocket-server</li><li>org.eclipse.jetty.websocket:javax-websocket-server-impl</li></ul>
spring-boot-starter-jooq	<ul><li>org.springframework.boot:spring-boot-starter</li><li>org.springframework.boot:spring-boot-starter-jdbc</li><li>org.springframework:spring-tx</li><li>org.jooq:jooq</li></ul>
spring-boot-starter-jta-atomikos	<ul><li>org.springframework.boot:spring-boot-starter</li><li>com.atomikos:transactions-jms</li><li>com.atomikos:transactions-jta *(excludes org.apache.geronimo.specs:geronimo-jta_1.0.1B_spec)*</li><li>com.atomikos:transactions-jdbc</li><li>javax.transaction:javax.transaction-api</li></ul>
spring-boot-starter-jta-bitronix	<ul><li>org.springframework.boot:spring-boot-starter</li><li>javax.jms:jms-api</li><li>javax.transaction:javax.transaction-api</li><li>org.codehaus.btm:btm *(excludes javax.transaction:jta)*</li></ul>
spring-boot-starter-log4j	<ul><li>org.slf4j:jcl-over-slf4j</li><li>org.slf4j:jul-to-slf4j</li><li>org.slf4j:slf4j-log4j12</li><li>log4j:log4j</li></ul>

Table B.1   Spring Boot starters *(continued)*

Starter *(Group ID: org.springframework.boot)*	Transitively depends on
spring-boot-starter-log4j2	▪ org.apache.logging.log4j:log4j-slf4j-impl ▪ org.apache.logging.log4j:log4j-api ▪ org.apache.logging.log4j:log4j-core ▪ org.slf4j:jcl-over-slf4j ▪ org.slf4j:jul-to-slf4j
spring-boot-starter-logging	▪ ch.qos.logback:logback-classic ▪ org.slf4j:jcl-over-slf4j ▪ org.slf4j:jul-to-slf4j ▪ org.slf4j:log4j-over-slf4j
spring-boot-starter-mail	▪ org.springframework.boot:spring-boot-starter ▪ org.springframework:spring-context ▪ org.springframework:spring-context-support ▪ com.sun.mail:javax.mail
spring-boot-starter-mobile	▪ org.springframework.boot:spring-boot-starter ▪ org.springframework.boot:spring-boot-starter-web ▪ org.springframework.mobile:spring-mobile-device
spring-boot-starter-mustache	▪ org.springframework.boot:spring-boot-starter ▪ org.springframework.boot:spring-boot-starter-web ▪ com.samskivert:jmustache
spring-boot-starter-redis	▪ org.springframework.boot:spring-boot-starter ▪ org.springframework.data:spring-data-redis ▪ redis.clients:jedis
spring-boot-starter-remote-shell	▪ org.springframework.boot:spring-boot-starter ▪ org.springframework.boot:spring-boot-starter-actuator ▪ org.crashub:crash.cli ▪ org.crashub:crash.connectors.ssh *(excludes org.codehaus.groovy:groovy-all)* ▪ org.crashub:crash.connectors.telnet *(excludes javax.servlet:servlet-api, log4j :log4j, commons-logging:commons-logging)* ▪ org.crashub:crash.embed.spring *(excludes org.springframework:spring-web, org.codehaus.groovy:groovy-all)* ▪ org.crashub:crash.plugins.cron *(excludes org.codehaus.groovy:groovy-all)* ▪ org.crashub:crash.plugins.mail *(excludes org.codehaus.groovy:groovy-all)* ▪ org.crashub:crash.shell *(excludes org.codehaus.groovy:groovy-all)* ▪ org.codehaus.groovy:groovy

Table B.1 Spring Boot starters *(continued)*

Starter *(Group ID: org.springframework.boot)*	Transitively depends on
spring-boot-starter-security	▪ org.springframework.boot:spring-boot-starter ▪ org.springframework:spring-aop ▪ org.springframework.security:spring-security-config ▪ org.springframework.security:spring-security-web
spring-boot-starter-social-facebook	▪ org.springframework.boot:spring-boot-starter ▪ org.springframework.boot:spring-boot-starter-web ▪ org.springframework.social:spring-social-config ▪ org.springframework.social:spring-social-core ▪ org.springframework.social:spring-social-web ▪ org.springframework.social:spring-social-facebook
spring-boot-starter-social-linkedin	▪ org.springframework.boot:spring-boot-starter ▪ org.springframework.boot:spring-boot-starter-web ▪ org.springframework.social:spring-social-config ▪ org.springframework.social:spring-social-core ▪ org.springframework.social:spring-social-web ▪ org.springframework.social:spring-social-linkedin
spring-boot-starter-social-twitter	▪ org.springframework.boot:spring-boot-starter ▪ org.springframework.boot:spring-boot-starter-web ▪ org.springframework.social:spring-social-config ▪ org.springframework.social:spring-social-core ▪ org.springframework.social:spring-social-web ▪ org.springframework.social:spring-social-twitter
spring-boot-starter-test	▪ junit:junit ▪ org.mockito:mockito-core ▪ org.hamcrest:hamcrest-core ▪ org.hamcrest:hamcrest-library ▪ org.springframework:spring-core *(excludes commons-logging:commons-logging)* ▪ org.springframework:spring-test
spring-boot-starter-thymeleaf	▪ org.springframework.boot:spring-boot-starter ▪ org.springframework.boot:spring-boot-starter-web ▪ org.thymeleaf:thymeleaf-spring4 ▪ nz.net.ultraq.thymeleaf:thymeleaf-layout-dialect
spring-boot-starter-tomcat	▪ org.apache.tomcat.embed:tomcat-embed-core ▪ org.apache.tomcat.embed:tomcat-embed-el ▪ org.apache.tomcat.embed:tomcat-embed-logging-juli ▪ org.apache.tomcat.embed:tomcat-embed-websocket

Table B.1 Spring Boot starters *(continued)*

Starter *(Group ID: org.springframework.boot)*	Transitively depends on
spring-boot-starter-undertow	<ul><li>io.undertow:undertow-core</li><li>io.undertow:undertow-servlet *(excludes org.jboss.spec.javax.servlet:jboss-servlet-api_3.1_spec)*</li><li>io.undertow:undertow-websockets-jsr</li><li>javax.servlet:javax.servlet-api</li><li>org.glassfish:javax.el</li></ul>
spring-boot-starter-validation	<ul><li>org.springframework.boot:spring-boot-starter</li><li>org.apache.tomcat.embed:tomcat-embed-el</li><li>org.hibernate:hibernate-validator</li></ul>
spring-boot-starter-velocity	<ul><li>org.springframework.boot:spring-boot-starter</li><li>org.springframework.boot:spring-boot-starter-web</li><li>commons-beanutils:commons-beanutils</li><li>commons-collections:commons-collections</li><li>commons-digester:commons-digester</li><li>org.apache.velocity:velocity</li><li>org.apache.velocity:velocity-tools</li><li>org.springframework:spring-context-support</li></ul>
spring-boot-starter-web	<ul><li>org.springframework.boot:spring-boot-starter</li><li>org.springframework.boot:spring-boot-starter-tomcat</li><li>org.springframework.boot:spring-boot-starter-validation</li><li>com.fasterxml.jackson.core:jackson-databind</li><li>org.springframework:spring-web</li><li>org.springframework:spring-webmvc</li></ul>
spring-boot-starter-websocket	<ul><li>org.springframework.boot:spring-boot-starter</li><li>org.springframework.boot:spring-boot-starter-web</li><li>org.springframework:spring-messaging</li><li>org.springframework:spring-websocket</li></ul>
spring-boot-starter-ws	<ul><li>org.springframework.boot:spring-boot-starter</li><li>org.springframework.boot:spring-boot-starter-web</li><li>org.springframework:spring-jms</li><li>org.springframework:spring-oxm</li><li>org.springframework.ws:spring-ws-core</li><li>org.springframework.ws:spring-ws-support</li></ul>

appendix C
Configuration properties

Although Spring Boot handles a lot of the grunt work when it comes to configuring the components in your application, you may want to fine-tune some of those components. That's where configuration properties come in handy.

Chapter 3 describes the `@ConfigurationProperties` annotation and how it can be used to expose properties that you can configure external to application code. Just as you can use `@ConfigurationProperties` in components that you create, many of Spring Boot's auto-configured components are also annotated with `@ConfigurationProperties`, making it possible to configure them via any supported property source.

For example, to specify the port that an embedded Tomcat or Jetty server should listen for requests on, you can set the `server.port` property. This can be set as a property in application.properties, in application.yml, in an operating system environment variable, or any of the other options listed in section 3.2.

This appendix lists all of the configuration properties offered by Spring Boot components. Note that the applicability of these properties is dependent upon the component being declared as a bean in the Spring application context (most likely by way of auto-configuration). Setting a property for an inactive component will have no effect.

- `flyway.baseline-description`
  The description to tag an existing schema with when executing baseline.

- `flyway.baseline-on-migrate`
  Whether to automatically call baseline when migrate is executed against a non-empty schema with no metadata table. (Default value: `false`)

- `flyway.baseline-version`
  Sets the version to tag an existing schema with when executing baseline. (Default value: `1`)

195

- `flyway.check-location`
  Check that migration scripts location exists. (Default value: `false`)

- `flyway.clean-on-validation-error`
  Whether to automatically call `clean` or not when a validation error occurs. (Default value: `false`)

- `flyway.enabled`
  Enable flyway. (Default value: `true`)

- `flyway.encoding`
  Sets the SQL migration encoding. (Default value: `UTF-8`)

- `flyway.ignore-failed-future-migration`
  Whether to ignore failed future migrations when reading the metadata table. (Default value: `false`)

- `flyway.init-sqls`
  SQL statements to execute to initialize a connection immediately after obtaining it.

- `flyway.locations`
  Locations of migrations scripts. (Default value: `db/migration`)

- `flyway.out-of-order`
  Whether or not "out of order" migrations are allowed. (Default value: `false`)

- `flyway.password`
  Login password of the database to migrate.

- `flyway.placeholder-prefix`
  Sets the prefix of every placeholder. (Default value: `${`)

- `flyway.placeholder-replacement`
  Whether placeholders should be replaced. (Default value: `true`)

- `flyway.placeholder-suffix`
  Sets the prefix of every placeholder. (Default value: `${`)

- `flyway.placeholders.[placeholder name]`
  Sets a placeholder value.

- `flyway.schemas`
  A case-sensitive list of schemes managed by Flyway. Defaults to the default schema of the connection.

- `flyway.sql-migration-prefix`
  The filename prefix for SQL migrations. (Default value: `V`)

- `flyway.sql-migration-separator`
  The filename separator for SQL migrations. (Default value: `__`)

- `flyway.sql-migration-suffix`
  The filename suffix for SQL migrations. (Default value: `.sql`)

- `flyway.table`
  The name of the schema metadata table to be used by Flyway. (Default value: `schema_version`)

- `flyway.target`
  The target version up to which Flyway should consider migrations. (Defaults to the latest version)

- `flyway.url`
  JDBC URL of the database to migrate. If not set, the primary configured data source is used.

- `flyway.user`
  Login user of the database to migrate.

- `flyway.validate-on-migrate`
  Whether to automatically validate when running migrate. (Default value: `true`)

- `liquibase.change-log`
  Change log configuration path. (Default value: `classpath:/db/changelog/db.changelog-master.yaml`)

- `liquibase.check-change-log-location`
  Check that the change log location exists. (Default value: `true`)

- `liquibase.contexts`
  Comma-separated list of runtime contexts to use.

- `liquibase.default-schema`
  Default database schema.

- `liquibase.drop-first`
  Drop the database schema first. (Default value: `false`)

- `liquibase.enabled`
  Enable Liquibase support. (Default value: `true`)

- `liquibase.password`
  Login password of the database to migrate.

- `liquibase.url`
  JDBC URL of the database to migrate. If not set, the primary configured data source is used.

- `liquibase.user`
  Login user of the database to migrate.

- `multipart.enabled`
  Enable support of multi-part uploads. (Default value: `true`)

- `multipart.file-size-threshold`
  Threshold after which files will be written to disk. Values can use the suffixes "MB" or "KB" to indicate a megabyte or kilobyte size. (Default value: `0`)

- `multipart.location`
  Intermediate location of uploaded files.

- `multipart.max-file-size`
  Max file size. Values can use the suffixes "MB" or "KB" to indicate a megabyte or kilobyte size. (Default value: `1MB`)

- `multipart.max-request-size`
  Max request size. Values can use the suffixes "MB" or "KB" to indicate a megabyte or kilobyte size. (Default value: `10MB`)

- `security.basic.authorize-mode`
  Security authorize mode to apply.

- `security.basic.enabled`
  Enable basic authentication. (Default value: `true`)

- `security.basic.path`
  Comma-separated list of paths to secure. (Default value: `[/**]`)

- `security.basic.realm`
  HTTP basic realm name. (Default value: `Spring`)

- `security.enable-csrf`
  Enable cross-site request forgery support. (Default value: `false`)

- `security.filter-order`
  Security filter chain order. (Default value: `0`)

- `security.headers.cache`
  Enable cache control HTTP headers. (Default value: `false`)

- `security.headers.content-type`
  Enable `X-Content-Type-Options` header. (Default value: `false`)

- `security.headers.frame`
  Enable `X-Frame-Options` header. (Default value: `false`)

- `security.headers.hsts`
  HTTP Strict Transport Security (HSTS) mode (`none`, `domain`, `all`).

- `security.headers.xss`
  Enable cross-site scripting (XSS) protection. (Default value: `false`)

- `security.ignored`
  Comma-separated list of paths to exclude from the default secured paths.

- `security.oauth2.client.access-token-uri`
  The URI used to fetch an access token.

- `security.oauth2.client.access-token-validity-seconds`
  How long an access token is to be valid before expiring.

- `security.oauth2.client.additional-information.[key]`
  Set additional information that token granters would like to add to the token.

- `security.oauth2.client.authentication-scheme`
  The method for transmitting the bearer token. One of `form`, `header`, `none`, or `query`. (Default value: `header`)

- `security.oauth2.client.authorities`
  The authorities to be granted to an authenticated client.

- `security.oauth2.client.authorized-grant-types`
  The grant types allowed to the client.

- `security.oauth2.client.auto-approve-scopes`
  The scope to automatically approve for a client.

- `security.oauth2.client.client-authentication-scheme`
  The method for transmitting authentication credentials when authenticating the client. One of `form`, `header`, `none`, or `query`. (Default value: `header`)

- `security.oauth2.client.client-id`
  OAuth2 client ID.

- `security.oauth2.client.client-secret`
  OAuth2 client secret. A random secret is generated by default.

- `security.oauth2.client.grant-type`
  The grant type for obtaining an access token for this resource.

- `security.oauth2.client.id`
  The application's client ID.

- `security.oauth2.client.pre-established-redirect-uri`
  The redirect URI that has been pre-established with the server. If present, the redirect URI will be omitted from the user authorization request because the server doesn't need to know it.

- `security.oauth2.client.refresh-token-validity-seconds`
  How long a refresh token will be valid before expiring.

- `security.oauth2.client.registered-redirect-uri`
  Comma-separated list of redirect URIs registered for the client.

- `security.oauth2.client.resource-ids`
  Comma-separated list of resource IDs associated with the client.

- `security.oauth2.client.scope`
  Scope assigned to the client.

- `security.oauth2.client.token-name`
  The token name.

- `security.oauth2.client.use-current-uri`
  Whether the current URI (if set) in the request should be used in preference to the pre-established redirect URI. (Default value: `true`)

- `security.oauth2.client.user-authorization-uri`
  The URI to which the user is to be redirected to authorize an access token.

- `security.oauth2.resource.id`
  Identifier of the resource.

- `security.oauth2.resource.jwt.key-uri`
  The URI of the JWT token. Can be set if the value is not available and the key is public.

- `security.oauth2.resource.jwt.key-value`
  The verification key of the JWT token. Can either be a symmetric secret or PEM-encoded RSA public key. If the value is not available, you can set the URI instead.

- `security.oauth2.resource.prefer-token-info`
  Use the token info; can be set to `false` to use the user info. (Default value: `true`)

- `security.oauth2.resource.service-id`
  The service ID. (Default value: `resource`)

- `security.oauth2.resource.token-info-uri`
  URI of the token decoding endpoint.

- `security.oauth2.resource.token-type`
  The token type to send when using the `userInfoUri`.

- `security.oauth2.resource.user-info-uri`
  URI of the user endpoint.

- `security.oauth2.sso.filter-order`
  Filter order to apply if not providing an explicit `WebSecurityConfigurerAdapter` (otherwise the order can be provided there instead).

- `security.oauth2.sso.login-path`
  Path to the login page—the page that triggers the redirect to the OAuth2 Authorization Server. (Default value: `/login`)

- `security.require-ssl`
  Enable secure channel for all requests. (Default value: `false`)

- `security.sessions`
  Session creation policy. (Default values: `always`, `never`, `if_required`, `stateless`).

- `security.user.name`
  Default user name. (Default value: `user`)

- `security.user.password`
  Password for the default user name.

- `security.user.role`
  Granted roles for the default user name.

- `server.address`
  Network address to which the server should bind.

- `server.compression.enabled`
  Whether or not compression should be enabled. (Default value: `false`)

- `server.compression.excluded-user-agents`
  Comma-separated list of user agents for which responses should not be compressed. (Default values: `text/html,text/xml,text/plain,text/css`)

- `server.compression.mime-types`
  Comma-separated list of MIME types that should be compressed.

- `server.compression.min-response-size`
  Minimum response size (in bytes) that is required for compression to be performed. (Default value: `2048`)

- `server.context-parameters.[param name]`
  Sets a servlet context parameter.

- `server.context-path`
  Context path of the application.

- `server.display-name`
  Display name of the application. (Default value: `application`)

- `server.jsp-servlet.class-name`
  The class name of the servlet to use for JSPs. (Default value: `org.apache.jasper.servlet.JspServlet`)

- `server.jsp-servlet.init-parameters.[param name]`
  Sets a JSP servlet initialization parameter.

- `server.jsp-servlet.registered`
  Whether or not the JSP servlet should be registered with the embedded servlet container. (Default value: `true`)

- `server.port`
  Server HTTP port.

- `server.servlet-path`
  Path of the main dispatcher servlet. (Default value: /)

- `server.session.cookie.comment`
  Comment for the session cookie.

- `server.session.cookie.domain`
  Domain for the session cookie.

- `server.session.cookie.http-only`
  HttpOnly flag for the session cookie.

- `server.session.cookie.max-age`
  Maximum age of the session cookie in seconds.

- `server.session.cookie.name`
  Session cookie name.

- `server.session.cookie.path`
  Path of the session cookie.

- `server.session.cookie.secure`
  "Secure" flag for the session cookie.

- `server.session.persistent`
  Persist session data between restarts. (Default value: `false`)

- `server.session.timeout`
  Session timeout in seconds.

- `server.session.tracking-modes`
  Session tracking modes (one or more of the following: `cookie`, `url`, `ssl`).

- `server.ssl.ciphers`
  Supported SSL ciphers.

- `server.ssl.client-auth`
  Whether client authentication is wanted (`want`) or needed (`need`). Requires a trust store.

- `server.ssl.enabled`
  Whether SSL is enabled or not. (Default value: `true`)

- `server.ssl.key-alias`
  Alias that identifies the key in the key store.

- `server.ssl.key-password`
  Password used to access the key in the key store.

- `server.ssl.key-store`
  Path to the key store that holds the SSL certificate (typically a .jks file).

- `server.ssl.key-store-password`
  Password used to access the key store.

- `server.ssl.key-store-provider`
  Provider for the key store.

- `server.ssl.key-store-type`
  Type of the key store.

- `server.ssl.protocol`
  SSL protocol to use. (Default value: `TLS`)

- `server.ssl.trust-store`
  Trust store that holds SSL certificates.

- `server.ssl.trust-store-password`
  Password used to access the trust store.

- `server.ssl.trust-store-provider`
  Provider for the trust store.

- `server.ssl.trust-store-type`
  Type of the trust store.

- `server.tomcat.access-log-enabled`
  Whether or not the access log is enabled. (Default value: `false`)

- `server.tomcat.access-log-pattern`
  Format pattern for access logs. (Default value: `common`)

- `server.tomcat.accesslog.directory`
  Directory in which log files are created. Can be relative to the tomcat base dir or absolute. (Default value: `logs`)

- `server.tomcat.accesslog.enabled`
  Enable access log. (Default value: `false`)

- `server.tomcat.accesslog.pattern`
  Format pattern for access logs. (Default value: `common`)

- `server.tomcat.accesslog.prefix`
  Log filename prefix. (Default value: `access_log`)

- `server.tomcat.accesslog.suffix`
  Log filename suffix. (Default value: `.log`)

- `server.tomcat.background-processor-delay`
  Delay in seconds between the invocation of `backgroundProcess` methods. (Default value: `30`)

- `server.tomcat.basedir`
  Tomcat base directory. If not specified, a temporary directory will be used.

- `server.tomcat.internal-proxies`
  Regular expression that matches proxies that are to be trusted. Default: "10\\d{1,3}\\d{1,3}\\d{1,3}| 192\168\\d{1,3}\\d{1,3}| 169\254\\d{1,3}\\d{1,3}| 127\.\d{1,3}\\d{1,3}\\d{1,3}| 172\1[6-9]{1}\\d{1,3}\\d{1,3}| 172\2[0-9]{1}\\d{1,3}\\d{1,3}| 172\3[0-1]{1}\\d{1,3}\\d{1,3}"

- `server.tomcat.max-http-header-size`
  Maximum size in bytes of the HTTP message header. (Default value: `0`)

- `server.tomcat.max-threads`
  Maximum number of worker threads. (Default value: `0`)

- `server.tomcat.port-header`
  Name of the HTTP header used to override the original port value.

- `server.tomcat.protocol-header`
  Header that holds the incoming protocol, usually named `X-Forwarded-Proto`. Configured as a `RemoteIpValve` only if `remoteIpHeader` is also set.

- `server.tomcat.protocol-header-https-value`
  Value of the protocol header that indicates that the incoming request uses SSL. (Default value: `https`)

- `server.tomcat.remote-ip-header`
  Name of the HTTP header from which the remote IP is extracted. Configured as a `RemoteIpValve` only if `remoteIpHeader` is also set.

- `server.tomcat.uri-encoding`
  Character encoding to use to decode the URI.

- `server.undertow.access-log-dir`
  Undertow access log directory. (Default value: `logs`)

- `server.undertow.access-log-enabled`
  Whether or not the access log is enabled. (Default value: `false`)

- `server.undertow.access-log-pattern`
  Format pattern for access logs. (Default value: `common`)

- `server.undertow.accesslog.dir`
  Undertow access log directory.

- `server.undertow.accesslog.enabled`
  Enable access log. (Default value: `false`)

- `server.undertow.accesslog.pattern`
  Format pattern for access logs. (Default value: `common`)

- `server.undertow.buffer-size`
  Size of each buffer in bytes.

- `server.undertow.buffers-per-region`
  Number of buffers per region.

- `server.undertow.direct-buffers`
  Allocate buffers outside the Java heap.

- `server.undertow.io-threads`
  Number of I/O threads to create for the worker.

- `server.undertow.worker-threads`
  Number of worker threads.

- `spring.activemq.broker-url`
  URL of the ActiveMQ broker. Auto-generated by default.

- `spring.activemq.in-memory`
  Specify if the default broker URL should be in memory. Ignored if an explicit broker has been specified. (Default value: `true`)

- `spring.activemq.password`
  Login password of the broker.

- `spring.activemq.pooled`
  Specify if a `PooledConnectionFactory` should be created instead of a regular `ConnectionFactory`. (Default value: `false`)

- `spring.activemq.user`
  Login user of the broker.

- `spring.aop.auto`
  Add `@EnableAspectJAutoProxy`. (Default value: `true`)

- `spring.aop.proxy-target-class`
  Whether subclass-based (CGLIB) proxies are to be created (`true`) as opposed to standard Java interface-based proxies (`false`). (Default value: `false`)

- `spring.application.admin.enabled`
  Enable admin features for the application. (Default value: `false`)

- `spring.application.admin.jmx-name`
  JMX name of the application admin MBean. (Default value: `org.springframe-work.boot:type=Admin,name=SpringApplication`)

- `spring.artemis.embedded.cluster-password`
  Cluster password. Randomly generated on startup by default.

- `spring.artemis.embedded.data-directory`
  Journal file directory. Not necessary if persistence is turned off.

- `spring.artemis.embedded.enabled`
  Enable embedded mode if the Artemis server APIs are available. (Default value: `true`)

- `spring.artemis.embedded.persistent`
  Enable persistent store. (Default value: `false`)

- `spring.artemis.embedded.queues`
  Comma-separated list of queues to create on startup. (Default value: `[]`)

- `spring.artemis.embedded.server-id`
  Server ID. By default, an auto-incremented counter is used. (Default value: `0`)

- `spring.artemis.embedded.topics`
  Comma-separated list of topics to create on startup. (Default value: `[]`)

- `spring.artemis.host`
  Artemis broker host. (Default value: `localhost`)

- `spring.artemis.mode`
  Artemis deployment mode, auto-detected by default. Can be explicitly set to `native` or `embedded`.

- `spring.artemis.port`
  Artemis broker port. (Default value: `61616`)

- `spring.autoconfigure.exclude`
  Auto-configuration classes to exclude.

- `spring.batch.initializer.enabled`
  Create the required batch tables on startup if necessary. (Default value: `true`)

- `spring.batch.job.enabled`
  Execute all Spring Batch jobs in the context on startup. (Default value: `true`)

- `spring.batch.job.names`
  Comma-separated list of job names to execute on startup. By default, all jobs found in the context are executed.

- `spring.batch.schema`
  Path to the SQL file to use to initialize the database schema. (Default value: `classpath:org/springframework/batch/core/schema-@@platform@@.sql`)

- `spring.batch.table-prefix`
  Table prefix for all the batch metadata tables.

- `spring.cache.cache-names`
  Comma-separated list of cache names to create if supported by the underlying cache manager. Usually this disables the ability to create additional caches on the fly.

- `spring.cache.ehcache.config`
  The location of the configuration file to use to initialize EhCache.

- `spring.cache.guava.spec`
  The spec to use to create caches. Check CacheBuilderSpec for more details on the spec format.

- `spring.cache.hazelcast.config`
  The location of the configuration file to use to initialize Hazelcast.

- `spring.cache.infinispan.config`
  The location of the configuration file to use to initialize Infinispan.

- `spring.cache.jcache.config`
  The location of the configuration file to use to initialize the cache manager. The configuration file is dependent on the underlying cache implementation.

- `spring.cache.jcache.provider`
  Fully qualified name of the CachingProvider implementation to use to retrieve the JSR-107 compliant cache manager. Only needed if more than one JSR-107 implementation is available on the classpath.

- `spring.cache.type`
  Cache type, auto-detected according to the environment by default.

- `spring.dao.exceptiontranslation.enabled`
  Enable the `PersistenceExceptionTranslationPostProcessor`. (Default value: true)

- `spring.data.elasticsearch.cluster-name`
  Elasticsearch cluster name. (Default value: `elasticsearch`)

- `spring.data.elasticsearch.cluster-nodes`
  Comma-separated list of cluster node addresses. If not specified, starts a client node.

- `spring.data.elasticsearch.properties`
  Additional properties used to configure the client.

- `spring.data.elasticsearch.repositories.enabled`
  Enable Elasticsearch repositories. (Default value: `true`)

- `spring.data.jpa.repositories.enabled`
  Enable JPA repositories. (Default value: `true`)

- `spring.data.mongodb.authentication-database`
  Authentication database name.

- `spring.data.mongodb.database`
  Database name.

- `spring.data.mongodb.field-naming-strategy`
  Fully qualified name of the `FieldNamingStrategy` to use.

- `spring.data.mongodb.grid-fs-database`
  GridFS database name.

- `spring.data.mongodb.host`
  Mongo server host.

- `spring.data.mongodb.password`
  Login password of the Mongo server.

- `spring.data.mongodb.port`
  Mongo server port.

- `spring.data.mongodb.repositories.enabled`
  Enable Mongo repositories. (Default value: `true`)

- `spring.data.mongodb.uri`
  Mongo database URI. When set, the host and port are ignored. (Default value: `mongodb://localhost/test`)

- `spring.data.mongodb.username`
  Login user of the Mongo server.

- `spring.data.rest.base-path`
  The base path to expose repository resources under.

- `spring.data.rest.default-page-size`
  The default size of a page in paged data. (Default value: `20`)

- `spring.data.rest.limit-param-name`
  The name of the URL query string parameter that indicates how many results to return at once. (Default value: `size`)

- `spring.data.rest.max-page-size`
  The maximum size of pages. (Default value: `1000`)

- `spring.data.rest.page-param-name`
  The name of the URL query string parameter that indicates what page to return. (Default value: `page`)

- `spring.data.rest.return-body-on-create`
  Whether to return a response body after creating an entity. (Default value: `false`)

- `spring.data.rest.return-body-on-update`
  Whether to return a response body after updating an entity. (Default value: `false`)

- `spring.data.rest.sort-param-name`
  The name of the URL query string parameter that indicates what direction to sort results. (Default value: `sort`)

- `spring.data.solr.host`
Solr host. Ignored if `zk-host` is set. (Default value: `http://127.0.0.1:8983/solr`)

- `spring.data.solr.repositories.enabled`
Enable Solr repositories. (Default value: `true`)

- `spring.data.solr.zk-host`
ZooKeeper host address in the form HOST:PORT.

- `spring.datasource.abandon-when-percentage-full`
The percentage threshold above which connections that have been abandoned (timed out) will be closed and reported.

- `spring.datasource.allow-pool-suspension`
Whether or not pool suspension is allowed. There is a performance impact when pool suspension is enabled. Unless you need it (for a redundancy system, for example) do not enable it. This property only applies when using the Hikari data pool. (Default value: `false`)

- `spring.datasource.alternate-username-allowed`
Whether or not an alternate username is allowed.

- `spring.datasource.auto-commit`
Whether or not updates are auto-committed.

- `spring.datasource.catalog`
The default catalog name.

- `spring.datasource.commit-on-return`
Whether or not the connection pool should commit any pending transaction when a connection is returned.

- `spring.datasource.connection-init-sql`
A SQL string that will be executed on all new connections when they are created, before they are added to the connection pool.

- `spring.datasource.connection-init-sqls`
A list of SQL statements to be executed when a physical connection is first created. (For use with the DBCP connection pool.)

- `spring.datasource.connection-properties.[key]`
Sets a property to be used when creating a connection. (For the DBCP connection pool.)

- `spring.datasource.connection-test-query`
A SQL query to be executed to test the validity of connections.

- `spring.datasource.connection-timeout`
The connection timeout (in milliseconds).

- `spring.datasource.continue-on-error`
  Do not stop if an error occurs while initializing the database. (Default value: `false`)

- `spring.datasource.data`
  Data (DML) script resource reference.

- `spring.datasource.data-source-class-name`
  The fully qualified class name of the data source to use to get connections.

- `spring.datasource.data-source-jndi`
  The JNDI location of the data source to use to get connections.

- `spring.datasource.data-source-properties.[key]`
  Sets a property to be used when creating the data source. (For the Hikari connection pool.)

- `spring.datasource.db-properties`
  Sets a property to be used when creating the data source. (For the Tomcat connection pool.)

- `spring.datasource.default-auto-commit`
  Whether or not to auto-commit on connections.

- `spring.datasource.default-catalog`
  The default catalog for connections.

- `spring.datasource.default-read-only`
  The default read-only state for connections.

- `spring.datasource.default-transaction-isolation`
  The default transaction isolation for connections.

- `spring.datasource.driver-class-name`
  Fully qualified name of the JDBC driver. Auto-detected based on the URL by default.

- `spring.datasource.fair-queue`
  Whether or not to return connections in a FIFO fashion.

- `spring.datasource.health-check-properties.[key]`
  Sets a property to be included in the health check. (For the Hikari connection pool.)

- `spring.datasource.idle-timeout`
  The maximum amount of time (in milliseconds) that a connection is allowed to sit idle in the pool. (Default value: `10`)

- `spring.datasource.ignore-exception-on-pre-load`
  Whether or not to ignore connections while initializing the datasource pool.

- `spring.datasource.init-sql`
  A custom query to run when a connection is first created.

- `spring.datasource.initial-size`
  The number of connections that will be established when the connection pool is started.

- `spring.datasource.initialization-fail-fast`
  Whether or not the construction of the pool should throw an exception if the minimum number of connections cannot be created. (Default value: `true`)

- `spring.datasource.initialize`
  Populate the database using data.sql. (Default value: `true`)

- `spring.datasource.isolate-internal-queries`
  Whether internal queries should be isolated. (Default value: `false`)

- `spring.datasource.jdbc-interceptors`
  A semicolon-separated list of classnames extending the `JdbcInterceptor` class. These interceptors will be inserted as an interceptor into the chain of operations on a `java.sql.Connection` object. (For the Tomcat connection pool.)

- `spring.datasource.jdbc-url`
  The JDBC URL to create connections with.

- `spring.datasource.jmx-enabled`
  Enable JMX support (if provided by the underlying pool). (Default value: `false`)

- `spring.datasource.jndi-name`
  JNDI location of the datasource. Class, URL, username, and password are ignored when set.

- `spring.datasource.leak-detection-threshold`
  The threshold, in milliseconds, for detecting connection leaks with the Hikari connection pool.

- `spring.datasource.log-abandoned`
  Whether to log stack traces for application code that abandoned a statement or connection. For use with the DBCP connection pool. (Default value: `false`)

- `spring.datasource.log-validation-errors`
  Whether validation errors should be logged when using the Tomcat connection pool.

- `spring.datasource.login-timeout`
  The timeout (in seconds) for connecting to the database.

- `spring.datasource.max-active`
  The maximum number of active connections in the connection pool.

- `spring.datasource.max-age`
  The maximum age of a connection in the connection pool.

- `spring.datasource.max-idle`
  The maximum number of idle connections in the connection pool.

- `spring.datasource.max-lifetime`
  The maximum lifetime (in milliseconds) of a connection in the connection pool.

- `spring.datasource.max-open-prepared-statements`
  The maximum number of open prepared statements.

- `spring.datasource.max-wait`
  The maximum number of milliseconds that the pool will wait for a connection to be returned before throwing an exception.

- `spring.datasource.maximum-pool-size`
  The maximum size that the pool is allowed to reach, including both idle and in-use connections.

- `spring.datasource.min-evictable-idle-time-millis`
  The minimum amount of time an object may sit idle in the pool before it is eligible for eviction by the idle object evictor (if any).

- `spring.datasource.min-idle`
  The minimum number of established connections that should be kept in the pool at all times. (For DBCP and Tomcat connection pools.)

- `spring.datasource.minimum-idle`
  The minimum number of idle connections that HikariCP tries to maintain in the pool.

- `spring.datasource.name`
  The datasource name.

- `spring.datasource.num-tests-per-eviction-run`
  The number of objects to examine during each run of the idle object evictor thread (if any).

- `spring.datasource.password`
  Login password of the database.

- `spring.datasource.platform`
  Platform to use in the schema resource (schema-${platform}.sql). (Default value: `all`)

- `spring.datasource.pool-name`
  The connection pool name.

- `spring.datasource.pool-prepared-statements`
  Whether to pool statements or not.

- `spring.datasource.propagate-interrupt-state`
  Whether to propagate interrupt state for interrupted threads waiting for a connection.

- `spring.datasource.read-only`
  Set a datasource as read-only when using the Hikari connection pool.

- `spring.datasource.register-mbeans`
  Whether or not the Hikari connection pool should register JMX MBeans.

- `spring.datasource.remove-abandoned`
  Whether abandoned connections should be removed if they exceed the abandoned timeout.

- `spring.datasource.remove-abandoned-timeout`
  The time in seconds before a connection can be considered abandoned.

- `spring.datasource.rollback-on-return`
  Whether any pending transactions should be rolled back when a connection is returned to the pool.

- `spring.datasource.schema`
  Schema (DDL) script resource reference.

- `spring.datasource.separator`
  Statement separator in SQL initialization scripts. (Default value: ;)

- `spring.datasource.sql-script-encoding`
  SQL scripts encoding.

- `spring.datasource.suspect-timeout`
  How long in seconds before logging a suspected abandoned connection.

- `spring.datasource.test-on-borrow`
  Whether a connection should be tested upon being borrowed from the connection pool.

- `spring.datasource.test-on-connect`
  Whether a connection should be tested upon creation.

- `spring.datasource.test-on-return`
  Whether a connection should be tested upon return to the connection pool.

- `spring.datasource.test-while-idle`
  Whether a connection should be tested while idle.

- `spring.datasource.time-between-eviction-runs-millis`
  The number of milliseconds to sleep between runs of the idle connection validation, abandoned cleaner, and idle pool resizing.

- `spring.datasource.transaction-isolation`
  Set the default transaction isolation level when using the Hikari connection pool.

- `spring.datasource.url`
  JDBC URL of the database.

- `spring.datasource.use-disposable-connection-facade`
  Whether the connection will be wrapped with a facade that will disallow the connection to be used after `Connection.close()` is called.

- `spring.datasource.use-equals`
  Whether to use `String.equals()` instead of `==` when comparing method names.

- `spring.datasource.use-lock`
  Whether a lock should be used when operations are performed on the connection object.

- `spring.datasource.username`
  Login user of the database.

- `spring.datasource.validation-interval`
  How often, in milliseconds, to run connection validation.

- `spring.datasource.validation-query`
  The SQL query that will be used to validate connections from this pool before returning them to the caller or pool.

- `spring.datasource.validation-query-timeout`
  The timeout in seconds before a connection validation query fails.

- `spring.datasource.validation-timeout`
  The timeout in seconds before a connection validation fails. (For use with the Hikari connection pool.)

- `spring.datasource.validator-class-name`
  The fully qualified class name for an optional validator class that will be used in place of test queries.

- `spring.datasource.xa.data-source-class-name`
  XA datasource fully qualified name.

- `spring.datasource.xa.properties`
  Properties to pass to the XA data source.

- `spring.freemarker.allow-request-override`
  Set whether `HttpServletRequest` attributes are allowed to override (hide) controller-generated model attributes of the same name.

- `spring.freemarker.allow-session-override`
  Set whether `HttpSession` attributes are allowed to override (hide) controller-generated model attributes of the same name.

- `spring.freemarker.cache`
  Enable template caching.

- `spring.freemarker.charset`
  Template encoding.

- `spring.freemarker.check-template-location`
  Check that the templates location exists.

- `spring.freemarker.content-type`
  `Content-Type` value.

- `spring.freemarker.enabled`
  Enable MVC view resolution for this technology.

- `spring.freemarker.expose-request-attributes`
  Set whether all request attributes should be added to the model prior to merging with the template.

- `spring.freemarker.expose-session-attributes`
  Set whether all `HttpSession` attributes should be added to the model prior to merging with the template.

- `spring.freemarker.expose-spring-macro-helpers`
  Set whether to expose a `RequestContext` for use by Spring's macro library, under the name `springMacroRequestContext`.

- `spring.freemarker.prefer-file-system-access`
  Prefer filesystem access for template loading. Filesystem access enables hot detection of template changes. (Default value: `true`)

- `spring.freemarker.prefix`
  Prefix that gets prepended to view names when building a URL.

- `spring.freemarker.request-context-attribute`
  Name of the `RequestContext` attribute for all views.

- `spring.freemarker.settings`
  Well-known FreeMarker keys that will be passed to FreeMarker's configuration.

- `spring.freemarker.suffix`
  Suffix that gets appended to view names when building a URL.

- `spring.freemarker.template-loader-path`
  Comma-separated list of template paths. (Default value: `["classpath:/templates/"]`)

- `spring.freemarker.view-names`
  Whitelist of view names that can be resolved.

- `spring.groovy.template.allow-request-override`
  Set whether `HttpServletRequest` attributes are allowed to override (hide) controller-generated model attributes of the same name.

- `spring.groovy.template.allow-session-override`
  Set whether `HttpSession` attributes are allowed to override (hide) controller-generated model attributes of the same name.

- `spring.groovy.template.cache`
  Enable template caching.

- `spring.groovy.template.charset`
  Template encoding.

- `spring.groovy.template.check-template-location`
  Check that the templates location exists.

- `spring.groovy.template.configuration.auto-escape`
  Whether or not model variables are escaped when rendered in the template. (Default value: `false`)

- `spring.groovy.template.configuration.auto-indent`
  Whether or not the template renders indentation automatically. (Default value: `false`)

- `spring.groovy.template.configuration.auto-indent-string`
  The string used for indentation when auto-indentation is enabled. Either `SPACES` or `TAB`. (Default value: `SPACES`)

- `spring.groovy.template.configuration.auto-new-line`
  Whether or not new lines should be rendered by the template. (Default value: `false`)

- `spring.groovy.template.configuration.base-template-class`
  The template base class.

- `spring.groovy.template.configuration.cache-templates`
  Whether or not templates should be cached. (Default value: `true`)

- `spring.groovy.template.configuration.declaration-encoding`
  The encoding used to write the declaration header.

- `spring.groovy.template.configuration.expand-empty-elements`
  Whether elements without a body should be written in the short form (e.g., `<br/>`) or expanded form (e.g., `<br></br>`). (Default value: `false`)

- `spring.groovy.template.configuration.locale`
Set the template locale.

- `spring.groovy.template.configuration.new-line-string`
The string to render for a new line when auto-newlines are enabled. (Default is the value of the system's `line.separator` property)

- `spring.groovy.template.configuration.resource-loader-path`
The path to the Groovy templates. (Default value: `classpath:/templates/`)

- `spring.groovy.template.configuration.use-double-quotes`
Whether attributes should use double quotes or single quotes. (Default value: `false`)

- `spring.groovy.template.content-type`
`Content-Type` value.

- `spring.groovy.template.enabled`
Enable MVC view resolution for this technology.

- `spring.groovy.template.expose-request-attributes`
Set whether all request attributes should be added to the model prior to merging with the template.

- `spring.groovy.template.expose-session-attributes`
Set whether all `HttpSession` attributes should be added to the model prior to merging with the template.

- `spring.groovy.template.expose-spring-macro-helpers`
Set whether to expose a `RequestContext` for use by Spring's macro library, under the name `springMacroRequestContext`.

- `spring.groovy.template.prefix`
Prefix that gets prepended to view names when building a URL.

- `spring.groovy.template.request-context-attribute`
Name of the `RequestContext` attribute for all views.

- `spring.groovy.template.resource-loader-path`
Template path. (Default value: `classpath:/templates/`)

- `spring.groovy.template.suffix`
Suffix that gets appended to view names when building a URL.

- `spring.groovy.template.view-names`
Whitelist of view names that can be resolved.

- `spring.h2.console.enabled`
Enable the console. (Default value: `false`)

- `spring.h2.console.path`
  Path at which the console will be available. (Default value: `/h2-console`)

- `spring.hateoas.apply-to-primary-object-mapper`
  Specify if HATEOAS support should be applied to the primary `ObjectMapper`. (Default value: `true`)

- `spring.hornetq.embedded.cluster-password`
  Cluster password. Randomly generated on startup by default.

- `spring.hornetq.embedded.data-directory`
  Journal file directory. Not necessary if persistence is turned off.

- `spring.hornetq.embedded.enabled`
  Enable embedded mode if the HornetQ server APIs are available. (Default value: `true`)

- `spring.hornetq.embedded.persistent`
  Enable persistent store. (Default value: `false`)

- `spring.hornetq.embedded.queues`
  Comma-separated list of queues to create on startup. (Default value: `[]`)

- `spring.hornetq.embedded.server-id`
  Server ID. By default, an auto-incremented counter is used. (Default value: `0`)

- `spring.hornetq.embedded.topics`
  Comma-separated list of topics to create on startup. (Default value: `[]`)

- `spring.hornetq.host`
  HornetQ broker host. (Default value: `localhost`)

- `spring.hornetq.mode`
  HornetQ deployment mode, auto-detected by default. Can be explicitly set to `native` or `embedded`.

- `spring.hornetq.port`
  HornetQ broker port. (Default value: `5445`)

- `spring.http.converters.preferred-json-mapper`
  Preferred JSON mapper to use for HTTP message conversion.

- `spring.http.encoding.charset`
  Charset of HTTP requests and responses. Added to the `Content-Type` header if not set explicitly. (Default value: `UTF-8`)

- `spring.http.encoding.enabled`
  Enable HTTP encoding support. (Default value: `true`)

- `spring.http.encoding.force`
  Force the encoding to the configured charset on HTTP requests and responses. (Default value: `true`)

- `spring.jackson.date-format`
  Date format string (yyyy-MM-dd HH:mm:ss) or a fully qualified date format class name.

- `spring.jackson.deserialization`
  Jackson on/off features that affect the way Java objects are deserialized.

- `spring.jackson.generator`
  Jackson on/off features for generators.

- `spring.jackson.joda-date-time-format`
  Joda date/time format string (yyyy-MM-dd HH:mm:ss). If not configured, `date-format` will be used as a fallback if it's configured with a format string.

- `spring.jackson.locale`
  Locale used for formatting.

- `spring.jackson.mapper`
  Jackson general purpose on/off features.

- `spring.jackson.parser`
  Jackson on/off features for parsers.

- `spring.jackson.property-naming-strategy`
  One of the constants on Jackson's `PropertyNamingStrategy` (`CAMEL_CASE_TO_LOWER_CASE_WITH_UNDERSCORES`). Can also be a fully qualified class name of a`PropertyNamingStrategy` subclass.

- `spring.jackson.serialization`
  Jackson on/off features that affect the way Java objects are serialized.

- `spring.jackson.serialization-inclusion`
  Controls the inclusion of properties during serialization. Configured with one of the values in Jackson's `JsonInclude.Include` enumeration.

- `spring.jackson.time-zone`
  Time zone used when formatting dates. Configured using any recognized time zone identifier, such as `America/Los_Angeles` or `GMT+10`.

- `spring.jersey.filter.order`
  Jersey filter chain order. (Default value: `0`)

- `spring.jersey.init`
  Init parameters to pass to Jersey via the servlet or filter.

- `spring.jersey.type`
  Jersey integration type. Can be either `servlet` or `filter`.

- `spring.jms.jndi-name`
  Connection factory JNDI name. When set, takes precedence to others' connection factory auto-configurations.

- `spring.jms.listener.acknowledge-mode`
  Acknowledge mode of the container. By default, the listener is transacted with automatic acknowledgment.

- `spring.jms.listener.auto-startup`
  Start the container automatically on startup. (Default value: `true`)

- `spring.jms.listener.concurrency`
  Minimum number of concurrent consumers.

- `spring.jms.listener.max-concurrency`
  Maximum number of concurrent consumers.

- `spring.jms.pub-sub-domain`
  Specify if the default destination type supports publish/subscribe (if it is a topic as opposed to a queue). (Default value: `false`)

- `spring.jmx.default-domain`
  JMX domain name.

- `spring.jmx.enabled`
  Expose management beans to the JMX domain. (Default value: `true`)

- `spring.jmx.server`
  MBeanServer bean name. (Default value: `mbeanServer`)

- `spring.jooq.sql-dialect`
  SQLDialect JOOQ used when communicating with the configured datasource, such as `POSTGRES`.

- `spring.jpa.database`
  Target database to operate on, auto-detected by default. Can be alternatively set using the `databasePlatform` property.

- `spring.jpa.database-platform`
  Name of the target database to operate on, auto-detected by default. Can be alternatively set using the `Database` enum.

- `spring.jpa.generate-ddl`
  Initialize the schema on startup. (Default value: `false`)

- `spring.jpa.hibernate.ddl-auto`
  DDL mode (`none`, `validate`, `update`, `create`, `create-drop`). This is actually a shortcut for the `hibernate.hbm2ddl.auto` property. Default to `create-drop` when using an embedded database; `none` otherwise.

- `spring.jpa.hibernate.naming-strategy`
  The fully qualified class name of a Hibernate naming strategy.

- `spring.jpa.open-in-view`
  Register `OpenEntityManagerInViewInterceptor`. Binds a JPA `EntityManager` to the thread for the entire processing of the request. (Default value: `true`)

- `spring.jpa.properties`
  Additional native properties to set on the JPA provider.

- `spring.jpa.show-sql`
  Enable logging of SQL statements when using the Bitronix Transaction Manager. (Default value: `false`)

- `spring.jta.allow-multiple-lrc`
  Whether the transaction manager should allow enlistment of multiple LRC resources in a single transaction when using the Bitronix Transaction Manager. (Default value: `false`)

- `spring.jta.asynchronous2-pc`
  Whether two-phase commit should be executed asynchronously when using the Bitronix Transaction Manager. (Default value: `false`)

- `spring.jta.background-recovery-interval`
  How often, in minutes, to run the recovery process when using the Bitronix Transaction Manager. (Default value: `1`)

- `spring.jta.background-recovery-interval-seconds`
  How often, in seconds, to run the recovery process when using the Bitronix Transaction Manager. (Default value: `60`)

- `spring.jta.current-node-only-recovery`
  Whether recovery should filter out recovered XIDs that don't contain this JVM's unique ID when using the Bitronix Transaction Manager. (Default value: `true`)

- `spring.jta.debug-zero-resource-transaction`
  Whether creation and commit call stacks of transactions executed without a single enlisted resource should be tracked and logged when using the Bitronix Transaction Manager. (Default value: `false`)

- `spring.jta.default-transaction-timeout`
  The default transaction timeout, in seconds, when using the Bitronix Transaction Manager. (Default value: `60`)

- `spring.jta.disable-jmx`
  Whether the registration of JMX MBeans should be disabled when using the Bitronix Transaction Manager. (Default value: `false`)

- `spring.jta.enabled`
Enable JTA support. (Default value: `true`)

- `spring.jta.exception-analyzer`
The exception analyzer to use when using the Bitronix Transaction Manager. Can be `null` for the default exception analyzer or the fully qualified class name of a custom exception analyzer.

- `spring.jta.filter-log-status`
Whether mandatory logs should be written when using the Bitronix Transaction Manager. Enabling this parameter lowers space usage of the fragments but makes debugging more complex. (Default value: `false`)

- `spring.jta.force-batching-enabled`
Whether disk forces are batched when using the Bitronix Transaction Manager. Disabling batching can seriously lower the transaction manager's throughput. (Default value: `true`)

- `spring.jta.forced-write-enabled`
Whether logs are forced to disk when using the Bitronix Transaction Manager. Do not set to `false` in production because without disk force, integrity is not guaranteed. (Default value: `true`)

- `spring.jta.graceful-shutdown-interval`
Maximum number of seconds the transaction manager will wait for transactions to be done before aborting them at shutdown time when using the Bitronix Transaction Manager. (Default value: `60`)

- `spring.jta.jndi-transaction-synchronization-registry-name`
The name that the transaction synchronization registry should be bound under in JNDI when using the Bitronix Transaction Manager. (Default value: `java:comp/TransactionSynchronizationRegistry`)

- `spring.jta.jndi-user-transaction-name`
The name the user transaction should be bound under in JNDI when using the Bitronix Transaction Manager. (Default value: `java:comp/UserTransaction`)

- `spring.jta.journal`
The journal name, when using the Bitronix Transaction Manager. Can be `disk`, `null`, or a fully qualified class name. (Default value: `disk`)

- `spring.jta.log-dir`
Transaction logs directory.

- `spring.jta.log-part1-filename`
The journal fragment file 1 name. (Default value: `btm1.tlog`)

- `spring.jta.log-part2-filename`
  The journal fragment file 2 name. (Default value: `btm2.tlog`)

- `spring.jta.max-log-size-in-mb`
  The maximum size in megabytes of the journal fragments. Larger logs allow transactions to stay longer in-doubt. If, however, the size is too small, the transaction manager will pause longer when a fragment is full. For use with the Bitronix Transaction Manager. (Default value: `2`)

- `spring.jta.resource-configuration-filename`
  The Bitronix Transaction Manager configuration filename.

- `spring.jta.server-id`
  The ID that uniquely identifies the Bitronix Transaction Manager instance.

- `spring.jta.skip-corrupted-logs`
  Whether corrupted log files should be skipped. (Default value: `false`)

- `spring.jta.transaction-manager-id`
  Transaction manager unique identifier.

- `spring.jta.warn-about-zero-resource-transaction`
  Whether to warn about transactions executed without a single enlisted resource when using the Bitronix Transaction Manager. (Default value: `true`)

- `spring.mail.default-encoding`
  Default `MimeMessage` encoding. (Default value: `UTF-8`)

- `spring.mail.host`
  SMTP server host.

- `spring.mail.jndi-name`
  Session JNDI name. When set, takes precedence over any other mail settings.

- `spring.mail.password`
  Login password of the SMTP server.

- `spring.mail.port`
  SMTP server port.

- `spring.mail.properties`
  Additional JavaMail session properties.

- `spring.mail.protocol`
  Protocol used by the SMTP server. (Default value: `smtp`)

- `spring.mail.test-connection`
  Test that the mail server is available on startup. (Default value: `false`)

- `spring.mail.username`
  Login user of the SMTP server.

- `spring.messages.basename`
  Comma-separated list of basenames, each following the `ResourceBundle` convention. Essentially a fully qualified classpath location. If it doesn't contain a package qualifier (such as `org.mypackage`), it will be resolved from the classpath root. (Default value: `messages`)

- `spring.messages.cache-seconds`
  Loaded resource bundle files cache expiration, in seconds. When set to `-1`, bundles are cached forever. (Default value: `-1`)

- `spring.messages.encoding`
  Message bundles encoding. (Default value: `UTF-8`)

- `spring.mobile.devicedelegatingviewresolver.enable-fallback`
  Enable support for fallback resolution. (Default value: `false`)

- `spring.mobile.devicedelegatingviewresolver.enabled`
  Enable device view resolver. (Default value: `false`)

- `spring.mobile.devicedelegatingviewresolver.mobile-prefix`
  Prefix that gets prepended to view names for mobile devices. (Default value: `mobile/`)

- `spring.mobile.devicedelegatingviewresolver.mobile-suffix`
  Suffix that gets appended to view names for mobile devices.

- `spring.mobile.devicedelegatingviewresolver.normal-prefix`
  Prefix that gets prepended to view names for normal devices.

- `spring.mobile.devicedelegatingviewresolver.normal-suffix`
  Suffix that gets appended to view names for normal devices.

- `spring.mobile.devicedelegatingviewresolver.tablet-prefix`
  Prefix that gets prepended to view names for tablet devices. (Default value: `tablet/`)

- `spring.mobile.devicedelegatingviewresolver.tablet-suffix`
  Suffix that gets appended to view names for tablet devices.

- `spring.mobile.sitepreference.enabled`
  Enable `SitePreferenceHandler`. (Default value: `true`)

- `spring.mongodb.embedded.features`
  Comma-separated list of features to enable.

- `spring.mongodb.embedded.version`
  Version of Mongo to use. (Default value: `2.6.10`)

- `spring.mustache.cache`
  Enable template caching.

- `spring.mustache.charset`
  Template encoding.

- `spring.mustache.check-template-location`
  Check that the templates location exists.

- `spring.mustache.content-type`
  `Content-Type` value.

- `spring.mustache.enabled`
  Enable MVC view resolution for this technology.

- `spring.mustache.prefix`
  Prefix to apply to template names. (Default value: `classpath:/templates/`)

- `spring.mustache.suffix`
  Suffix to apply to template names. (Default value: `.html`)

- `spring.mustache.view-names`
  Whitelist of view names that can be resolved.

- `spring.mvc.async.request-timeout`
  Amount of time (in milliseconds) before asynchronous request handling times out. If this value is not set, the default timeout of the underlying implementation is used, such as 10 seconds on Tomcat with Servlet 3.

- `spring.mvc.date-format`
  Date format to use (such as dd/MM/yyyy).

- `spring.mvc.favicon.enabled`
  Enable resolution of favicon.ico. (Default value: `true`)

- `spring.mvc.ignore-default-model-on-redirect`
  If the content of the "default" model should be ignored during redirect scenarios. (Default value: `true`)

- `spring.mvc.locale`
  Locale to use.

- `spring.mvc.message-codes-resolver-format`
  Formatting strategy for message codes (`PREFIX_ERROR_CODE`, `POSTFIX_ERROR_CODE`).

- `spring.mvc.view.prefix`
  Spring MVC view prefix.

- `spring.mvc.view.suffix`
  Spring MVC view suffix.

- `spring.rabbitmq.addresses`
  Comma-separated list of addresses to which the client should connect.

- `spring.rabbitmq.dynamic`
  Create an `AmqpAdmin` bean. (Default value: `true`)

- `spring.rabbitmq.host`
  RabbitMQ host. (Default value: `localhost`)

- `spring.rabbitmq.listener.acknowledge-mode`
  Acknowledge mode of container.

- `spring.rabbitmq.listener.auto-startup`
  Start the container automatically on startup. (Default value: `true`)

- `spring.rabbitmq.listener.concurrency`
  Minimum number of consumers.

- `spring.rabbitmq.listener.max-concurrency`
  Maximum number of consumers.

- `spring.rabbitmq.listener.prefetch`
  Number of messages to be handled in a single request. It should be greater than or equal to the transaction size (if used).

- `spring.rabbitmq.listener.transaction-size`
  Number of messages to be processed in a transaction. For best results, it should be less than or equal to the prefetch count.

- `spring.rabbitmq.password`
  Login to authenticate against the broker.

- `spring.rabbitmq.port`
  RabbitMQ port. (Default value: `5672`)

- `spring.rabbitmq.requested-heartbeat`
  Requested heartbeat timeout in seconds; 0 for none.

- `spring.rabbitmq.ssl.enabled`
  Enable SSL support. (Default value: `false`)

- `spring.rabbitmq.ssl.key-store`
  Path to the key store that holds the SSL certificate.

- `spring.rabbitmq.ssl.key-store-password`
  Password used to access the key store.

- `spring.rabbitmq.ssl.trust-store`
  Trust store that holds SSL certificates.

- `spring.rabbitmq.ssl.trust-store-password`
  Password used to access the trust store.

- `spring.rabbitmq.username`
  Login user to authenticate to the broker.

- `spring.rabbitmq.virtual-host`
  Virtual host to use when connecting to the broker.

- `spring.redis.database`
  Database index used by the connection factory. (Default value: 0)

- `spring.redis.host`
  Redis server host. (Default value: `localhost`)

- `spring.redis.password`
  Login password of the Redis server.

- `spring.redis.pool.max-active`
  Max number of connections that can be allocated by the pool at a given time. Use a negative value for no limit. (Default value: 8)

- `spring.redis.pool.max-idle`
  Max number of idle connections in the pool. Use a negative value to indicate an unlimited number of idle connections. (Default value: 8)

- `spring.redis.pool.max-wait`
  Maximum amount of time (in milliseconds) a connection allocation should block before throwing an exception when the pool is exhausted. Use a negative value to block indefinitely. (Default value: -1)

- `spring.redis.pool.min-idle`
  Target for the minimum number of idle connections to maintain in the pool. This setting only has an effect if it is positive. (Default value: 0)

- `spring.redis.port`
  Redis server port. (Default value: 6379)

- `spring.redis.sentinel.master`
  Name of Redis server.

- `spring.redis.sentinel.nodes`
  Comma-separated list of host:port pairs.

- `spring.redis.timeout`
  Connection timeout in milliseconds. (Default value: 0)

- `spring.resources.add-mappings`
  Enable default resource handling. (Default value: `true`)

- `spring.resources.cache-period`
  Cache period for the resources served by the resource handler, in seconds.

- `spring.resources.chain.cache`
  Enable caching in the resource chain. (Default value: `true`)

- `spring.resources.chain.enabled`
  Enable the Spring resource handling chain. (Disabled by default unless at least one strategy has been enabled.)

- `spring.resources.chain.html-application-cache`
  Enable HTML5 application cache manifest rewriting. (Default value: `false`)

- `spring.resources.chain.strategy.content.enabled`
  Enable the content version strategy. (Default value: `false`)

- `spring.resources.chain.strategy.content.paths`
  Comma-separated list of patterns to apply to the version strategy. (Default value: `[/**]`)

- `spring.resources.chain.strategy.fixed.enabled`
  Enable the fixed version strategy. (Default value: `false`)

- `spring.resources.chain.strategy.fixed.paths`
  Comma-separated list of patterns to apply to the version strategy.

- `spring.resources.chain.strategy.fixed.version`
  Version string to use for the version strategy.

- `spring.resources.static-locations`
  Locations of static resources. Defaults to `classpath:[/META-INF/resources/, /resources/, /static/, /public/]` plus `context:/` (the root of the servlet context).

- `spring.sendgrid.password`
  SendGrid password.

- `spring.sendgrid.proxy.host`
  SendGrid proxy host.

- `spring.sendgrid.proxy.port`
  SendGrid proxy port.

- `spring.sendgrid.username`
  SendGrid username.

- `spring.social.auto-connection-views`
  Enable the connection status view for supported providers. (Default value: `false`)

- `spring.social.facebook.app-id`
  Application ID.

- `spring.social.facebook.app-secret`
  Application secret.

- `spring.social.linkedin.app-id`
  Application ID.

- `spring.social.linkedin.app-secret`
  Application secret.

- `spring.social.twitter.app-id`
  Application ID.

- `spring.social.twitter.app-secret`
  Application secret.

- `spring.thymeleaf.cache`
  Enable template caching. (Default value: `true`)

- `spring.thymeleaf.check-template-location`
  Check that the templates location exists. (Default value: `true`)

- `spring.thymeleaf.content-type`
  `Content-Type` value. (Default value: `text/html`)

- `spring.thymeleaf.enabled`
  Enable MVC Thymeleaf view resolution. (Default value: `true`)

- `spring.thymeleaf.encoding`
  Template encoding. (Default value: `UTF-8`)

- `spring.thymeleaf.excluded-view-names`
  Comma-separated list of view names that should be excluded from resolution.

- `spring.thymeleaf.mode`
  Template mode to be applied to templates. See also `StandardTemplateModeHandlers`.
  (Default value: `HTML5`)

- `spring.thymeleaf.prefix`
  Prefix that gets prepended to view names when building a URL. (Default value:
  `classpath:/templates/`)

- `spring.thymeleaf.suffix`
  Suffix that gets appended to view names when building a URL. (Default value:
  `.html`)

- `spring.thymeleaf.template-resolver-order`
  Order of the template resolver in the chain. By default, the template resolver is
  first in the chain. Ordering starts at 1 and should only be set if you have defined
  additional `TemplateResolver` beans.

- `spring.thymeleaf.view-names`
Comma-separated list of view names that can be resolved.

- `spring.velocity.allow-request-override`
Set whether `HttpServletRequest` attributes are allowed to override (hide) controller-generated model attributes of the same name.

- `spring.velocity.allow-session-override`
Set whether `HttpSession` attributes are allowed to override (hide) controller-generated model attributes of the same name.

- `spring.velocity.cache`
Enable template caching.

- `spring.velocity.charset`
Template encoding.

- `spring.velocity.check-template-location`
Check that the templates location exists.

- `spring.velocity.content-type`
`Content-Type` value.

- `spring.velocity.date-tool-attribute`
Name of the DateTool helper object to expose in the Velocity context of the view.

- `spring.velocity.enabled`
Enable MVC view resolution for this technology.

- `spring.velocity.expose-request-attributes`
Set whether all request attributes should be added to the model prior to merging with the template.

- `spring.velocity.expose-session-attributes`
Set whether all `HttpSession` attributes should be added to the model prior to merging with the template.

- `spring.velocity.expose-spring-macro-helpers`
Set whether to expose a `RequestContext` for use by Spring's macro library, under the name `springMacroRequestContext`.

- `spring.velocity.number-tool-attribute`
Name of the NumberTool helper object to expose in the Velocity context of the view.

- `spring.velocity.prefer-file-system-access`
Prefer filesystem access for template loading. Filesystem access enables hot detection of template changes. (Default value: `true`)

- `spring.velocity.prefix`
Prefix that gets prepended to view names when building a URL.

- `spring.velocity.properties`
Additional velocity properties.

- `spring.velocity.request-context-attribute`
Name of the `RequestContext` attribute for all views.

- `spring.velocity.resource-loader-path`
Template path. (Default value: `classpath:/templates/`)

- `spring.velocity.suffix`
Suffix that gets appended to view names when building a URL.

- `spring.velocity.toolbox-config-location`
Velocity Toolbox config location, such as /WEB-INF/toolbox.xml. Automatically loads a Velocity Tools toolbox definition file and exposes all defined tools in the specified scopes.

- `spring.velocity.view-names`
Whitelist of view names that can be resolved.

- `spring.view.prefix`
Spring MVC view prefix.

- `spring.view.suffix`
Spring MVC view suffix.

appendix D
Spring Boot dependencies

Whether you're building your project with Maven or Gradle or you're working with the Spring Boot CLI, Spring Boot provides dependency management support for several libraries that are commonly used in Spring applications. Table D.1 lists all of the library dependencies supported by Spring Boot version 1.3.0.

In many cases, these dependencies will automatically be added to your project's build and classpath by one of the Spring Boot starters (described in appendix A). If, however, you need a library that isn't covered by the starters you're using, you can explicitly declare the dependency in your Maven or Gradle build specification.

For instance, suppose you want to include the H2 embedded database in your project. In a Gradle build, you'd need to declare the following:

```
compile("com.h2database:h2")
```

The same dependency can be declared in a Maven build like this:

```
<dependency>
  <groupId>com.h2database</groupId>
  <version>h2</version>
</dependency>
```

Notice that in both cases, you shouldn't need to specify the version. Spring Boot's dependency management will take care of that for you. You may, however, explicitly provide the version if you want to override the version chosen by Spring Boot.

If you're using the Spring Boot CLI to run your application, you can use the @Grab annotation from Groovy like this:

```
@Grab("h2")
```

When using the @Grab annotation to include any of the libraries in table D.1, you only need to specify the artifact. Spring Boot extends @Grab to infer the group and version for you.

Table D.1   Library dependencies supported by Spring Boot

Group	Artifact	Version
antlr	antlr	2.7.7
ch.qos.logback	logback-access	1.1.3
ch.qos.logback	logback-classic	1.1.3
com.atomikos	transactions-jdbc	3.9.3
com.atomikos	transactions-jms	3.9.3
com.atomikos	transactions-jta	3.9.3
com.fasterxml.jackson.core	jackson-annotations	2.6.3
com.fasterxml.jackson.core	jackson-core	2.6.3
com.fasterxml.jackson.core	jackson-databind	2.6.3
com.fasterxml.jackson.dataformat	jackson-dataformat-csv	2.6.3
com.fasterxml.jackson.dataformat	jackson-dataformat-xml	2.6.3
com.fasterxml.jackson.dataformat	jackson-dataformat-yaml	2.6.3
com.fasterxml.jackson.datatype	jackson-datatype-hibernate4	2.6.3
com.fasterxml.jackson.datatype	jackson-datatype-hibernate5	2.6.3
com.fasterxml.jackson.datatype	jackson-datatype-jdk7	2.6.3
com.fasterxml.jackson.datatype	jackson-datatype-jdk8	2.6.3
com.fasterxml.jackson.datatype	jackson-datatype-joda	2.6.3
com.fasterxml.jackson.datatype	jackson-datatype-jsr310	2.6.3
com.fasterxml.jackson.module	jackson-module-parameter-names	2.6.3
com.gemstone.gemfire	gemfire	8.1.0
com.github.mxab.thymeleaf.extras	thymeleaf-extras-data-attribute	1.3
com.google.code.gson	gson	2.3.1
com.googlecode.json-simple	json-simple	1.1.1
com.h2database	h2	1.4.190
com.hazelcast	hazelcast	3.5.3
com.hazelcast	hazelcast-spring	3.5.3
com.jayway.jsonpath	json-path	2.0.0
com.jayway.jsonpath	json-path-assert	2.0.0
com.samskivert	jmustache	1.11
com.sendgrid	sendgrid-java	2.2.2

Table D.1   Library dependencies supported by Spring Boot *(continued)*

Group	Artifact	Version
com.sun.mail	javax.mail	1.5.4
com.timgroup	java-statsd-client	3.1.0
com.zaxxer	HikariCP	2.4.2
com.zaxxer	HikariCP-java6	2.3.12
commons-beanutils	commons-beanutils	1.9.2
commons-collections	commons-collections	3.2.1
commons-dbcp	commons-dbcp	1.4
commons-digester	commons-digester	2.1
commons-pool	commons-pool	1.6
de.flapdoodle.embed	de.flapdoodle.embed.mongo	1.50.0
io.dropwizard.metrics	metrics-core	3.1.2
io.dropwizard.metrics	metrics-ganglia	3.1.2
io.dropwizard.metrics	metrics-graphite	3.1.2
io.dropwizard.metrics	metrics-servlets	3.1.2
io.projectreactor	reactor-bus	2.0.7.RELEASE
io.projectreactor	reactor-core	2.0.7.RELEASE
io.projectreactor	reactor-groovy	2.0.7.RELEASE
io.projectreactor	reactor-groovy-extensions	2.0.7.RELEASE
io.projectreactor	reactor-logback	2.0.7.RELEASE
io.projectreactor	reactor-net	2.0.7.RELEASE
io.projectreactor	reactor-stream	2.0.7.RELEASE
io.projectreactor.spring	reactor-spring-context	2.0.6.RELEASE
io.projectreactor.spring	reactor-spring-core	2.0.6.RELEASE
io.projectreactor.spring	reactor-spring-messaging	2.0.6.RELEASE
io.projectreactor.spring	reactor-spring-webmvc	2.0.6.RELEASE
io.undertow	undertow-core	1.3.5.Final
io.undertow	undertow-servlet	1.3.5.Final
io.undertow	undertow-websockets-jsr	1.3.5.Final
javax.cache	cache-api	1.0.0
javax.jms	jms-api	1.1-rev-1

Table D.1 Library dependencies supported by Spring Boot *(continued)*

Group	Artifact	Version
javax.mail	javax.mail-api	1.5.4
javax.servlet	javax.servlet-api	3.1.0
javax.servlet	jstl	1.2
javax.transaction	javax.transaction-api	1.2
jaxen	jaxen	1.1.6
joda-time	joda-time	2.8.2
junit	junit	4.12
log4j	log4j	1.2.17
mysql	mysql-connector-java	5.1.37
net.sf.ehcache	ehcache	2.10.1
net.sourceforge.nekohtml	nekohtml	1.9.22
nz.net.ultraq.thymeleaf	thymeleaf-layout-dialect	1.3.1
org.apache.activemq	activemq-amqp	5.12.1
org.apache.activemq	activemq-blueprint	5.12.1
org.apache.activemq	activemq-broker	5.12.1
org.apache.activemq	activemq-camel	5.12.1
org.apache.activemq	activemq-client	5.12.1
org.apache.activemq	activemq-console	5.12.1
org.apache.activemq	activemq-http	5.12.1
org.apache.activemq	activemq-jaas	5.12.1
org.apache.activemq	activemq-jdbc-store	5.12.1
org.apache.activemq	activemq-jms-pool	5.12.1
org.apache.activemq	activemq-kahadb-store	5.12.1
org.apache.activemq	activemq-karaf	5.12.1
org.apache.activemq	activemq-leveldb-store	5.12.1
org.apache.activemq	activemq-log4j-appender	5.12.1
org.apache.activemq	activemq-mqtt	5.12.1
org.apache.activemq	activemq-openwire-generator	5.12.1
org.apache.activemq	activemq-openwire-legacy	5.12.1
org.apache.activemq	activemq-osgi	5.12.1

Table D.1   Library dependencies supported by Spring Boot *(continued)*

Group	Artifact	Version
org.apache.activemq	activemq-partition	5.12.1
org.apache.activemq	activemq-pool	5.12.1
org.apache.activemq	activemq-ra	5.12.1
org.apache.activemq	activemq-run	5.12.1
org.apache.activemq	activemq-runtime-config	5.12.1
org.apache.activemq	activemq-shiro	5.12.1
org.apache.activemq	activemq-spring	5.12.1
org.apache.activemq	activemq-stomp	5.12.1
org.apache.activemq	activemq-web	5.12.1
org.apache.activemq	artemis-jms-client	1.1.0
org.apache.activemq	artemis-jms-server	1.1.0
org.apache.commons	commons-dbcp2	2.1.1
org.apache.commons	commons-pool2	2.4.2
org.apache.derby	derby	10.12.1.1
org.apache.httpcomponents	httpasyncclient	4.1.1
org.apache.httpcomponents	httpclient	4.5.1
org.apache.httpcomponents	httpcore	4.4.4
org.apache.httpcomponents	httpmime	4.5.1
org.apache.logging.log4j	log4j-api	2.4.1
org.apache.logging.log4j	log4j-core	2.4.1
org.apache.logging.log4j	log4j-slf4j-impl	2.4.1
org.apache.solr	solr-solrj	4.10.4
org.apache.tomcat.embed	tomcat-embed-core	8.0.28
org.apache.tomcat.embed	tomcat-embed-el	8.0.28
org.apache.tomcat.embed	tomcat-embed-jasper	8.0.28
org.apache.tomcat.embed	tomcat-embed-logging-juli	8.0.28
org.apache.tomcat.embed	tomcat-embed-websocket	8.0.28
org.apache.tomcat	tomcat-jdbc	8.0.28
org.apache.tomcat	tomcat-jsp-api	8.0.28
org.apache.velocity	velocity	1.7

Table D.1 Library dependencies supported by Spring Boot (*continued*)

Group	Artifact	Version
org.apache.velocity	velocity-tools	2.0
org.aspectj	aspectjrt	1.8.7
org.aspectj	aspectjtools	1.8.7
org.aspectj	aspectjweaver	1.8.7
org.codehaus.btm	btm	2.1.4
org.codehaus.groovy	groovy	2.4.4
org.codehaus.groovy	groovy-all	2.4.4
org.codehaus.groovy	groovy-ant	2.4.4
org.codehaus.groovy	groovy-bsf	2.4.4
org.codehaus.groovy	groovy-console	2.4.4
org.codehaus.groovy	groovy-docgenerator	2.4.4
org.codehaus.groovy	groovy-groovydoc	2.4.4
org.codehaus.groovy	groovy-groovysh	2.4.4
org.codehaus.groovy	groovy-jmx	2.4.4
org.codehaus.groovy	groovy-json	2.4.4
org.codehaus.groovy	groovy-jsr223	2.4.4
org.codehaus.groovy	groovy-nio	2.4.4
org.codehaus.groovy	groovy-servlet	2.4.4
org.codehaus.groovy	groovy-sql	2.4.4
org.codehaus.groovy	groovy-swing	2.4.4
org.codehaus.groovy	groovy-templates	2.4.4
org.codehaus.groovy	groovy-test	2.4.4
org.codehaus.groovy	groovy-testng	2.4.4
org.codehaus.groovy	groovy-xml	2.4.4
org.codehaus.janino	janino	2.7.8
org.crashub	crash.cli	1.3.2
org.crashub	crash.connectors.ssh	1.3.2
org.crashub	crash.connectors.telnet	1.3.2
org.crashub	crash.embed.spring	1.3.2
org.crashub	crash.plugins.cron	1.3.2

Table D.1   Library dependencies supported by Spring Boot *(continued)*

Group	Artifact	Version
org.crashub	crash.plugins.mail	1.3.2
org.crashub	crash.shell	1.3.2
org.eclipse.jetty	jetty-annotations	9.2.14.v20151106
org.eclipse.jetty	jetty-continuation	9.2.14.v20151106
org.eclipse.jetty	jetty-deploy	9.2.14.v20151106
org.eclipse.jetty	jetty-http	9.2.14.v20151106
org.eclipse.jetty	jetty-io	9.2.14.v20151106
org.eclipse.jetty	jetty-jsp	9.2.14.v20151106
org.eclipse.jetty	jetty-jmx	9.2.14.v20151106
org.eclipse.jetty	jetty-plus	9.2.14.v20151106
org.eclipse.jetty	jetty-security	9.2.14.v20151106
org.eclipse.jetty	jetty-server	9.2.14.v20151106
org.eclipse.jetty	jetty-servlet	9.2.14.v20151106
org.eclipse.jetty	jetty-servlets	9.2.14.v20151106
org.eclipse.jetty	jetty-util	9.2.14.v20151106
org.eclipse.jetty	jetty-webapp	9.2.14.v20151106
org.eclipse.jetty	jetty-xml	9.2.14.v20151106
org.eclipse.jetty.orbit	javax.servlet.jsp	2.2.0.v201112011158
org.eclipse.jetty.websocket	javax-websocket-server-impl	9.2.14.v20151106
org.eclipse.jetty.websocket	websocket-server	9.2.14.v20151106
org.elasticsearch	elasticsearch	1.5.2
org.firebirdsql.jdbc	jaybird-jdk16	2.2.9
org.firebirdsql.jdbc	jaybird-jdk17	2.2.9
org.firebirdsql.jdbc	jaybird-jdk18	2.2.9
org.flywaydb	flyway-core	3.2.1
org.freemarker	freemarker	2.3.23
org.glassfish	javax.el	3.0.0
org.glassfish.jersey.containers	jersey-container-servlet	2.19
org.glassfish.jersey.containers	jersey-container-servlet-core	2.19
org.glassfish.jersey.core	jersey-server	2.22.1

Table D.1   Library dependencies supported by Spring Boot *(continued)*

Group	Artifact	Version
org.glassfish.jersey.ext	jersey-bean-validation	2.22.1
org.glassfish.jersey.ext	jersey-spring3	2.22.1
org.glassfish.jersey.media	jersey-media-json-jackson	2.22.1
org.hamcrest	hamcrest-core	1.3
org.hamcrest	hamcrest-library	1.3
org.hibernate	hibernate-core	4.3.11.Final
org.hibernate	hibernate-ehcache	4.3.11.Final
org.hibernate	hibernate-entitymanager	4.3.11.Final
org.hibernate	hibernate-envers	4.3.11.Final
org.hibernate	hibernate-jpamodelgen	4.3.11.Final
org.hibernate	hibernate-validator	5.2.2.Final
org.hibernate	hibernate-validator-annotation-processor	5.2.2.Final
org.hornetq	hornetq-jms-client	2.4.7.Final
org.hornetq	hornetq-jms-server	2.4.7.Final
org.hsqldb	hsqldb	2.3.3
org.infinispan	infinispan-jcache	8.0.1.Final
org.infinispan	infinispan-spring4	8.0.1.Final
org.javassist	javassist	3.18.1-GA
org.jdom	jdom2	2.0.6
org.jolokia	jolokia-core	1.3.2
org.json	json	20140107
org.jooq	jooq	3.7.1
org.jooq	jooq-meta	3.7.1
org.jooq	jooq-codegen	3.7.1
org.liquibase	liquibase-core	3.4.1
org.mariadb.jdbc	mariadb-java-client	1.2.3
org.mockito	mockito-core	1.10.19
org.mongodb	mongo-java-driver	2.13.3
org.postgresql	postgresql	9.4-1205-jdbc41
org.skyscreamer	jsonassert	1.2.3

Table D.1   Library dependencies supported by Spring Boot *(continued)*

Group	Artifact	Version
org.slf4j	jcl-over-slf4j	1.7.13
org.slf4j	jul-to-slf4j	1.7.13
org.slf4j	log4j-over-slf4j	1.7.13
org.slf4j	slf4j-api	1.7.13
org.slf4j	slf4j-jdk14	1.7.13
org.slf4j	slf4j-log4j12	1.7.13
org.slf4j	slf4j-simple	1.7.13
org.spockframework	spock-core	1.0-groovy-2.4
org.spockframework	spock-spring	1.0-groovy-2.4
org.springframework	spring-core	4.2.3.RELEASE
org.springframework	spring-framework-bom	4.2.3.RELEASE
org.springframework	springloaded	1.2.4.RELEASE
org.springframework.amqp	spring-amqp	1.5.2.RELEASE
org.springframework.amqp	spring-rabbit	1.5.2.RELEASE
org.springframework.batch	spring-batch-core	3.0.5.RELEASE
org.springframework.batch	spring-batch-infrastructure	3.0.5.RELEASE
org.springframework.batch	spring-batch-integration	3.0.5.RELEASE
org.springframework.batch	spring-batch-test	3.0.5.RELEASE
org.springframework.cloud	spring-cloud-cloudfoundry-connector	1.2.0.RELEASE
org.springframework.cloud	spring-cloud-core	1.2.0.RELEASE
org.springframework.cloud	spring-cloud-heroku-connector	1.2.0.RELEASE
org.springframework.cloud	spring-cloud-localconfig-connector	1.2.0.RELEASE
org.springframework.cloud	spring-cloud-spring-service-connector	1.2.0.RELEASE
org.springframework.data	spring-data-releasetrain	Gosling-SR1RELEASE
org.springframework.hateoas	spring-hateoas	0.19.0.RELEASE
org.springframework.integration	spring-integration-bom	4.2.1.RELEASE
org.springframework.integration	spring-integration-http	4.2.1.RELEASE
org.springframework.mobile	spring-mobile-device	1.1.5.RELEASE
org.springframework.plugin	spring-plugin-core	1.2.0.RELEASE
org.springframework.retry	spring-retry	1.1.2.RELEASE

Table D.1 Library dependencies supported by Spring Boot *(continued)*

Group	Artifact	Version
org.springframework.security	spring-security-bom	4.0.3.RELEASE
org.springframework.security	spring-security-jwt	1.0.3.RELEASE
org.springframework .security.oauth	spring-security-oauth	2.0.8.RELEASE
org.springframework .security.oauth	spring-security-oauth2	2.0.8.RELEASE
org.springframework.session	spring-session	1.0.2.RELEASE
org.springframework.session	spring-session-data-redis	1.0.2.RELEASE
org.springframework.social	spring-social-config	1.1.3.RELEASE
org.springframework.social	spring-social-core	1.1.3.RELEASE
org.springframework.social	spring-social-security	1.1.3.RELEASE
org.springframework.social	spring-social-web	1.1.3.RELEASE
org.springframework.social	spring-social-facebook	2.0.2.RELEASE
org.springframework.social	spring-social-facebook-web	2.0.2.RELEASE
org.springframework.social	spring-social-linkedin	1.0.2.RELEASE
org.springframework.social	spring-social-twitter	1.1.2.RELEASE
org.springframework.ws	spring-ws-core	2.2.3.RELEASE
org.springframework.ws	spring-ws-security	2.2.3.RELEASE
org.springframework.ws	spring-ws-support	2.2.3.RELEASE
org.springframework.ws	spring-ws-test	2.2.3.RELEASE
org.thymeleaf	thymeleaf	2.1.4.RELEASE
org.thymeleaf	thymeleaf-spring4	2.1.4.RELEASE
org.thymeleaf.extras	thymeleaf-extras-conditionalcomments	2.1.1.RELEASE
org.thymeleaf.extras	thymeleaf-extras-springsecurity4	2.1.2.RELEASE
org.webjars	hal-browser	9f96c74
org.yaml	snakeyaml	1.16
redis.clients	jedis	2.7.3
wsdl4j	wsdl4j	1.6.3

index